Dear Jan,

It was a pleasure to meet you.

Jewish Aviators
in World War II

*Personal Narratives
of American Men and Women*

Bruce H. Wolk

Foreword by Sheldon A. Goldberg

McFarland & Company, Inc., Publishers
Jefferson, North Carolina

LIBRARY OF CONGRESS CATALOGUING-IN-PUBLICATION DATA

Names: Wolk, Bruce H., author.
Title: Jewish aviators in World War II : personal narratives of American
    men and women / Bruce H. Wolk ; foreword by Sheldon A. Goldberg.
Description: Jefferson, North Carolina : McFarland & Company, Inc.
    Publishers, 2016 | Includes bibliographical references and index.
Identifiers: LCCN 2016002116 | ISBN 9780786499953 (softcover : acid free
    paper) ∞
Subjects: LCSH: World War, 1939–1945—Participation, Jewish. | Air pilots,
    Military—United States—Interviews. | Women air pilots—United
    States—Interviews. | World War, 1939–1945—Personal narratives,
    Jewish. | World War, 1939–1945—Aerial operations, American.
Classification: LCC D810.J4 W575 2016 | DDC 940.54/49730923924—dc23
LC record available at http://lccn.loc.gov/2016002116

BRITISH LIBRARY CATALOGUING DATA ARE AVAILABLE

ISBN (print) 978-0-7864-9995-3
ISBN (ebook) 978-1-4766-2355-9

Front cover photograph of P-47 fighter plane © 2016 DenGuy/iStock

Printed in the United States of America

McFarland & Company, Inc., Publishers
    Box 611, Jefferson, North Carolina 28640
    www.mcfarlandpub.com

In Memory

Staff Sergeant Laurence Wolk, 8th Air Force,
467th Bombardment Group, 791st Squadron

First Lieutenant John Wilson Roberts III, H Troop,
17th Cavalry, 198th Infantry Brigade, Americal Division

Acknowledgments

It would have been impossible to write this book without the kindness and support of the American-Jewish World War II veterans who were interviewed. They became first my teachers, then my friends.

My heartfelt appreciation and deepest gratitude to Lt. Col. Sheldon Goldberg, Ph.D., USAF (Ret.), docent and historian at the National Museum of American-Jewish Military History. Dr. Goldberg is a 30-year veteran of the USAF, and the recipient of two Distinguished Flying Crosses for valor as an F-4 weapons systems officer during the war in Southeast Asia. Dr. Goldberg provided me with invaluable editing assistance and critical historical review.

I would like to thank the Jewish War Veterans of America, specifically former national executive director Col. Herbert Rosenbleeth, USA (Ret.), and Cheryl Waldman, former national programs/public relations coordinator.

I would like to acknowledge Kimberly L. Johnson, coordinator of special collections, and Sarah K. Whittington, library assistant, of the Texas Woman's University; Renee Corcoran, director of the Nebraska Jewish Historical Society; Dr. Vivian Rogers-Price, research center director, and Jean Prescott, reference specialist, of the Mighty Eighth Air Force Museum; Herbert Weber, Willi Wachholz and Monika Wachholz of *Flieger-Lynchmorde*; *The Intermountain Jewish News*; Aaron Elson, Linda Dewey and Duane Giesler of the Kassel Mission Historical Society; Dennis West of the 483rd Bomb Group Association; Andy Wilkinson of the 467th Bomb Group Association; and Larry Grauerholz of the Armed Forces Escape and Evasion Society (AFEES).

Many individuals went out of their way to provide assistance for this book: Marcia Allen; Maurice Ashkinaz; CJ Backus; Norman Cohen; Mickey Corn; Philip Elbaum, LCSW; Michael Fuenfer, M.D.; Jack Latkin; Jonathan Newmark, M.D.; Lynne Riedesel; Allen Sabol; Rabbi Rafael Sonnenfeld; Morris Spector; William Wagner; and the family of Laurence Wolk.

Finally, to Jannette, who has always had faith in my humble journey.

Table of Contents

After the first mission, I figured we're never going to make 35. So I had an attitude, "This is it." It never bothered me too much—I figured I'd never get back. The most anyone in our crew had was a couple pieces of flak that hit the nose of the bomber and some frostbite. So we were lucky. But remember, we had three Jewish guys watching over everyone else! On every mission I said the Shema Yisrael,* you know, to myself. I was in my own world down in that turret. At 18, you don't have a wife and kids to worry about.

—SSGT Morton Israel, ball turret gunner.
For a period his bomber, most improbably,
had three Jewish crewmembers.

---

* *A sacred Jewish prayer: "Hear, O Israel, the Lord is our God, the Lord is One."*

Foreword
by Sheldon A. Goldberg

From before the time our country was the United States, Jewish men and women have participated in its defense. In 1654, beginning with the small Jewish community under the leadership of Asher Levy, Jews won the right to stand guard on the walls of New Amsterdam. Jews have served in every branch of the U.S. armed forces and fought in every war since this nation's founding.

Yet just as there are Holocaust deniers, so too are there those who have repeatedly claimed over the years that Jews never served, or if they served, never fought in America's wars.

Even Mark Twain, having learned the truth about Jewish participation in the Civil War, retracted his 1897 *Harper's* article in which he wrote, "[The Jew] is a frequent and faithful and capable officer in the civil service, but he is charged with an unpatriotic disinclination to stand by the flag as a soldier—like the Christian Quaker."

This book is the retelling of the personal narratives of Jewish men and women aviators who wore the uniform of the U.S. Army Air Forces, Navy, Marines or the Women Airforce Service Pilots. It is a testament to the service of American Jews who fought and died in our greatest national undertaking—World War II. It is a chronicle of heroism and honor that has not been told before, in many cases not even to the families of those who served.

Bruce Wolk's dedication and persistence in finding these Jewish members of America's "Greatest Generation," most of whom have since passed on, is a remarkable effort that opens an unknown chapter of Jewish and World War II history and to the literature of that time.

Sheldon Goldberg, Ph.D., is docent and historian of the National Museum of American-Jewish Military History.

1

Preface

This book chronicles the participation of American-Jewish airmen and women in World War II. When Jewish airmen entered the service, more often than not they were subjected to anti–Semitism. The discrimination could range from taunts and fistfights to instructors intentionally failing them in training to not receiving commendations for heroism in combat. In training and on active duty, some were questioned as to their loyalty to America, their courage under fire or whether they had the mechanical and engineering skills to pilot an aircraft or work on an engine.

When those Jews who were shot down and captured as POWs were placed into German Stalag Luft camps, anti–Semitism from their fellow airmen often followed them into the barracks. Toward the end of the war, depending on the camp, they could be segregated from the other airmen for the intended purpose of being shipped to concentration camps and executed—not as Allied airmen but as Jews. When the war was over, one of the prevailing attitudes some Americans had was that Jews had done the easy jobs in the service or that they had altogether avoided combat.

There has never been a book exploring the topic of the Jewish airmen in terms of their dual battle to be recognized and accepted within the ranks and to prove themselves in combat. In writing this book, I sought out as many Jewish World War II airmen and women as possible and conducted first-person interviews. I became interested in the topic not long after the death of my uncle, a childhood hero of mine, who was a ball turret gunner on a B-24 bomber with the 8th Air Force, 467th Bomb Group.

The interviewees relate service and combat experiences in all theaters of the war and stories of internment as prisoners of war in German camps. Included are accounts of how some airmen first came to suspect the Holocaust was raging below and how, in their own ways, they tried to exact revenge. The final chapter is devoted to the lives of the veterans after they returned from the war.

In the course of the interviews, a great deal of material was collected that could not be included due to limitations of space and focus. These topics—including American-Jewish life prior to World War II, the debate as to whether the Army Air Corps could have or should have bombed the concentration camps, and the combat role of Jews in the infantry and other branches of the service—have been fully covered in other works.

About 110 American-Jewish World War II veterans were interviewed; 103 consented to be in the book and 99 are mentioned by name or are directly quoted. The interviews were conducted between 2009 and 2015. The youngest veteran interviewed was 83, the oldest 95. Despite their ages, when talking of their service experiences, their memories of the period were clear and historically accurate. Contributing to their accuracy was the fact that several retained lists of their bomb group missions and day-to-day combat diaries.

Proceeds from the sale of this book will go to National Museum of American-Jewish Military History in Washington, D.C., in honor of the service and sacrifice of the men and women whose recollections made it possible.

Where We Came From

My mother didn't want me to go. She didn't want me to come [to America], but my father said, "Please, he's going to be killed here." So they dragged my mother off the ship.
>   —Private Raymond Paluch, 15th Air Force,
>   33rd Fighter Group, departing from Poland
>   on one of the last ships before the Nazi invasion

As he was dying of lung cancer, I would make one last visit to my Uncle Larry. He was bald and pasty-faced from several rounds of chemotherapy. His speech was labored and his hands shook. Still, he smoked.

He was sitting at the dining room table of his Florida condominium, slowly turning the pages of a World War II era photo album filled with black and white snapshots. He showed me his crewmates and his B-24 bomber, *Heaven Can Wait*. There were also snapshots of bombers flying in formation across flak-filled skies, guys in T-shirts and khakis horsing around outside of a wooden barracks and a beautiful English woman whose name was not given.

Though Uncle Larry was pleased to see me, it was also clear that he was spending time with a family I would never meet.

Following high school, Laurence Wolk took a production job at Grumman Aircraft on Long Island. He enlisted on January 11, 1943, and served in the Army Air Corps until October 25, 1945. Staff Sergeant Wolk was an armorer and ball turret gunner assigned to the 8th Air Force, 467th Bombardment Group and 791st Bomb Squadron. His pilot was Lt. Lowell J. Hanna.

I would learn much later that the name a crew gave to their bomber could be chosen on a whim or out of superstition, folly or love, but the much deeper connection was to the pilot. If Laurence Wolk could speak from his grave, I am sure he would say, "My plane? I was on Lowell Hanna's crew."

Wolk flew 30 missions out of RAF Rackheath, England, and was awarded the Distinguished Flying Cross, the Air Medal with three Oak Leaf clusters and various campaign ribbons. He was in the air on D–Day, possibly over Colleville-sur-Mer, France. On one mission his crew was forced to crash-land. As a gunner, he was credited with German fighter plane kills. If last names are a reliable indicator, he was the only crewmember on his bomber who was Jewish.

He never articulated his war story, the story of an American-Jewish airman who had been lucky enough to escape an airman's death. He never told anyone. Yet as he turned the pages of his album looking up at me from time to time, I could not help but believe he was trying to tell me something.

They—the men and women in this book—were immigrants themselves, or at best first-generation Americans, as was my uncle.

Theirs was an American story to be sure, but also a Jewish story. Most of their parents left the tiny *shtetls* or cities of Galicia, Poland, Russia or the Ukraine between 1899 and 1924 to seek a better life for themselves or their families far away from the pogroms, forced conscription and persecution they faced in their native lands. Even the German and Austrian Jews, though wealthier, cultured and perhaps more refined, were eventually forced to flee ahead of Nazi brutality.

The veterans came from families with differing perspectives of Judaism— some were raised Orthodox and some with no practice of Judaism at all. Some followed the kosher dietary laws, but for most, the adherence faded with each passing year—and certainly ended with the start of military service. Some celebrated bar mitzvahs, religious holidays and other cultural events, while others never participated in any observance remotely Jewish.

They, or their parents, entered North American ports up and down the east coast, then quickly fanned out across the nation to large cities, towns and backwater villages. Most of their fathers worked as tradesmen or as unskilled laborers; almost none boasted of wealth.

Of those who had been fortunate enough to build up modest retail, food or manufacturing businesses, the majority saw the

Staff Sergeant Laurence Wolk (courtesy Carol Wolk).

Great Depression wipe them out. In several cases, the poverty was so crushing it forced families onto public assistance, and sometimes led to family breakups where the future veterans would be shuffled off to relatives or placed in orphanages and foster homes.

There were those who experienced frequent anti–Semitism growing up, while others were heartily welcomed into the fabric of their communities, and were never subjected to bigotry. In school, they were much like other kids; some were talented athletes or they played musical instruments, others were artists, sculptors and writers.[1] A number aspired to be mathematicians, physicians, lawyers, accountants and educators but when war came, they felt a need to serve.

Though a small percentage had enlisted earlier, much like the rest of the American men and women entering the service, the clarion call was December 7, 1941. Every veteran interviewed could recall where he or she was on that Sunday and precisely what they were doing.

Jewish fraternities enlisted together, quitting college *en masse*; whole families, fathers, sons and daughters enlisted.[2] They loved this country and they had a need to prove themselves and their worth.

However, upon entering the service many Jews, even those who had never before experienced anti–Semitism, would soon learn that not all their fellow Americans loved them back. Their era had given rise to Father Coughlin, Huey Long and the German-American *Bund*. It was the time frame in which the steamship MS *St. Louis*, the so-called "Voyage of the Damned," with more than 900 Jewish passengers fleeing Europe, was turned away by the Roosevelt administration and sent back to Europe.[3]

In 1939, a Roper poll was conducted to measure American attitudes towards Jews.[4] Only 39 percent of Americans felt that Jews should be "treated like everyone else." Ten percent believed that all Jews should be deported. A Roper poll taken in 1938 showed that Americans overwhelmingly opposed raising the Jewish immigration quotas to help those Jews who were trying to flee Nazi Europe.

The sons and daughters of the immigrants had to fight for respect, not only for themselves as soldiers and sailors, but for all of the Jews they left at home. It is disappointing that so little is known of their service, given their surprising numbers. There were between 4.5 and 4.8 million Jews living in the United States in 1940, about three percent of the total population.[5] Of that number, 550,000 Jewish men and women served in the military in World War II.[6] Half of all Jewish men between 18 and 50 were in the service. For comparative purposes, in 1940 the total population of the United States was about 132.2 million.[7] During World War II, a total of 13 million men and women served in the military. Jews as a group in fact served at a slightly higher percentage than the population at large.

In World War II, American Jewish personnel suffered between 38,000 and 40,000 casualties; 11,000 Jewish personnel were killed in combat or combat related activities.[8] The statistics for Jewish versus non-Jewish deaths and casualties were virtually identical on a percentage basis, yet insidious humor during and long after World War II suggested that Jews served in the "Jewish Infantry," or it was referred to as the "Jewish Quartermaster Corps," where Jews had hand-picked assignments such as guarding Coney Island in Brooklyn. The quartermaster allusion was based on old stereotypes going back to the Eastern European immigrants, the Greenhorns: Jews always dodged the service; Jews were afraid to fight; Jews paid others to do their dirty work.

Following World War II, Hollywood tried to generate a more accurate image of Jews in the infantry. However, Jewish service in other branches of the military has gone virtually unexplored. This is especially true in regard to the air war.

The Jewish Airman

Dr. Vivian Rogers-Price, research center director of the Mighty Eighth Air Force Museum, referencing Roger A. Freeman's definitive book *Mighty Eighth*, stated that the best estimates are that there were 46,456 combat deaths, killed in action for the 8th, 9th, 12th and 15th Air Forces combined.[9] Some 22,000 to 26,000 of the deaths were suffered in the England-based 8th Air Force. There were about 8,300 airmen killed in action in the Pacific.[10] On a percentage basis, the casualties among aircrews were higher than was experienced by the U.S. Marines.

More than 150,000 Jews served in the Army Air Corps, or were involved in Army, Navy or Marine aviation.[11] There were also nine Jewish women in the WASP—the Women Airforce Service Pilots.

Jewish airmen earned many awards and decorations including the Navy Cross, the Silver Star, the Purple Heart and the Bronze Star as well as numerous campaign ribbons and battle stars. One veteran I interviewed even earned the Soldier's Medal for saving the lives of two comrades in a non-combat situation at an airfield. More than 2,000 Jewish personnel were awarded the Distinguished Flying Cross and more than 13,000 were awarded the Air Medal.[12] Only recently have several have been awarded the French Legion of Honor for their participation in the liberation of France.

The Interviews

Beginning in the fall of 2009, I initiated my research partly as a way to honor my uncle and partly to fight the ugly stereotypes that had plagued the

American-Jewish generation of servicemen and women before mine. I began with just one interview of a Jewish airman in my home town of Denver, Colorado. "Is there anyone else you know?" I would ask. One airman would call or email another, who then referred me to another and so on, crisscrossing the country, until I accumulated about 110 first-person interviews.

I was surprised by the high degree of networking among the airmen, especially through their bomb groups, veteran's organizations and informal "breakfast clubs." The attachments formed among crewmembers did not fade with the passage of time. Sadly, most of the veterans whose words appear on these pages have passed away. Their voices remain with me.

•• 2 ••

The War Within

A highlight of my life is that I met Hymie Rickover.[1] I always felt he had never made it all the way because he was Jewish. Over coffee, I told him I was Jewish. A big grin broke out across his face. From that point on, we talked about the Navy.

—Lt. Commander Jack Latkin, U.S. Navy Pilot,
World War II and Korea

Though many of the veterans interviewed had experienced bigotry in their personal lives, they were often surprised at how it carried over into the military. While some American-Jewish veterans claimed that they never encountered anti–Semitism at any point in their training, they were clearly in the minority. The intolerance could be verbal or physical, overt or subtle. It was not confined to just one branch of the service nor to rank.

It was a warm Sunday afternoon early in the spring of 1945 as a group of 240 newly minted officers were marched in perfect formation onto the parade ground of Maxwell Field in Montgomery, Alabama. Lieutenant Sidney Crane was among them. The parade ground usually served as a football field. On this day, the review stand was placed in what would have been the end zone. A scattering of officers, NCOs and civilians sat in the hot sun. In front of the reviewing stand was a dais with a podium and microphone.

This was the final phase of pilot training. The pilots would now learn to fly the B-17, and then head off to war, most probably in the Pacific.

A captain walked up to the microphone, a tall, thin man with a dyspeptic face, the kind of face you might expect from a training officer. His name was Captain Byron H. Barry.[2] He looked over the assembled troops and then screamed into the microphone:

"Crane, Sidney, Isadore, one step forward!"

"I stepped forward and saluted. And the next words out of his mouth, 'Crane, are you a Jew?' or maybe 'Are you a damn Jew?' I said, 'Yes, sir.' He announced to everyone that no goddamn Jew was going to fly a B-17. 'What do you have to say to that, Jew boy?' And I said, 'Thank you, sir.' And he said, into the microphone, 'What kind of a Jew crack is that?' And I said, 'Sir, if I fail, it won't be you, it will be me.'

"I was in shock. I couldn't imagine. I am at a school because I chose to go to combat. I had everything in front of me, and it came totally out of left field. While I was in formation, no one whispered a word to me, even though there were a number of Jews in the formation.

"Afterwards? Well, the funny thing is, the whole base came to know about 'Jew Crane.'[3] The word went throughout the whole station. I didn't have to say anything, but everybody on the base knew who I was.

"The base commander was in the stands that day. He might have been a full colonel. He didn't say anything. But he did something later.

"It wasn't just [idle] harassment. The next day I failed the flight test. We went up in an airplane and I never touched the controls. We landed and Barry put me down for failure, 'Not fit to fly an airplane.'

"Because I was failed, I was not to take part in the organized training events. I had to have a check ride. The next day, the base commander took me for a check ride. He let me do a number of things. He asked me how much time I had in a B-17, and I told him. When we came down, he said, 'Crane, you go back to your outfit—you can fly.'

"So Monday was the failure, Tuesday was the check ride, and Wednesday morning at 7:00 a.m., [0700 hours] we went to the flight office on the flight line, and Captain Barry said, 'What are you doing here?' I said, 'Apparently sir, the base commander thinks I can fly a B-17.' He said, 'He does, does he? Well, we'll see about that.' And he failed me again that day!

"The day after that, the base check pilot, whose job it was to check people, took me up. He passed me, and he said I had exceptional ability. I went back the day after that, which I think was a Friday.

"Friday, there was no Captain Barry there, it was a different man. Barry wasn't fit to be an instructor. He immediately lost the 50 percent flight pay that we got, and he was put in an office.

"The last day I was on the station, I found out where he was and made it my business to go over there. He said, 'What do you want, Jew boy?' I said, 'I want to thank you, sir.' And he said, 'Don't thank me for nothing—I didn't do anything for you.' I said, 'Yes, you did, you 'blank.' It was a case of you or me, and then it really wasn't a case at all.' He said, 'Get out of here, Jew boy.'

"The base commander took me up solely because of that interchange on the parade ground. I believe what the base commander's thought was, 'Crane was put on notice—he could've done a lot of things. He chose to fight.'"

Another training story was that of First Lieutenant Herbert Pearlman, who would become a B-17 pilot with the 379th Bombardment Group, 526th Squadron based at RAF Kimbolton Air Field, England:

"I had very little recognition [among my peers] of my having been Jewish. I had a friend named Ray P—[4] who was from Mississippi. He had been my roommate for quite a while, when we were in training. Ray and I were sitting on the floor of the ready room waiting for the weather to clear up. There was a lull in the conversation when I heard my good buddy say, 'and that dirty New York Jew.' I saw red. I jumped up and away from him dumping him on his back. I had my fists clenched and my face was flushed ... perplexed, he asked me what was wrong? I stuck my face up to his, as close as I could get, my nose was about even with his Adam's apple. I asked, 'Ray, do you know where I'm from?'

"He said, 'Sure, y'all from Noo Yawk!'

"Then I asked, 'Ray, do you know that I am Jewish?'

"He stepped back, his face paled, and his jaw dropped as he said something I could not hear. I ignored him completely for the next two weeks. One morning he blocked my way out of the [ready] room and said, 'I never met a Jew before in my life, to my knowledge. Back home there were stories about a Jew who lived in a shack in the woods near town, but I never saw him. My saying what I said was a natural cuss word that we all used back home without thinking. You got to admit you do the same thing in a way. I heard you say, 'G-d dammit,' but you did not really mean it. So I'll try to behave and let's be friends.' I saw the logic in what he said, and we shook hands, but we were never the best of friends as we were before."[5]

Sergeant Morris Spector was in the U.S. Army Air Corps in air traffic control and was part of the initial wave of occupying forces in a bombed-out, but still dangerous Germany.[6]

"I volunteered while I was still under-age, and yet I heard other guys who didn't join the Army Air Corps until Uncle Sam came and dragged them into the service, who would say things like, 'The Jews aren't in any dangerous places. They make sure that they get the cushy jobs. They make sure they're not going to be in danger.'

"I was down south in training and I went into this very small restaurant, wearing my Army uniform. There was a sign on the back wall that said, 'No Jews or dogs permitted.'

"So I said, 'You have many Jews in this town?' The guy behind the counter said, 'We ain't got no Jews in this here town.' And I said, 'Well, how would you know a Jew if one came in?' He said, 'I knows that because they's got horns in their head.' I said, 'I've seen lots of Jews, and they don't have horns on their head.' And he said, 'Well, that's because they had that operation—they called it a circumcision—they takes it off.' And I removed my cap from my head and I said, 'I'm Jewish. Where are my horns? Where are my scars?'

"Remember, I was only 16 or 17 or 18 at that time. I lied about my age to get in. I forged my birth certificate. I wanted to fly."

PFC Burt Mandel was assigned to the 6th Air Force, part of the Caribbean Defense Command.

"When we were in school we had a couple of Southern boys that were anti–Semitic, and we had a Jewish guy from the Bronx, New York who had a moustache, and I guess they held him down and shaved half of his moustache off one night. That was the first incident I had ever encountered with anti–Semitism.

"I was assigned to another outfit, when I was in Curacao, and I did have a guy who was anti–Semitic, and he was picking on another guy from New York City. I forget the Jewish guy's name, anyhow the guy was a little bit of a guy, and I think he was 5'1" or 5'2". And this other guy who came from Trenton, New Jersey, started to pick a fight with him one night, and I called him out on it, and I said, 'Why don't you pick on someone your own size you son-of-a-bitch?' I said, 'Let's get the hell out of here, and I'll take care of you outside!' I was not a tough kid, but just then, a Staff Sergeant walked into the barracks and the next day I found myself transferred. I had detached service to Aruba for six weeks. They wanted to get me out of the outfit for a while."

Sergeant Morris Spector (courtesy Morris E. Spector).

Several of the interviewees encountered the term "White Jew," which meant that though they were Jewish, they were somehow a different kind of Jew. Corporal Harold Isenstein was assigned as an armorer and gunner with the 15th Air Force, 455th Bomb Group, and 740th Squadron based in Cerignola, Italy.

"Shortly after I joined this outfit, I was coming into the mess hall, and I heard someone say something about 'Isenstein, another Jew bastard.' I stopped and said, 'What?' And he repeated it! Then the silence was deafening. After he repeated it, I slugged him. He got up and slugged me. Fortunately they separated us, because I'm only 5'6".

"But there was another time I was coming back with a friend of mine from the enlisted men's club. I was helping him walk because he was drunk, and he said to me, 'Ozzie, you're a White Jew, and I dropped him in a slit trench latrine.[7]

"What is a 'White Jew?' He was from Texas. He said that we weren't as bad as the African Americans, the blacks. To him, it was a compliment.

"There were also guys who would stick up for me. Yeah, when I had the fight in the mess hall, there was a big Swede, and he separated us, and he said something to the other guy; he said that I was with him, meaning that the guy would have to come through him to get to me. It was a nice gesture.

"During the war, the guy I fought with and I were overseas together for about two years. I found out he was from Philadelphia, and he was Italian, and as time wore on, we nodded to each other, but we never spoke, but we nodded at each other."

Staff Sergeant Robert (Bob) Lerner was a gunner on a B-26 medium bomber. He was assigned to the 9th Air Force, 386th Bomb Group that at first flew out of RAF Boxted, England and then RAF Great Dunmow, England.

"On my crew of six I was the only Jew, and there was one anti–Semite. He made a remark to me, and I should've got to him right then and there, but I didn't want to disrupt the crew. He said, 'You know how Jews are?' [Lerner made kissing sounds]. You know what that is? It's like kissing ass. He was a sergeant, just like I was—he was the flight engineer."

Many of the Jewish airmen who would become officers left college to enlist. By then, many of them had taken college level mathematics and physics. First Lieutenant James Ruttenberg was a navigator with the 15th Air Force. He flew with the 461st Bomb Group out of Cerignola, Italy.

"Like most kids in those days, I had dreams of being a flyer with the white silk scarf around my neck floating in the breeze, and a helmet and goggles. I was on my way downtown on the Chicago Rapid Transit to enlist in the Navy. I was reading the Chicago newspaper and I came across an article that said that the Army Air Force is opening enlistments that day. The scuttlebutt was that a Jewish fellow in the Navy had a couple strikes against him when he went in—that the Navy was not completely non-anti–Semitic.

"I would say that the number of Jews in the Army Air Corps that I came across was probably slightly higher than the percentage of Jews in the overall population of the country. Education was also something that was put into our veins by osmosis; I think the Jewish population was a little higher educated as a group than their peers. In fact, I found that in navigation school the percentage went up even more.

"I was called a 'Jew-boy' one time and got into a fight in basic training. I was somewhat of a hothead myself, and this guy just lit my fuse, and we ended up having to put on 16-ounce boxing gloves, which I'd never done in my life, and had regular three-minute boxing and one-minute rest periods by the time—we did that for two rounds—the third round, I could hardly lift my arms. So it ended up being something that just drizzled away. I ran into that all my life, but that was part of growing up for a Jewish boy."

Len Berman was a Petty Officer 3rd Class assigned to the aircraft carrier USS Wasp. He was a musician in the ship's jazz band, but as with everyone on ship, he had secondary duties as part of a gunnery crew when the ship was under attack.

Petty Officer 3rd Class Leonard S. Berman (courtesy Leonard S. Berman).

"The Navy band consisted of about 20 military band members, then we broke down into a jazz band of about 18 or something like that. Well, this guy who played the trumpet was always antagonizing me, calling me names and harassing me. My bunk was right above his, so he used to stick his legs up and push my body, call me names, and try to tease me because I was a Jew. I never really did anything—I told him to knock it off.

"Finally, one of my toughest buddies, who was also a trumpet player, said,

'Hey, I'll change bunks with you.' His name was Abe Schwartz, a very dear friend—he passed away many years ago, but he was a Brooklyn fellow. You know, those guys were tough. He agreed to swap bunks with me, so that I didn't have to have that ordeal when I was trying to sleep.

"When we landed—I think it was in Pearl Harbor, we were coming back from the war, on our way back to the states because our ship was damaged from the typhoon—we were both out on the dock, right near the ship. We [the anti–Semite and me] got into a fistfight because he started again. That time, I said, 'I'm not going to take this anymore.' So we started to box—you know, we were throwing fists at each other.

"I remember vividly, I smacked him one time. I got him just before the other sailors pulled us apart. But anyway, he didn't hurt me—I was fortunate—I got one good smack into him, and then the guys broke us up. From that point on, he never bothered me."

The USS Wasp was credited with shooting down the last *Kamikaze* of the war. The Japanese plane got through the carrier's anti-aircraft fire and many gunnery crews, including Berman's, defended against the attack. Berman said they nicked the plane's wing and it missed the carrier by 15 feet, crashing into the sea.

Albert Kleeman had the rank of ARM/2C while a radioman and gunner on a Navy PBM "Mariner," which was a medium-range patrol bomber. He was assigned to Squadron VPB 26 in the Pacific.

"One of the guys in the squadron had an anti–Semitic sort of thing, you know what I mean? The Navy was really not a Jewish outfit—I don't know if you knew that or not. It was probably the smallest amount of Jews in all the services. I don't think we were discouraged, but I kind of think that as I said, from my own experiences, and in all the bases I was stationed on, I never met many Jewish guys [in the Navy]."

Jack Latkin was a Navy pilot who would ultimately retire as a Lieutenant Commander. He also served in the Korean conflict.

"I always felt some anti–Semitism in the Navy, but it was just under the surface. Any place I went in the Navy, even as a cadet in pre-flight school they knew, or it came out somehow. They might say, 'Oh you're Jewish. I knew this Jewish kid in High School, but you're different.' They wouldn't say 'White Jew,' they just said you were different. I might have reacted a little different.

"When I first got to Pensacola, Florida, this was my final training station where I finally got my Navy wings. The first night I got there we went to the movies. We went to the movies a lot. I think they were a dime. Anyway, 'The Jolson Story' was the movie. When I came back from the movie, I was singing one of the songs, 'Oh How We Danced.' It was the first time I had ever heard the song. When I came back to the room, I met my roommate for the first time. He said, 'Oh you must have really liked the song.' I told him it was the first time I'd ever heard it. 'Oh,' he said, 'I thought you would know that song because you're Jewish.' Here this is the first night, a new room and a new barracks and he already knew I was Jewish!

"I also heard over the course of my time in the Navy that it was in the 'admiralties,' where the anti–Semitic feelings came from, more so than the level I was in. We all became really close at my level. They never kept me away from anything and I was never uninvited to anything.

Sol Schwartz was assigned to the USS Quincy as a radioman and gunner on an observation float plane (sea plane) called the "Kingfisher" or officially an OS2U. He held the rank of ARM/1C. Schwartz said there were about 18 Jews on the ship.[8]

"There was some anti–Semitism on the Quincy. The most serious event concerned one of the Jewish kids who in civilian life had been a member of local union 65, which was a plumbing and steam-fitting union. This kid was very tough. One evening some sailor was drunk and came over to this guy's bed, and called him a Jew bastard. He got out of bed, hit the drunk in the face and the drunk wound up in the hospital. The Jewish kid was transferred off the ship."

David H—was a Navy Petty Officer Second Class who served on a ship that went into service toward the end of the war. His primary duties were clerical while his secondary duties were to man an anti-aircraft station.

"Usually I was a Yeoman, typing out letters, reports, logs, and transfers. I took dictation and transcribed records. While on ship, I passed all the tests for Petty Officer Second class and I had served time in rank. So I asked the captain for a promotion to Petty Officer Second Class, for which I was qualified. The Captain was not well liked, and he never made anti–Semitic remarks directly toward me. However, shortly after I had asked him for a promotion, he was overheard saying on the bridge, 'No Jew will get a promotion on this ship.'"

The "Cheap Jews" Who Started the War— and Were Then Afraid to Fight

References to the "Cheap Jew" have always been puzzling to the Jewish people. The Jewish sacred texts prohibit usury and stress the requirement to perform acts of charity. Yet, the perception of Jews being cheap and Jews being unwilling to fight accompanied them into war.

Horace "Mickey" Baskin was a Technical Sergeant and radio operator and gunner with the 489th Bomb Group. He flew with the 8th Air Force out of RAF Halesworth, England on a B-24, "Liberator" bomber.

"My barracks had maybe 40 guys, and two or three were Jewish. There was a man in the barracks from Minnesota. Some anti–Semitic remark came up, and I asked him why? He said a Jewish man owned a shoe store in the small town that he lived in. One time the store owner refused to accept a return on a pair of shoes that didn't fit. That was it. I didn't ask if they were returned worn or not worn. He just said the Jewish shoe store refused to accept his shoes in return. It was kind of crazy. He was a pretty ignorant guy, I think."

First Lieutenant Robert "Bob" Simon was a navigator with the 8th Air Force, the 401st Bomb Group, and 613th Squadron. He flew out of RAF Deenethorpe in the Midlands:

"In our Bomb Group there was a First Lieutenant and pilot who always had an anti–Semitic attitude. In March to April 1945 there was Pesach [Passover]. There were [civilian] Jews not far from the base who invited Jewish servicemen to have Seder with them. We were officially given permission to attend. This pilot called me a slacker. My crew was delighted since it meant they were not on call for combat for two days."

First Lieutenant Robert H.M. Simon (sitting on wing, right) (courtesy Robert H.M. Simon).

First Lieutenant Maurice Ashkinaz was a bombardier with the 8th Air Force, the 448th Bomb Group that flew out of RAF Seething in Norfolk, England.

"After we'd fly about 20 missions, you had to go on rest and recuperation [R&R]. So we went on rest and recuperation in England to some castle.

"The four officers, the pilot, the copilot, the bombardier, and the navigator, stayed in one place. The enlisted men were in another place in the castle. So the four of us guys are sitting at breakfast one morning, and we're shooting the breeze and we're talking about the war.

"The copilot comes up with, 'All the Jews are financing the war. If the Jews weren't financing the war, we wouldn't be at war.' Now this is the guy that I'm flying with for like 20 missions, risking my life, and trying to protect his life. The pilot and the navigator said to him, 'Hey, what the hell you talking about? You don't even know what the hell you're goddamn talking about.' And he says to me, 'Oh, boy, well you're a White Jew.'

"I'm a good Jew—I guess that's what it means. So I turned around—you'll have to excuse some of my language—I turned around to him, and I said, 'You son-of-a-bitch. You should be wearing a Nazi uniform instead of what you're wearing. Don't you ever talk to me again! If you say one word to me from now on, I'll pull my gun and kill you.'

"The four of us bunked in the same Quonset hut. I said to him, 'When we're in the airplane, if you have something to say to me, if we're in the airplane that's okay. But when we're on the ground, if you say one word, I'm going to kill you.'"

Second Lieutenant Norman Smeerin was a B-24 pilot with the 15th Air Force, 450th Bomb Group. He flew out of southern Italy.

"Right after I got my commission, there were a couple of officers—second lieutenants—that made some remark one night in our barracks about the Jews causing the war. He was jumped on by many, many non-Jewish people—they really chewed him out—they bore down on him, which was very surprising to me, but that's what they did. They weren't [necessarily] defending me.

"See, my name wasn't particularly a Jewish name, and a lot of people didn't know that I was Jewish. Now there were some fellas that were there with Jewish names, and I don't know whether they had a worse time than I did.

"I was raised in this little town—[ours] was the only Jewish family there, I was the only Jewish boy in the town. And so I was brought up with non-Jews, but we never had an incident in 18 years in this little town—never. People loved my father—they thought he was next to God. It was wonderful.

There was about seven or eight churches in town, so everybody was very church-going. But they were always very—not solicitous, but they always respected the fact that we were Jewish. There never was any bad problems."

Fighter pilot, First Lieutenant George Lichter burned over the following incident:

"I was in a Jeep with four guys, three pilots and a driver. We were going to the flight line, and they were from another squadron. One of them held up a dollar bill for whatever reason and he said, 'A Jewish flag,' and I didn't call him on it. That's 60-some-odd years, and I'll never forget it. And I'm ashamed—why didn't I say anything? I'm ashamed of myself that I didn't."

Florence Elion Mascott was a member one of the last Women Airforce Service Pilots (WASP) classes to go into training. Unfortunately, her class was disbanded. She fell in love and married, and then left the service. She tells of her time in the program:

"In training, there was one girl who gave me a hard time. I don't know whether it's because she was 35, which was the oldest [allowed] to join the WASP. I was really the youngest one that was accepted. Anyhow, this girl just was not very nice to me. I was so naïve and lived such a sheltered life at home, that I didn't even know that she wasn't being nice to me…. I'm the only one [Jewish cadet in my class] that I know of. If I go through the roster now, some of the names sound Jewish, but I don't think they were. In the WASP, there wasn't any kind of background check in that way. They checked to see if we were good citizens, criminal records and all. But I had no problem getting in, and it was a known fact I was Jewish."

First Lieutenant Courtney Shanken was a B-24 navigator with the 15th Air Force, 450th Bombardment Group, and 722nd Bomb Squadron. The 450th flew on some of the most horrendous missions in Europe; many bomber crews were lost. To make 50 missions unscathed was a major accomplishment. Both Courtney and his twin brother Earl served in the Army Air Corps.

"I do recall one occasion where my brother Earl and I and [a] Jewish bombardier on my crew, Lou Siegel … and by the way we had a third Jew on our crew, our Ball Turret gunner was Harold Saperstein … went to the operations room to meet with the new squadron commander to help him put together the line-up for the formation. You have to understand that the three of us had already flown 50 combat missions in Italy.

"He [the commander] says, 'Who would be good for position number four? I'm new, help me pick out the best crew for number four.'

"I need to explain. The number four position in the formation had to be the best pilot. The pilot in the number four has to be the most experienced and best because he holds the formation together. Number two is to the left of the lead plane and number three is to the right of the lead plane. Usually number one and two had the most sophisticated radar and number one, of course, is the commander's plane. Number four puts its nose underneath the tail of the lead plane. He's got planes all around him. When the formation was under attack from German fighters the number four position was always subject to friendly fire. My bomber, named the *Patricia Ann*, was shot down by friendly fire. Flying in formation was extremely difficult. We could be wing-tip to wing-tip when we were under attack.

"So we mentioned a pilot by the name of K—, who was a very good pilot. The new commander said, 'K—sounds like a Jewish name. They haven't got any guts. I don't want him there.' The commander was stupid. He was an ignoramus."

Arthur Sherman had two job titles. He was a B-24 bombardier with the 464th Bombardment Group, 779th Bomb Squadron of the 15th Air Force up until his eleventh mission over Austria when he was injured by flak. Following his recuperation, he was re-assigned to headquarters in Bari, Italy. He would eventually become an intelligence officer with the 483rd Bombardment Group. He was the only Jewish officer in headquarters.

Over time, First Lieutenant Sherman struck a close working relationship and friendship with his commanding general. As the war was winding down, Sherman and his general were discussing the possibility of his making the military his career.

"I talked to Brigadier General Charles W. L—about staying in the service. He said, 'You've got three strikes against you. Number one, you don't drink [because I had a head wound]. Number two, you didn't go to West Point, and number three, you're Jewish.' He was only pointing out the problems I would face. He was good to his men."

First Lieutenant Stanley Newman, a pilot with the 10th Photo Reconnaissance Group would go on to have a successful career in the Air Force, and would serve in both the Korean Conflict and Vietnam War. He was also mentored by a superior officer.

"The squadron I was assigned to was a mixed bag. Most didn't seem to care one way or the other that I was Jewish. But there was a minority of them that obviously didn't like me and there was some of the snide variety of comments.

"My flight leader, on the other hand, warmly welcomed me and took me under his wing. Years later [after the war], I asked him about anti–Semitism in our unit. He stated that there were several anti–Semites who did their best to undercut me but he and several friends I had made defended me. Generally speaking, I don't think many of them would have sat shiva [the mourning period in Judaism] for me. Post WWII, I wasn't aware of anti–Semitism in the Air Force or Air National Guard. Quite to the contrary."

Jewish personnel, whether devout or atheist, could come face-to-face with negative perceptions no matter the degree to which they felt at ease in the military. Sergeant Marvin G. Freeman was a cryptographer assigned to the 8th Air Force, 385th Bomb Group that flew out of England at the RAF Great Ashfield. His mission was to convey top secret coded orders to the bomber group at command level.

"I'm kind of a light-skinned small-nosed Jew [chuckle]. I had blond hair and a light complexion. I've got to be careful. My father looked like a Negro in the summertime. My mother was very white, and I've got my mother's complexion.

"When I joined my outfit, we were sent to this airbase in England. I was in a headquarters group, and there were maybe 30 of us. There was one other

Jew, this fellow, G—, and myself. He was a little bit of a wise guy. I think there was more anti–Semitism against him than anybody else.

"There were occasions when a guy in our group said he just didn't like Jews. I never associated with the guy … one fellow was in a crap game or a poker game, and he lost a lot of money to a Jewish fellow on the base. I was out, probably playing table tennis or something—I came back to the barracks, and one of the guys came up to me and said, 'Marv, don't come in now. So-and-so is having an anti–Semitic tirade.' I don't think he said it that nicely. So I left and came back like an hour later."

First Lieutenant Stanley F.H. Newman (courtesy Stanley F.H. Newman).

Sergeant Edward Penzer was in communications with the 14th Air Force in the China Burma

India (CBI) Theater of Operations. While overseas, he was on detached service with the Royal Air Force. His anecdote reflects Freeman's comments:

"I was dumbfounded when they sent me to the RAF unit. Very diplomatically they asked me, 'Are you R.C. [Roman Catholic] or Church of England?' I told them I was neither. Then they asked me, 'What is your Christian name?' I didn't know what they were talking about! I told them my name was Edward. I chose not to identify myself as a Jew. I was in close quarters with four other men and I had a lot of expensive equipment to look after. I enjoyed them though."

Penzer recalled an incident from when he first reported to his duty station in New Delhi, India:

"Our head sergeant was either a Staff Sergeant or Master Sergeant who was an Irishman. He was smart enough to hide his anti–Semitism. I showed him a picture of my girlfriend at that time. She had blond hair and blue eyes, but she was Jewish. My sergeant said, 'She'll never marry you,' meaning that a woman who looked like that would never marry a Jew. I had blond hair and blue eyes myself and a straight nose. I later found out through a friend who was stationed in England that the girl had gotten engaged—and she didn't tell me!"

Sergeant Milton Fields was assigned to the little known Persian Gulf Command in World War II,[9] where he was assigned to Iran and Iraq. He was quite devout and in addition to his military duties he volunteered to help the Jewish Chaplain as a para-chaplain (lay leader).

"I avoided anti–Semitism in training by changing my name to Fields from Finkelstein in January of 1942 but I never denied my Judaism. When I was assigned to Iraq, there was a southern gentleman who in civilian life had been a representative from one of the school textbook companies. He was a major, and extremely prejudiced towards blacks and Jews and when I conducted organized services for the Jewish guys when we were in Basra, Iraq, I would have to go to him every week and ask permission for us to be excused. There were about 10 to 12 of us, and we would take a truck and drive into Basra, to the local synagogue, and we used their facilities to hold our services."

Fields explained that prior to a major Jewish holiday he asked the major, as usual, for permission to be excused to take the men to worship. The officer grunted his approval. When Fields returned, he was put up for court-martial as the major claimed Fields went AWOL. Fields was cleared of the charges and the major was transferred.

Bernice Falk Haydu was a WASP, Class 44–4 in Sweetwater, Texas. She was kind enough to send me the following recollection:

"I was always afraid there might be an incident [in training] … I encountered anti–Semitism before entering the WASP program. I graduated high school in 1938. The job market was extremely difficult. I would travel from East Orange where we lived by bus to Newark to get the Newark Evening News when it was first printed in the morning to examine the help wanted and pursue it quickly. It was not unusual to read, 'Jews need not apply.' Usually when you applied for a job in those days you were asked your religion. In my first job they did not ask but as I was working there I could hear remarks against the Jews. I was only 17 and frankly I did not know how to handle the situation so I would just keep quiet."

Second Lieutenant Norman Smeerin remembered an evaluation during training:

"As a Jew going into the service, and being in the service, we were sent to a classification center after we'd finished our preflight training and before we got any flight training. They classified you there as a navigator, bombardier, or pilot. If you were going to be a navigator or bombardier, they sent you to one school. If you were going to be a pilot, they sent you to flying school. So my preference was pilot—I didn't have a second or third preference.

"We were taking our final physical, and we were stripped down, no clothes on and they did all the things that they had do to give you a physical. Then they put you in a little room with a man at a card table and one steel chair. Now we had no clothes on, and we're sitting in this steel chair. This man at the table is a psychologist or a psychiatrist, and he's evaluating us.

"So he says, 'I see here that you want to be a pilot.' I said yes. He says, 'But you're Jewish.' I said yes. He said, 'Well, don't you know that Jews make better bombardiers and navigators—they don't make good pilots?' I challenged him, and I said, 'No, I didn't know that, and I think I'd be a very good pilot. That's really why I enlisted in the Air Force.' So anyway, I was lucky— he checked me through, and I got to go to pilot training.

"I'm commenting on this because most of the Jewish officers—there was only one other Jewish pilot in our squadron, and there were several Jewish navigators and bombardiers.

"They thought that Jews were good at numbers, they think that Jews are the merchants, Jews are the bankers, Jews are the number people and they also thought of Jews as being kind of klutzes I think."

Herbert Shanker, a Technical Sergeant, flight engineer/gunner with the 8th Air Force, 303rd Bomb Group, flew out of RAF Molesworth, England on a B-17.

"I think almost all the navigators in the 8th Air Force were Jewish. I guess they were good at arithmetic! Now that I look back, it seems like three out of four times, navigators were Jewish.[10] As far as anti–Semitism, some jerk made some remark about, 'The Jews are sitting home.' So he realizes I was there, or that I was Jewish. He was the usual disgruntled know-it-all. I was in training with 12 to 15 guys that did the whole first year of gunnery school and [Flight Engineer] school. About three or four of us were Jewish, the other eight or nine were whatever. But we had a wonderful group."

Gideon Lichtman was a fighter pilot who would not only serve in World War II, but went on to become one of the first pilots in the Israeli Air Force. In World War II, Lichtman flew the P-51 and was with the 3rd Air Commando Group stationed at Clark Field in the Philippines.

"My name is Gideon, and [because] I was Jewish [they] called me 'A.B.' for Abe, so you can go from there. I was always very well aware of the anti–Semitism while I was a cadet. I can give you an example. Each instructor had six cadets or students. And I had a guy who had an Irish name; I forgot his name, O'Malley or something. And he spent very little time instructing me on anything. We had to go through 20, 40, and 60-hour checks. After 20 hours, you went for a check, 40 hours, and so forth. If you didn't meet the requirements, you had to go through the 'Washing Machine,' they called it, which meant that if you didn't pass, you were washed out.

"Now my instructor, as I indicated—I was the first one to solo after I think about 12 hours of flight time, 11 or 12 hours—no, it was 8 hours of flight time. Then the other guy soloed, and you had to go through various maneuvers in order to be put up for soloing. Despite the fact that I wasn't taught certain things, there was a lot of conversation among the cadets themselves. I would hear them talk about what they did and how they did it and so forth, so I learned a lot from listening to them.

"They were learning how to do loops and rolls, Immelmans and Chandelles—the names of different maneuvers. I was learning nothing because my instructor didn't teach it to me, but I learned by talking. I didn't have the expertise that they had; for obvious reasons, the instructor didn't show me.

"So I was put into the washing machine. Luckily for me, you got a check by another instructor, and then another—all of whom were civilians, and then the final check before washout was by a Second Lieutenant who was a commissioned pilot. The commissioned officer took me up and told me to do a loop. I said, 'I never learned how to do a loop.' So he did a loop and said, 'Now you do it.' So I did it, and then he [did] the same with the other maneuvers…. So he got furious and brought me back to the squadron and chewed the instructor out, and I got another instructor, and I breezed through."

"Well, let me put it to you this way—I was the only Jew among the six. I'll put it to you better—there were a lot of Jews who were flying and didn't tell anybody they were Jewish. They had dog tags with 'P' on them for Protestant, because they knew the situation. They were a lot more hip to what was going on in society than I was at the time. They had absolutely no problems. I'm not saying this because I'm bitter, but this was a fact. I had an 'H' on my dog tag for 'Hebrew.'"

Looking back, Lichtman was convinced that there were a lot of qualified Jewish pilots that did not make it because they had H on their dog tags.

Lieutenant (JG) Lester Levitt was a Navy fighter pilot who would ultimately be assigned to the USS Yorktown where he flew the renowned F6F "Hellcat."

"When I finally finished my advanced training—now you know, this is months and months already I'm flying, and this was in Corpus Christi [Texas] in one of the outlying fields—[the instructor] was giving me a check for my last flight. He sits in the front, and I sat in the back. He keeps giving me stuff to do—a roll, a dive, a spin, whatever and I did everything beautifully, so I thought. He said, 'Okay, take it in.' I took it in, landed, and I got out of the plane and looked over at the instructor and I said, 'How was it?'

"He goes, 'Thumbs Down!' I said, 'What did I do?' He wouldn't talk to me. In the back of my mind, I thought it was something with the Jews, but it wasn't [obvious]. So I immediately went up to the commander, and I said, 'I just got a down,' and to me that meant they were going to kick me out of the Navy, and I wasn't going let that happen. So he [the commander] said, 'What happened?' I said, 'I had a good flight, and my instructor gave me a down.' He said, 'Meet me out on the flight line, and I'll take you up.' He immediately took me up, gave me the same flights, everything, and then we came down. I said, 'How did I do?' He said, 'You did perfect.' I said, 'What about the instructor's down?' He said, 'I'll take care of that.' I don't know what he did after that, but that's as close as I came to washing out of that place.

"There was not even another Jew in our group. I don't know if they knew I had an 'H' on my dog tags. But they don't look at your dog tags. He might've found out, I don't know. I never felt that somebody was persecuting me—never felt that at all. I just thought I was going out there and doing my job.

"I remember when we're at war, we're on the carrier, and all of us pilots are on the fantail [the rear] of the USS Yorktown. We're just shooting the breeze. We didn't have nothing to do. One kid starts talking about the Jews of Florida, you know, the Jewish population there. I finally interrupted him, and I said, 'Don't go there.' He said, 'Why not?' 'I'm Jewish.' 'Oh, but you're not like them.' You know, the good Jew."

Marvin Leventon was initially trained as an air cadet and then failed to make the transition to pilot. He would become a Technical Sergeant, radio operator/gunner with the 5th Air Force, 386th Bomb Group.

"My initial training was in Akron, Ohio. That was in the summer of 1942. In fact it's funny—we got ten hours of dual instruction in a Cub. After I finished up, my instructor says, 'You're Jewish aren't you?' and I said yeah. He said, 'Well, Jews usually don't make good pilots, but you're one of the others that I expect to hear big things from you one of these days in a P-51.' Now whether that was a compliment or not, I don't know. [Eventually] I went down in classification. They decided they had too many pilots. So I had some radio background and they made me a radio operator."

Arthur Toppston's story raises a more serious set of questions. Toppston was a Technical Sergeant with the 8th Air Force, 93rd Bomb Group that flew most of its missions out of RAF Hardwick-on-the-wash, England. He was a radio operator and gunner on a B-24 bomber.

"I got out of radio school, and then went on to gunnery school. We were assigned to a crew. I was the only Jewish fellow on the crew. Some people in the squadron were negative toward me, but most of my crew was OK. We had one guy who was anti–Semitic and an alcoholic, and nobody liked him. I'm sure the pilot wouldn't have had him if he could've gotten rid of him, but he couldn't.

"Anyway, when they extended our range, we were able to reach Germany, and I was in on one of the first two missions to Berlin. I felt exhilarated. I'm sure the other crewmembers did as well. I was the only Jew, and I was exhilarated to get back at the Germans.

"There was a guy in the command post of my squadron, the northeast post in France that used to keep me from getting commendations. He was definitely anti–Jewish, and he was a Master Sergeant. And he used to eliminate my name, so the rest of the crew went up for a commendation, he would eliminate my name."

Toppston complained to his pilot, who was a captain, about the withholding of commendations. The captain took up the fight, berated the Master Sergeant and possibly people above him. All of Toppston's commendations were restored including the Distinguished Flying Cross.

First Lieutenant Alfred Benjamin was a navigator with the 8th Air Force, 384th Bomb Group. His airbase was RAF Grafton Underwood near to Kettering, England.

"On active duty, I would hear remarks like 'Jew them down,' things like that—things that bothered me, but were not enough to cause any trouble. I had four battle stars, a Purple Heart, air medal with four oak leaf clusters. I would have had a Distinguished Flying Cross, but I ran into a little problem with discrimination about that.

"My commander who took over my squadron was really anti–Semitic.

My pilot said, 'You know, we got this nice smart Jewish boy who's my navigator, and I want him to be your navigator [on lead missions].' This commander says, 'Well, I'll use him, but I really don't like Jews.' He [the commander] was the one who had to recommend me [for commendations].

"You know, I did eight lead missions, and if you did lead missions, you certainly earned the Distinguished Flying Cross, because that's the way it is. I mean in the beginning everybody got a Distinguished Flying Cross. In the end, I didn't get one, and I've been a little P.O.'d about that, but I let it go by. At this point in time, it doesn't really matter much."

It is not possible to calculate how many commendations were arbitrarily withheld from the more than one-half million Jews who served in the military during the Second World War.

Payback

Samuel Nilva initially volunteered for flight training as a cadet. He would eventually end up as a criminal investigator for the Military Police.

"There was another Jewish fellow from New York [in with me]. This anti–Semitic guy … I think his name was 'P' but it doesn't make any difference. Anyway, this guy kept calling my friend 'Ikey.'[11] So I said to P—one day, 'You know, why don't we have a nice little talk, you and I? We can go to mess a little bit later.' He said, 'Sure, what do you want to talk about?' I said, 'I want you to call me Ikey.' He says, 'Why?' I says, 'So I can break your nose.' 'What do you mean?' he says. 'Because if I hear you say that [to my friend] one more time, I'm going to get a dishonorable discharge because I'm going to break every bone in your body.' That was the end of it."

First Lieutenant George Lichter flew P-47s and P-51s out of RAF Station Little Walden near Essex, England.

"The motor pool met at a spot in Cambridge [England] to go to back to the base every night at 10:30 or 11:00. The trucks would leave for different bases.
"I had a few to drink, but I wasn't drunk—and I was an officer. There are three guys waiting for a bus, and they are very loud, and it's 'the Jew bastards,' 'those kikes, they made this war,' and 'fucking Jews.' So I go over to them, and I say, 'Look, you're very loud, and I don't like the language you used—I want you to shut up.' They said, 'It's a free country—we can talk all we want.'
"I didn't know what to do. I'm an officer—they're enlisted men—three

guys. They said, 'We'll talk all we want, and we'll say anything we want to say.' I said, 'Let me have your dog tags.' The middle guy makes an obscene gesture, and the other guys do the same thing. He says, 'If you think you're man enough to take us, come and get us.'

"I was smoking, I took the cigarette, flicked it out. I went *boom*—I'm left-handed—and I smashed him in the face as hard as I could. I was strong then and there was an iron picket fence at least six feet high—it was taller than us. I dove on him and started beating the shit out of him. The other guys didn't jump me—whether they were scared or what, I don't know.

"I finally got pulled off, and there was a colonel, a major and a captain that came over. There was a crowd by this time. One of the guys from my squadron gave me my hat, and when I put it on, I felt the pain because I had crashed into the picket fence and didn't even feel it—didn't even know it until I touched my head.

"The colonel was doing the talking. He says, 'What happened? Do you know what you just did is a court martial offense, lieutenant?' I said, 'They were cursing, they were using foul language, and most of it was anti–Jewish and anti–Semitic, and I'm a Jew. I wouldn't take that from anyone. I asked for their dog tags, and they said 'Come and get them if you think you're man enough,' so I went to get them.' The colonel says, 'Let me handle this.'

"I'm talking there must have been 50 to 100 people watching this fight. He goes over to the men and says, 'The lieutenant doesn't want to press any charges, so let's break it up now.' Everybody started to walk away, and he ended it very nicely. I wish I knew who he was. The colonel was from another base and I didn't know him, but he really took care of me because it was a terrible offense for an officer, but I reacted as a Jew, absolutely as a Jew. I mean I was in pain."

Sol Shafner was a Staff Sergeant and crew chief in the 20th Air Force, 346th Bomb Group.

"I enlisted with a Jewish kid, Benny D—. He was a radio operator on B-24s. I had one guy in my outfit that was an anti–Semite, and we had a fistfight about it. He was always mocking the Jewish people, and we fought a couple rounds, and that was the end of it. I think my First Sergeant was a Jewish guy. He used to give me fits—I hated that son of a bitch!"

Captain and P-47 fighter pilot Harold Steinberg was with the 9th Air Force, 365th Fighter Group. The following happened after a very tough mission around D–Day.

"I once had an incident in which I had a deal with this anti–Semite. He said something like do you know who is [responsible for the war].... I pulled a loaded automatic on that son of a bitch, too. They grabbed me, and that was the end of that fight you know. I never bothered him again, and he never bothered me. I told him, 'You asshole, if you're ever in trouble, and I know it's you, you're liable to have a problem with having support from me.' He was a P-47 pilot in our squadron, one of the original 36 guys. But like I said, he bought the apple [was killed in combat]."

Corporal Dick Bosley was a truck driver assigned to Tinian Island in the Pacific. He tells a funny story, especially from a Jewish perspective.

"When I graduated truck-driving school from Camp Lee, Virginia, I was put in charge of five guys who were all from Kentucky and Tennessee. They were real hillbillies and anti–Semitic. Before we shipped out and we were still in the states, the five of them got syphilis and they circumcised them! Well these guys were all of 21 years old. Do you know how that hurt them? They were lying in their beds for weeks. Eventually I got them to like me. Some of the guys I kept in touch with after the war."

First Lieutenant Irvin Harris was a pilot with the 8th Air Force, 302nd Troop Carrier Squadron (C-47).

"I didn't make an issue of my religion. Nobody made an issue of their religion as far as I can recall. Nobody went around saying, 'I'm Catholic,' 'I'm Protestant' or 'I'm Jewish.' There was a certain amount of clinging and seeking out people of your own ilk, but it was only a rare occasion that a conflict would arise.

"I had an opportunity during the war to take an R&R. I was stationed in France at the time, and the R&R was to take place in the City of Cannes, the Côte d'Azur. My R&R buddy was another guy from the squadron who I knew to be somewhat anti–Semitic. I never raised the issue with him.

"But when we got to Cannes, and we were sharing a room together, I brought the subject up that I thought it was unique that he, of all people, would be assigned to the same room with me. And of course, he wanted to know why—he was curious about why I felt that way. So I told him that it was no secret that you had anti–Semitic feelings.

"He says, 'Why, are you a Jew?' I said, 'I certainly am.' So then he became very apologetic. And he had, you know, good things now to say about Jews, that he knew a Jew so-and-so, he knew one Jew here and one Jew there. These are not the kind of remarks that would give him credentials or that would absolve him of any of his anti–Semitic feelings.

"Once we separated and went our own way, I'm sure that I didn't set him straight or cured any of his anti–Semitic feelings. I'm sure that they were much too deep for me to have to give him a course on equality of religions and all of his aches and pains will come eventually someday, as I expect they will. Somewhere along the line, he will learn that he has done wrong, and that he made people regret that they ever met him.'"

First Lieutenant Leonard Luck was a navigator with the 9th Air Force, 15th Troop Carrier Group.

"When I was in navigation school, we had barracks, and each barracks was divided into three units, and each unit had three cadets living in them and the guy who slept next to me didn't talk to me. I say to him one day, 'What's the deal? You don't talk to me?' He said, 'I don't talk to Jewish people.' Well, by the time I got through with him, I became his best buddy. He was shot down and killed, and his mother used to send us Christmas cards every year. We became best friends. He had never known a Jew before in his life. He probably thought I had horns or something, I don't know. He was a nice guy and I straightened him out, that's all.

"We used to have regular reunions … and for some reason they wanted me to make the prayer over the meal and at the reunion and I did [it] in Hebrew! Another guy who had joined our outfit later, a guy named Jacobsen was sitting at my table. I made the blessing or something and this other guy from the group says, 'What kind of language is that?' And Jacobsen says, 'It's Jewish!' And the guy says, 'I didn't know there were any Jews here,' and Jacobsen says, 'There were two of them!'"

George Lichter, the fighter pilot who had gotten into a fistfight at the depot, told a very different kind of story from his last days of training when he invited two of his buddies to his home for Thanksgiving.

"One of my closest friends was from Felts Mills, a little town in upstate New York. His name was Vernon R –. We were buddies, we palled around, we drank together, and we got in fights together.

"We're having dinner, and it was before Thanksgiving, November of 1943. My parents had a big turkey on the table, and they had all sorts of delicious food, and bread of course. He's looking for something and I said, 'What are you looking for?' He says, 'Where's the butter?' I said, 'We don't have butter with our meals, we're Jewish, and there are dietary laws.' I didn't care about it and, my parents didn't, but my grandmother was living with us by then. He didn't say anything.

"When we got overseas, we had to sign a paper that said every pilot volunteered to fight against all the enemies of the United States. So we get overseas, and Leo S—[an army intelligence officer who was Jewish] comes to me one day, and he says, 'Lieutenant, I know you're friendly with Vernon R—. I want to ask you a question in real confidence. May I?' I said, 'Of course.' He said, 'All you pilots agreed to fight against all the enemies of the United States and so on.' I said, 'Yes.' He says, 'Well, Vernon R—signed that, and he agreed to fly against all the enemies of the United States,' and then in his own hand-writing he wrote, 'Except the Jews.'

"I'm so sorry he's dead now—that I never confronted him and never asked him. I couldn't because it was in confidence. It's obvious to me that he had never met a Jew in his life, and he was told Jews are rotten—he was brought up that way. Now he realizes that I'm a pilot, my parents are lovely and generous and are feeding him and giving him food to take back. There was a lovely table, and my grandmother was there, and my parents were lovely people. So he decided the Jews weren't so bad—that he's not going to fight against the Jews, who he was taught were enemies of the United States."

Second Lieutenant Paul Kaufman was an officer on a B-17 bomber and was with the 388th Bombardment Group, 560th Bomb Squadron. Kaufman's bomber, *The Millie-K*, got shot down over Merseburg, Germany in July 1944. He bailed out and was quickly captured and imprisoned in a POW camp.

On his homecoming, Kaufman's family had arranged to meet him at the pier, but due to fog the ship was delayed in the harbor. His father, as was true of many other fathers, could not afford to take another day off.

"We finally arrived at Pier 60. Nobody was there to meet us. There was a man handing out flyers to select people. One of my buddies got a flyer and I asked to see it. It said something like: 'So and so died in Europe, Colin Kelly died in Guadalcanal, etc. … and Nathan Goldstein, the son-of-a-bitch got four brand new tires.'[12] I said to myself, will it ever end?"

•• 3 ••

The Stars on My Wings— Europe

If the flak was bad you took a zigzag course. If the flak exploded near you, you had bad luck.

—First Lieutenant Bob Simon

D–Day

June 6, 1944, D–Day, was not the first major battle of the Second World War nor would it be the last. However, D–Day sent a clear signal to the Axis that they could not win, and we would not let them. It was perhaps the most pivotal period of the war in Europe—and arguably the most brutal.

There would be other beach landings and many diversionary air missions during that period from early to mid–June. All would be dangerous. Less than a year following D–Day, Hitler and many of his high ranking officers were dead and his war machinery was dismantled. We start this chapter with D–Day and the accounts of the Jewish airmen who were there.

Fighter pilot and Captain Harold Steinberg flew the P–47 fighter with the 9th Air Force, 365th Fighter Group.

"We flew the first mission to Omaha Beach on D–Day. When we took off, it was still just barely starting to be daybreak—it wasn't dawn yet. We got into France to destroy whatever we could see. When we were coming out you could get an inkling of the immensity of the operation. It seemed like you could almost walk on the water from one ship to another. I mean the immensity of that operation absolutely boggled our minds. You could see what the ground troops were doing. You couldn't see too much progress at the time and there were a lot of casualties.

"We flew directly over the beach to make sure that there weren't going to be any Nazi aircraft coming back to fly over and to strafe the troops. That wasn't going to happen and it didn't happen, as a matter of fact. We did our job. There were so many of us.

"The only incident that I was aware of was when the German fighters got into what we called the 'Lufberry.' The Lufberry is a maneuver where they formed a circle of planes to protect each other. There was this one German fighter plane, a Messerschmitt Bf-109, and he got into a line of our P-47s, and he shot down one of our guys, a guy by the name of R—. I was above the Bf-109 and I dove down to get a lot of airspeed, and I came back up. I shot and hit him, and he just rolled over, and down he went. But you didn't see many enemy aircraft there—I mean we were overwhelming, and squadrons and squadrons were patrolling.

"We were armed with eight-50 caliber machine guns. I remember that four of us were flying, and we saw a tanker truck. So we came in from four different directions. This driver, he took off, and led it straight down the road, and as the driver took a turn, the other fighter hit him with all eights ... we backed him up into a building where he blew up.

"We were 19 or 20 years old. We were fearless. What we feel now that we're older certainly isn't what we felt then. There was intensity to what we were doing. I mean you're talking about life and death."

First Lieutenant George Lichter, like Harold Steinberg, was also an 8th Air Force fighter pilot but with the 361st Fighter Group.

"We switched from P-47s to the P-51 about a month before the invasion, and we only had about three to three and one-half hours of orientation in a P-51 before we went into combat.[1] They painted invasion stripes on it, a month or two before the invasion [D–Day].

"We didn't know when the invasion would take place, but you know, the night before the invasion [June 5th, 1944], we were briefed and we went out to our planes. We were sitting in our cockpits, ready to take off at 1:00 a.m. in the morning, and I guess they gave us a take-off around 2:00 a.m.

First Lieutenant George Lichter in a P-47 (courtesy George Lichter).

Then at first light, we were up with our lights on, and they ordered us, 'If you run into [spot] other aircraft, turn your lights off.' I mean the whole thing was so stupid, it seemed to me, because we were flying in the dark in the middle of the night, but what could we do? They wanted us in the air, I guess, to prevent us from being bombed by the Germans while we were on the ground, or them attacking us in the air when they saw the invasion coming.

"In the morning, of course at first light, we went down and looked for what they called 'targets of opportunity.' Anything that moved was a target of opportunity, and particularly trucks and cars or trains.

"We loved going after trains, especially those going towards the coast. We did strafing; we didn't do dive-bombing because we didn't have bombs. We were using just the guns. We'd shoot up trains; we'd shoot up truck convoys, anything heading towards the front. We loved to hit a locomotive and see that steam come shooting up.

"But we had trouble with some of them. We strafed one train, and it was an ammunition train, and it exploded. One of the guys [P-51 pilot] flew through it and it knocked him out. We didn't see him get hit because there was so much smoke. The explosion probably went up 1,500 feet in the air, and we didn't see him. He bailed out, and became a prisoner of war. I met him after the war—that's how I knew—otherwise I didn't know he was alive."

Staff Sergeant Homer Goodman was a gunner on a B-17 Bomber with the 8th Air Force, 100th Bombardment Group, nicknamed "The Bloody 100th."

"We named our plane *Hell in Heaven*. The nose art was a devil in the clouds. Our first bombing run was on June 6, 1944, D–Day. The Germans had bunkers up there, with thick cement walls and they were shooting down on the Americans. We bombed the hell out of them. Our bombs were thousand-pound bombs.[2] When they would hit, they'd make a hole 20 feet or 30 feet deep.... There's holes all over in Normandy, and the French never covered them up—they made a park there, and you can walk through and see where all the holes are from the bombs. Our group bombed the whole coast, all the way—the whole coast of France."

Obviously, an invasion of the size and ambition of D–Day included all kinds of crews performing numerous duties. Leonard Luck was a navigator on a C-47 troop transport.[3] He was a First Lieutenant and flew with the 9th Air Force, 15th Troop Carrier Group.

"On D–Day we were going in early and we had 21 airplanes [in our group] which went in, and we were there six hours before D–Day. Our purpose was to drop pathfinder paratroopers who were trained to get on the ground and set up drop zones and mark them with color. They had radio beacons so that, theoretically, we would have three drop zones for the 101st Division, three drop zones for the 82nd Division, and then the main columns of paratroopers would come in, and they would hone in on these Pathfinder paratroopers who were already on the ground. This sounded real good in theory, but unfortunately, the weather got bad and the thing got screwed up some. But anyway, in the long run it worked out.

"We had no armament and no gunner. If we would have picked up flak in our gas tanks, that would have been the end of us. On D–Day, we did not encounter enemy fighter planes, but when we went in over the Channel Islands, all hell broke loose from flak.[4] They didn't hit us.

"Our lead plane lost an engine due to the flak. We were flying off his right wing, and he couldn't keep his altitude because he had 18 men on-board and only one engine. So he signaled that he was leaving the formation and we went in to the drop-zone. We went in and just dropped our troops. I ran into one of the paratroopers who was in our airplane at a reunion. He said we put them right on the drop zone, which was fortunate, because this 'Gee' thing [a special radio signal] that we had, we were supposed to be able to drop within 50 yards of the target, well, the Germans blocked the signal. When we crossed the channel, we had no signal … but I had gotten a couple of fixes, so that I was able to dead reckon in … well, he felt that we put him on the money. I don't know whether we did, but it was close enough."

In order for D–Day and the subsequent offensive to be successful, it was necessary for there to be many diversionary actions to confuse German intelligence both before and after the event. It was a strategy needed to spread their defense.

Technical Sergeant Norman Zalkin was a radio operator and gunner on a B-17 Bomber. He was with the 15th Air Force, 99th Bombardment Group and on D–Day their group was charged with going after targets in northern Italy. At the same time, First Lieutenant and navigator Nat Bailen, a Jewish kid from Kentucky, also with the 15th Air Force, but with the 455th Bombardment Group, flying the B-24, was going after German submarine positions in France.

First Lieutenant Courtney Shanken served with the 15th Air Force, 450th Bombardment Group, and 722nd Bombardment Squadron (B-24). He was involved in diversionary activities weeks prior to June 6, 1944.

"I recently received the French Legion of Honor, France's highest military award, for missions we flew two weeks prior to D–Day.[5] Our squadron was assigned the job of wiping out railroad centers at Marseilles, the submarine repair facilities at Toulon and the railroad center in Nice. By the time of D–Day itself, I had already finished my missions on May 27, 1944.

"Eisenhower in his memoirs states that there was a dual purpose for the diversionary flights. First, we wanted the Germans to think maybe that the invasion would come from the south. Second, we wanted to stop the ability of the Germans to re-supply to the north."

The battle for Saint-Lô, soon after D–Day in Normandy and close to the beaches, is a reminder that we cannot reduce war to video games. First Lieutenant Robert Cohn was a B-17 pilot who flew with the 8th Air Force, 452nd Bombardment Group.

"D–Day was June 6, 1944 and I started flying missions on June the 8 or 9. We then went after Saint-Lô.[6] We had 1,500 bombers [along with fighter planes] trying to bomb a one-mile-square area in order that the Allied troops could break through. Well, we killed more Americans on that mission than anything else.[7] We dropped bombs off the target. Troops were in a place that the bombardier didn't know they were, I guess. Well, this we didn't find out about until much later, much later being defined as a month or so. After Saint-Lô, we went after all kinds of industrial plants in France and Germany."

Technical Sergeant Herbert Shanker was a flight engineer aboard a B-17 bomber named *The 8 Ball*. He was assigned to the 303rd Bombardment Group. They flew out of RAF Molesworth, England. The bomber was active on D–Day around the area of Caen, France in support of the invasion. Caen was relatively close to the Normandy beachhead. The 303rd would also be involved with operations around Saint-Lô area through July 24, 1944, when there was a major Allied breakthrough.

It is important to point out that the June 6, 1944, invasion was not an isolated event in terms of liberating France. There was a second D–Day that occurred on August 15, 1944, with numerous diversionary missions.

Navy Radioman, ARM/1C Sol Schwartz, was assigned to an OS2U Kingfisher seaplane that was catapulted from the deck of the USS Quincy.

"We flew at about 100 to 120 miles per hour. Due to our slow speed [too slow for a beach invasion] we did not participate in activities on D–Day. Instead, we were assigned to fly out of a British seaplane base in Gulfport, England. We flew diversionary missions that day to confuse the Germans.

"Our job was to go ahead of the fleet or from our ship and look for submarines or other dangerous situations and at times to direct artillery fire on German targets. In Porquerolles Bay, in the South of France, we directed bombardments from August 15 to August 25. We helped capture a fort on August 18, 1944, on Port Cros Island which held a German garrison, by directing fire from the Quincy. We were also involved in directing fire on August 15 in the capture of the French seaside town of Hyères."

Staff Sergeant Leon Waldman was with the 15th Air Force, 483rd Bombardment Group, and 840th Bombardment Squadron (B-17).

"On my 49th mission, it was D–Day for southern France which was August 15, 1944. We bombed the beaches at St. Tropez. Three divisions came up from Italy into southern France."

While bombing St. Tropez sounds incongruous to our 21st Century ears, more than 200,000 troops landed on St. Tropez and though the action was lighter than on Omaha Beach, more than 3,000 Allied troops died in that invasion.

Gravel from Hell

In the comfort of his living room former Staff Sergeant Homer Goodman presented a jagged piece of black iron in a clear plastic case. He removed it from the case and let me touch it. It was approximately one inch by two and one-half inches. He then showed me a dented Zippo cigarette lighter. It sounds like parody, but Goodman's cigarette lighter, perfectly positioned in his pocket, stopped the piece of metal from killing him.

Flak was a splendid, albeit evil technology. An artillery shell packed with metal was fired from an artillery gun and then, at a pre-determined altitude, the shell would explode. The hot metal chunks cut through anything. Though fighter plane attacks carry somewhat romantic imagery, it was flak that did the greater damage.

"That thing was white-hot when it came through the ball turret of the ship," said Goodman. "My cousin gave me a lighter before I went overseas, and I used to carry it in my watch pocket. This piece of shrapnel stuck in that lighter. It would have tore my whole gut out.

"On our second mission, our left waist gunner, an Irish kid by the name of Tom S—, a real nice kid, had a 22-millimeter shell come through the ship and hit him in the leg and it blew up. It tore his leg right off. We had no place to put a tourniquet on him—just right here [the groin], you know. We put a parachute on him. We were going to throw him out and we thought maybe the Germans would help him—we couldn't do nothing for him—he was bleeding like crazy. We were just ready to throw him out, and we looked down there, and his blood froze because the cabin was so cold [the airmen wore insulated suits and felt slippers].

"You never could come back for one guy, so we went the whole mission, dropped our bombs, came back at the same altitude, made a quick descent, and there was an ambulance waiting for him. He was good for about five or six years, but he passed away from complications from that thing. That was only our second mission and I thought, 'Oh, shit, what am I getting into here?'"

Those who were in combat described the sound of flak striking an aircraft as gravel hitting a metal roof. Those who could hear those bits of metal brushing the fuselage were those who lived to talk about it.

First Lieutenant and pilot Herbert Pearlman flew a B-17 with the 379th Bombardment Group. He talked about how his crew, like many others, would wear good luck amulets of all sorts. While making a bomb run, Pearlman said that the bombers would have to spend several minutes flying straight and level from the initial point (IP) to the targets despite flak and fighter planes. It was a terrifying prospect because the German gunners displayed incredible accuracy, given the technology of the day.

Pearlman talked of a particularly rough mission where he felt something strike the insole of his left boot. His leg went numb and his foot became hot. It was not until after landing that he discovered a piece of flak that had pierced his boot and gently rested against his sock. Others were not so lucky.

Staff Sergeant Bernard Witt was with the 8th Air Force, 487th Bombardment Group, and 839th Bombardment Squadron as a B-24 ball turret

Staff Sergeant Witt (standing, second from left) and his flight crew (courtesy Sylvia Witt and Linda Howard).

gunner. Witt sent me a copy of "The Lucky Bastard Club," a certificate that was well known in the 8th Air Force. It was an unofficial document that congratulated the airmen on the completion of their missions.[8] For Witt, it was 34 missions. In some ways, the document was more valued than the ribbons and various medals he had earned. It meant the hell was over.

What was it like to be a "Lucky Bastard"? Witt provided the diary of his co-pilot that contains a few hints.[9] The first entry, May 24, 1944, was a target near Paris, and the second was written during the D–Day invasion period.

"Raid #3. After several days layoff on account of weather we finally got it going again. Our target was an airport just south of Paris. Bomb load 12–500 lb. G.P. [general purpose bombs]. Gas load 23,500 pounds. Alt. [Altimeter] 22,000 feet. We were in the lead squadron…. The flak was very heavy but very inaccurate. The lead bombardier missed the target so we flew on to our secondary target which was another airfield named POIX. We finally dropped our bombs after dodgeing [sic] about ten other groups. The results were good.

"We were turning away from the target when we were hit by flak which entered behind the left blister window in the nose compartment narrowly missing Ted W—, continued up through the instrument panel knocking out the airspeed indicator and several lines including the altimeter. George S— [the pilot], was standing between Ted and my seat. The flak passed between the three of us taking some skin off Ted's face on the way and finally coming to rest above the radio desk. Believe me that was the closest any of us ever came to seeing St. Peter. Don't see how it got by me and especially by George standing between the seats…."

June 7, 1944

"Raid #8. Raid #8 was on June 7 [D–Day +1] and was to knock out a roundhouse and marshalling yards at Chateabriant [sic] in Southern France. The Germans are using this railroad to bring up their [supplies] to the front. The mission was at 12,000 feet. The weather was bad with an under cast over the continent. The channel was clear and I saw more boats of different types than I've ever seen in my life. We [flew] around over the target about an hour before dropping our bombs. I'm afraid the results were not so good. Coming back we got into some heavy flak [all we saw all day] and [a bomber] who was flying on our wing got knocked down. Only 2 chutes are reported to have been seen from the burning and spinning aircraft. We got an 8 inch flak hole in the leading edge of the wing between the fuselage and No. 3 engine. Pretty close!"

First Lieutenant and 8th Air Force navigator Bob Simon stated:

"If the flak was bad you took a zigzag course. If the flak exploded near you, you had bad luck … after our first mission to Berlin, I looked down at the floor where my desk was. I saw a spent piece of flak near my foot. It made a hole in the skin of the plane and landed there. I picked it up and have it to this day."

Staff Sergeant Morton Israel was a gunner on a B-17. He was with the 8th Air Force (another "Lucky Bastard") and the 446th Bombardment Group.

"We were over Neunkirchen rail yard in Germany, November 30, 1944.[10] The plane beside us—and you flew very close like 25 feet apart for safety— the plane beside us blew up. That day I was in the waist gun. The plane blew up, and there was complete silence. We got splattered by debris and so forth, and we thought everybody on that plane was killed. I mean we didn't see any parachutes or anything go up—it just blew up. When we came down, we were all interviewed, and we talked very little about this.

"Our crew was very close. We just sort of kept it quiet. About 20 years later at a convention, Captain C—[the pilot of the plane that exploded] showed up, and he had become a preacher. He doesn't know how he survived. This crew had 11—the other 10 got killed instantly—they never found a piece of bone even. He remembers waking up in a field, and he was captured, and after the war he came back.

"The flak might have hit the bomb bay. It affected everybody on my crew more than anything else. My co-pilot started to sort of crack up or whatever—I remember my pilot saying to the co-pilot, 'Shut up, Norm.' And after that, everything was quiet. I mean when you see this happen, it's a different kind of feeling."

As the stories of these bomber crews are recounted, it is important to understand that World War II bombing missions could be flown with hundreds of bombers from several different squadrons or even bombardment groups. The formations were very tight and strictly controlled. Aircraft literally flew within *feet* of one another. To "freelance," to arbitrarily dodge flak, would have been calamity.

Gideon Lichtman, a P-51 fighter pilot, put the mission of the bomber pilot into perspective:

"I admire bomber pilots because they take off, they head on a [compass] reading, get into a certain altitude, maybe 15,000 feet, and they fly straight and level. Anti-aircraft comes up and shoots half of them down, and they keep going back for more until they got their 28 or 30 missions. You know, it requires huge balls to do that, knowing that half of you are going to get killed."

However, being a fighter pilot, Lichtman displayed the feistiness common to every fighter pilot the world over.

"A fighter pilot, on the other hand, is all over the skies going straight up, straight down, rolling, looping, and doing all kinds of things, so you can avoid all that kind of stuff. But despite that, there were guys who became fighter pilots who used to shit in their pants every time they got ready to fly a mission!"

Second Lieutenant Norman Smeerin was a B-24 pilot with the 15th Air Force, 450th Bombardment Group, based around Cerignola, Italy. They went after transportation centers such as railroad yards and bridges. Their missions could be as long as 10 hours to targets as far as Linz and Vienna, Austria.

"By the time I got over there and started flying, it was January of 1945 and the Germans had lost air control. We also had air cover from P-51s. They would pick us up as soon as we got into enemy territory, they would fly cover for us until we got to the target. But over the target they would leave us because of flak. There was no reason for them to stick around. No enemy plane was going to come after us over the target area because the area was covered with anti-aircraft fire.

"I unfortunately saw several wingmen go down from flak. When we flew over the target, the whole idea was to get a close concentration of our bombs. So if we were going for a marshaling yard, and they had 12 rows of train rails in it, we wanted to hit all those rails. So we would close up the formation to where we were practically wing-over-wing....

"We had a lot of holes from [anti-aircraft] artillery, and one time we lost our hydraulic system. The closest I came to being injured was when a piece of shrapnel about the thickness of your thumb and about three inches long came in the window on the pilot side, broke the window, and dropped down behind the pilot's head—it was that close to hitting him."

Second Lieutenant Norman Smeerin (courtesy Jaynie Smeerin and Laurie Kabb).

As with Smeerin, First Lieutenant and B-24 navigator

James Ruttenberg was part of a crew that frequently went after targets in Austria. He was with the 15th Air Force, 461st Bombardment Group.

"We were on an all-out mission to Wiener Neustadt, Austria, which is like Gary is to Chicago; it was all steel mills and factories. When we got there, the weather was quite overcast, and in those days our radar couldn't penetrate that stuff well enough to do bombings. So our squadron rallied off to some secondary targets that were in Zagreb in Yugoslavia. There were some train yards, where there wasn't supposed to be much flak. Our intelligence got that one wrong because it was so thick we could almost get out and walk on it. Our plane got shot up pretty badly. We lost most of one of the tails and we also lost an engine.

"My pilot asked me for a heading to the nearest airbase that we could get to across the Adriatic. And I gave him a heading from Yugoslavia to the Tuskegee Airbase, which was our farthest north airfield at the time.[11] We went across the Adriatic with three engines, and then lost our second engine when we were almost all the way across. The Tuskegee Airmen picked us up and flew cover for us, because a single bomber flying by itself, especially a wounded one, was a real easy target for enemy fighters.[12]

"When we went onto our bomb runs, we would generally don flak suits hoping that, if some flak did come through into the airplane, this would protect our vital parts. They were heavier than hell and with all the other crap you were wearing, when you put that on, you just about weren't able to keep your knees from buckling, but we used them. In fact, if you could get a hold of some extra ones, you'd take them on the flight with you and put them on the floor and stand on them so that you'd have something protecting you from the bottom-up.

"The amazing thing was that we were four or five miles in the air, and the German gunners were on the ground with a cannon pointing up at us. Their equipment was so good that they were able to pinpoint our altitude, our speed, and put those shells right up there with us. The bomb run was where we were the most vulnerable. Because you started at an initial point and had to fly straight and level so that the bombardier could set the bombsight. During that time, when we were flying absolutely straight and level at one altitude, we were the most vulnerable. We lost many more planes to flak than we did to fighters."

As with many other airmen, Technical Sergeant Murray Codman who flew with the 8th AF, 447th Bomb Group, and 710th Squadron had his superstitious rituals. He never cut his hair and always got reprimanded by his pilot for looking less than military. He was also "responsible" for naming his plane. Codman got drunk one night, found a can of paint and wrote *Big Shorty* on the nose. The pilot yelled at him over that one, too, but the name stuck.

Codman made it through 35 missions and he also became a member of "The Lucky Bastard Club."

"There was one other Jewish fellow on my crew. He was a radioman and he was killed. Three of my guys went down on their first mission. Of my original crew who went over only three of us came back. Our bomber was never shot down, but we were shot up. We had a new plane but we only flew half our missions [in that plane]. One mission we stopped counting the bullet holes at 150.

"The closest I ever came to being hit was when flak hit a metal box right next to me ... on one mission one of my crew took flak in the leg and they had to amputate. My co-pilot had a piece of flak knock into his officer's bars and he never put on his bars again. Flak was pure luck."

Paratroopers and glider planes were usually the first on the ground in advance of a major battle. The troops had to be ready for combat the minute they jumped, or in the case of gliders, when they were released from the aircraft. Though the "transport equation," the actual trip to the drop zones, is often overlooked, it called for flight crews to exhibit tremendous courage under fire. The crew was forced to dodge flak, enemy fighter planes and be wary of the physical dangers of the drop zone.

The following account was shared by First Lieutenant Irvin Harris who was a C-47 pilot with the 8th Air Force, 302nd Troop Carrier Squadron:

"Glider landings were almost always a very dangerous operation, because there were hedge rows, there were trees, there were unknown objects on the ground that the gliders would encounter, not to mention the German troops that were down there waiting for them.[13]

"Ground fire was routine. What made it all the more hazardous—we couldn't drop the gliders from a height any higher than 700 feet over the ground, because it would take the gliders that much longer to get to the ground, which would then again give the Germans that much longer time to shoot at them. And so 700 feet was what we stuck with, and the troopers would bail out at that altitude or lower, and the gliders would disengage from us at that altitude or lower.

"But the gliders had to have as much as they could possibly get from us in order to find a likeable landing zone. Never having been to that area before, they had to quickly survey the area, get their eyes on a spot, and hopefully not have to change that plan. [They had to] get the nose of that glider up, and drive the jeep out, get the troops out, and start functioning according to their battle plan."

If there was a flak expert among all of the veterans I interviewed, it would surely be First Lieutenant Herbert Kaster, who was an aircraft armament officer assigned to the 8th Air Force, 303rd Bombardment Group. He helped set up a B-17 sheet metal repair shop to fix the bombers that hobbled into base from flak damage.

"You have to remember that planes came back from missions shot up, and they had many problems. And one of them was that the hydraulic lines had been shot out of the landing gear so that you couldn't operate the landing gear.

"We had an old RAF base and we had grass areas where planes could land, rather than on these concrete runways. In most cases they successfully crash landed the planes, but they demolished the bottom of the plane because the ball turret was just torn out all the way back across the B-17.

"And yeah, I've seen B-17s come in with the gunner trapped in the ball turret with a faulty landing gear, and they couldn't get him out of the ball turret, and the plane crashed with the guy in the ball turret and he got killed. He was ground up in it—there was nothing you could do.

"But you know they tried. The plane would land, and the door would open, and the ambulances would rush up. And meanwhile there's guys, wounded men, trapped in the plane, and they had to come out. I saw where a pilot would be killed [by flak], and the copilot is flying. The navigator might become wounded and the bombardier would take over and so forth—all kinds of stories."

First Lieutenant Maurice Ashkinaz was a bombardier with the 8th Air Force, 448th Bombardment Group.

"One of the missions, we were flying deputy lead—deputy lead means we were flying to the right of the lead airplane and slightly below him. As we were flying into the target, naturally there were all kinds of anti-aircraft fire and so forth, and about a minute before bombs-away, this lead ship got hit in the bomb bays by anti-aircraft and blew up. When you see anti-aircraft fire in the movies from World War II, with all the black smoke and everything else, that's like eating pancakes. The black smoke doesn't hurt you—it's when it blows up and fire comes out of it. That was one of the things I can remember quite vividly.

"There was a superstition that you flew 18 missions with God in the airplane. Don't ask me why it was 18 missions[14] … but that was the superstition. After the 18 missions, you fly alone, because God is too busy with the new guys coming in, so He can't fly with you anymore. Let me say this—I flew— I don't remember exactly, but I think I flew about 15 missions without washing my underwear.

"All the things that we went through in combat, all of these things build up. It was all part of the war—that's the only thing I can explain to you. We never discussed anything—nobody discussed a thing."

Bad Dreams at 20,000, 10,000 Feet and on the Ground

B-17 gunner Staff Sergeant Homer Goodman's crew was credited with "knocking down" several enemy aircraft.

"Our fighter planes used to give us escort as the bombers went into Germany. But they could only go so far because of the amount of gas they carried; they had to turn around and go back to their bases and leave us out in the open. Then it was up to the gunners when the Germans attacked you to shoot them down.

"Let me tell you something—I was no killer to begin with. Here's this guy is coming at me. I see blinking and he was shooting at me. I'm thinking the guy in that plane is a human being, you know? Probably somebody's kid, maybe a father, maybe he had a family, maybe—then I'm going to kill the son-of-a-bitch. But I'd rather it be him than me. Well, while you're shooting at him, you'd think about it all the time.

"After I got out of the service, for two or three years, I would sit bolt-up in the middle of the night in bed thinking about this. My wife would say, 'Calm down, it's a bad dream.'"

Staff Sergeant Yale Feingold was a gunner assigned to the 8th Air Force, 95th Bombardment Group. He flew out of RAF Horham, England on a B-17. Feingold echoed Goodman's sentiments that one does not forget combat.

"I shot down one airplane, and was credited and got an award and everything for it. But I can still see it, to this day, as I just think of it right now talking to you, I can see the airplane that I shot at, and it blew up. I know I killed one man in the war, I know that. I can still see that airplane as it came toward me, and it came up from under the belly, and I just open-fired on it, and I got it in my sights, and I just held the triggers, and the plane just blew up, disintegrated."

Feingold talked of the incredible amount of luck it took just to survive. His luck would run out as his bomber was shot down over Germany. He would be taken prisoner on his 25th mission but he lived to tell his story.

"Most all of our missions were pretty far into German territory ... we flew on the first bombing mission to Berlin. We were very lucky. None of us were ever injured and none of us were hurt in any way. We flew the 24 missions without a scratch. We all survived the war—we were a lucky crew. The missions were bad, but we were fortunate and we survived.

"But yeah, there was a lot of sadness. You got up early in the morning, and you were awakened at maybe 2:00 a.m. or 3:00 a.m. You had an early breakfast, and you started the mission at maybe 6:00 a.m. or 7:00 a.m. You said goodbye to people in the barracks you were flying with, and when you came back, they were gone—they were just empty beds.

"I lost some friends. I witnessed some of their planes actually being shot out of the sky, many of them. It was horrible. I can still see them. I was fortunate—or unfortunate—I don't know what you want to call it."

Second Lieutenant and navigator Jack Sorkin, flew with the 8th Air Force, 92nd Bombardment Group.

"One day we lost three airplanes, just as they were getting off the ground on a bombing mission. I remember Jack P—as one of the pilots who went down. He was Jewish. One of the pilots, for some reason, didn't gain altitude and crashed into the woods at the end of the runway. The second plane saw that first plane go down, turned around, and taxied back while the third plane was on the takeoff; those two collided, so there was a loss of three airplanes. I think there were only three survivors out of the 30 total crewmembers.

"I wasn't scheduled for a mission that day, but I remember being in bed—it was early in the morning of course—and almost being blown out of bed by the explosions."

Technical Sergeant Horace "Mickey" Baskin flew on a B-24 Liberator, from RAF Halesworth, England. Baskin was a radio operator and a gunner with the 8th Air Force, 489th Bombardment Group.

"Our bomber's name was *Linda Lee*, because in our first month of training in Tucson, our pilot's wife had a baby girl named Linda and the second month in training, the bombardier's wife had a son named Lee. So we named our aircraft *Linda Lee*. The artwork on the plane, showed a baby straddling a bomb.

"I flew 32 missions ... my first mission was May 30, 1944. My last mission was September 11, 1944. That's strange isn't it, September 11th?

"The end of July 1944, we were supposed to bomb an aircraft component factory in Kempton, Germany, a suburb of Munich. However, the target was overcast, so we hit the secondary target, which was Munich, and on the way back, through a navigational error we flew over Frankfurt, where we lost five planes from our squadron.[15] We lost one engine on our bomber and our hydraulic fluid was half shot out. When we came to land, we discovered that we had a flat tire when we let our gear down.

"My pilot, Boyd M –, made a beautiful landing, put it down on the right wheel, let the nose down, and then eased the left wheel down very slowly, and we rolled to a halt without having to use our brakes.

"The Rostock mission wasn't too good either. When we bombed Rostock, we lost an engine and dropped out of formation—we couldn't keep up

Technical Sergeant Horace "Mickey" Baskin (seated, front center) (courtesy Horace "Mickey" Baskin).

with formation. Fortunately, [on] the way back was over water. A P-51 picked us up and said, 'I'll take you home as far as I can go.' He took us back practically all the way to England. He said, 'If you run into any clouds, fly through them.'

"I feared enemy aircraft more than flak. Although I found out later, after the war was over—I didn't realize it—that we lost more aircraft to flak than we did enemy fighters. Yet every time I was in a mission where there were fighters, I saw more planes go down from fighter planes. It was just, you know, maybe timing. Oh, gosh, we used to count parachutes when guys were bailing out of damaged bombers—we really did.

"We had ten men in our crew. I and the navigator are the only ones still alive. Really a day doesn't go by when I don't think of the guys I served with. We got together over the years, you know, when we were 60 years old and at 70 years old, we got together and we had reunions. I still think of them every day, and I still see them [in their] youth. A combat crew, a bomber crew of ten men—they're family—they're more than family."

Technical Sergeant Norman Zalkin and his crew would learn that there was nothing but luck that separated the living from the dead. Though moments such as he describes are not flashy in the same sense as his missions to bomb the oilfields in Ploesti, every airman came to realize that being safe in a combat zone was a relative concept.

"April 4, 1944, was a mission that stands out, and I'm turning to the page of my diary and looking at it. On that day, we started to fly a mission, and taxied to go to the runway. The bombardier accidentally hit the emergency switch, and all the bombs dropped on the ground ... we didn't hear the bombs drop, but the next thing I knew was I saw the pilot and the co-pilot running from the plane. The tail gunner who was in the radio room with me—we opened the door to the bomb bay, and all the bombs were on the ground. That was amazing, because I'm still here. I said many prayers after that one. We could have been killed or something like that, they didn't go off."

Lee Levitan was with the 9th Air Force, 387th Bomb Group and 557th Bomb Squadron. He was part of a B-26 crew and was known as a Gee-Box Navigator. Under normal circumstances, the B-26 carried six crewmen, but they could carry as many as eight if they were the lead flight.

On one mission, December 23, 1944, in support of ground troops trapped at the Bastogne, they were jumped on by 20 to 30 German Bf-109s and FW-190s. They lost six bombers in the air and another 10 crash landed.

But the mission that will never erase itself from his memory was on Valentine's Day, 1945. The squadron was sent to Koblenz to destroy the Crown Prince Wilhelm Bridge. The "brass" had assured them it would be a milk run with little anti-aircraft, no fighters and no opposition.

The reality was that the Germans had placed 88mm anti-aircraft batteries of three guns each around the target; there were 94 such positions. As was true with most bombing runs, when the squadron approached the IP, the initial point of the bomb run, it was the bombardier who steered the bomber, not the pilot. The plane had no choice but to fly steady and with no evasive action for 12 to 15 minutes. Time took on a different dimension.

"With flak, when you see a gray or black puff you're still OK," said Levitan. "When you can see the explosion, the red flash, it's really close, then when you hear it explode you know you're in trouble. On that day, the Germans really poured it on. I looked over at the plane next to us; flak hit them and I saw the pilot and co-pilot slump forward.

"I was at my navigator's table with charts in front of me. There was a pencil sitting on the table. It rolled off and I bent down to pick it up and flak blasted through the fuselage where my head had been. Had I not bent down, I would not be talking to you today.

"We counted 109 holes in the fuselage when the mission was over. I lost six of my good friends on that mission. I was a youngster then, but I won't lie, I was scared. It was luck not to be hit or shot.

"I had a little thing I used to do. There was a Johnny Mercer song called: *Accentuate the Positive*. I sang it during those missions. It kind of gave me courage. Also you were busy doing your job. It takes your mind away from the danger at that moment. I felt bad for the guys on the ground in the Bas-togne at the Bulge in their foxholes. But in the air, there's no place to hide."

Captain Harold Steinberg, the fighter pilot who described his D–Day experiences above, shared the following memory in regard to close calls:

"One time while on a mission, I heard a bang. I knew I was hit by flak, or it felt like it was flak. So I called my wingman over [we were in formation] and I said, 'Wayne, get under the airplane, look around, I can't see any damage on top. Go under and see what the hell happened. I got hit with something.' He goes under, he looks around, and he says, 'Hershe,' he says, 'There's noth-ing wrong—I can't see a goddamn thing.'

"So I thought OK, well, we'll fly back. So we flew back. We parked the planes. I was going out on a mission for the next day. The ground crew went to hang bombs on my plane, 500-pound bombs. They couldn't get the bomb to hang up in there—it couldn't lock. They looked in there, and there was a round, an incendiary shell, that had lodged into the root of the wing. It was right near the gas tanks and all it did was burn, but it didn't do anything, so I was very fortunate. It was very fortunate all the way around. I was very, very, very lucky, very, very fortunate. There were guys who only flew one mission and never came back."

Staff Sergeant Sidney Stein would quickly learn about humility and to appreciate the skills of his crew in combat. He was with the 8th Air Force, 93rd Bombardment Group. The 93rd was active during the Battle of the Bulge.

"We were all bachelors on the plane, and the pilot's name was Byron, so we named the plane *Byron's Bachelors*. I don't think we had any kind of tattoo or picture on the plane itself.

"The worst mission was when the bombardier got hit. He got the Purple Heart for that mission. The B-24 had four engines and we had two of them knocked out, and we had to drop out of formation, which meant you were very vulnerable to enemy fighters. The pilot who I thought was probably the greatest pilot in the Air Force, and I guess all crewmembers thought their pilots were the greatest, but our pilot got on the intercom and says, 'Nobody jump, nobody leave this plane until I tell you to go. If I tell you to get out, get out, because I'm going to beat you to the exit—I'm [chuckle] diving out of this darn thing.'

"Fortunately, we didn't have to ever parachute out of the plane. We came in with two engines gone, full of flak, full of holes, full of wounded men aboard. He landed the damn thing, not at our home base, but at I guess a base closer to the channel that a lot of the planes that were wounded and beat up made landings at. I was scared, I'll tell you the truth. After the first mission, you lose your cockiness, I guarantee you."

Isadore "Iz" Kozatch remembered his crew as young kids at war, and not as the invincible heroes of The Greatest Generation. Kozatch, a Technical Sergeant and flight engineer with the 15th Air Force, 485th Bombardment Group, related the story of an airman who packaged himself as a hero after the war, and who ultimately rode this notoriety to a lofty position.

"One time we had hysterics on the airplane. We were flying over Vienna, and it was very rough as the planes were blowing up all around us from flak. We dropped about 1,000 feet [from the concussions of the flak], and our bombardier starts hollering, 'Captain, flak on the left, flak on the right, turn back, turn back!' And the captain says, 'Shut up, you son-of-a-bitch!' The bombardier's a second lieutenant. He couldn't do anything right and after the war he became a newspaper editor and was famous and won the Pulitzer prize, but he wasn't worth a crap on the airplane."

Mr. Kozatch explained that one occasion he saved the life of the same bombardier though it was hardly "medal stuff." The bombardier decided to perform some tasks around the plane at 30,000 feet without an oxygen tank. This was against policy. Kozatch found the officer in an unconscious state and revived him by sharing oxygen from his own tank. Kozatch shared:

"I saw airplanes blow up, spin out of control and people bailing out. We used to write reports on how many guys bailed out, what was the number of the airplane, how did it blow up, and all that. But we were never hit—it's all providence.

"Our plane didn't have a nickname. We were a replacement crew, so they gave you all the old crappy airplanes. We never had all that bull crap with the names—a lot of it was BS![16] We just wanted to get to the mission, get over it, get our 50 missions, and then get home—that was the big push.

"One of my friends was a Jewish guy about 180 pounds or so that worked in the office at the base. He used to drink my whiskey—we used to get issued 2 or 3 ounces of whiskey when we came down from a mission. The medics would be out at the end of the runway and pour you two or three ounces of whiskey, and some of the guys would drink it. Well, I don't drink. So underneath the table where the guys were sitting, there'd always be empty bottles. I'd take an empty bottle and a funnel and pour my shot in, then I would take it back to my tent to my friend. If he didn't get a letter from his wife, he'd drown his sorrows. Oh, that was a fun deal!"

Staff Sergeant Leon Waldman was the right waist gunner on a B-17. He was assigned to the 15th Air Force, 483rd Bombardment Group, 840th Squadron.

On July 18th, 1944, the 483rd was scheduled to go on a mission to an airfield near Memmingen, Germany. The bombardment group was given the task of wiping out the runways and airdrome. Reconnaissance had spotted enemy fighter aircraft on the runways and it was essential that the Allied bombers maintain air supremacy in the region. The mission had been described as easy, the kind of operation on which many of the desk-bound officers at headquarters clamored to fly in order to give them credit for a combat mission.

"Memmingen, Germany is about 60 miles west-southwest of Munich. It was a little airfield and everyone thought it was going to be a milk run. The group took off from Sterparone Airfield [Italy] then proceeded up the Adriatic and we headed over the Alps.

"On this mission, the 332nd Fighter Group [the Red Tails; the Tuskegee Airmen] was assigned to escort us. We were over the Po valley above Venice, when the 332nd saw German fighter planes and they took off after them.

"The weather turned terrible, and the rest of the bomb wing went off in different directions to bomb secondary targets or to turn back home. We were the lead group and we proceeded by ourselves with no escort. There had been a recall to return to base, which was a radio signal. The other groups turned back. However, the signal was never verified [as being authentic]. We proceeded to the target with no escort.

"I was the right waist gunner on my plane. I had a limited, 90-degree view, not like the ball turret or tail gunners who had a full view. I looked out over the right wing and I saw what I thought was a dark cloud and then it looked like a flock of locusts or birds. I soon realized they were German fighter planes, more planes than I had ever seen.

"The fighter planes swung around and began to attack our rear squadrons and they knocked them out. I remember that our executive officer, a lieutenant colonel who by our standards was elderly, decided to fly on one of bombers as a tail gunner. He was killed. There were planes and bodies that littered the ground below. I only had poor chances to shoot, because I could only get off short bursts.

"On that mission our group lost 14 of 26 planes. I was lucky as I was off the right wing of the lead plane. The remaining 12 remaining planes were saved by P-38s that showed up."

The bombers of the 483rd fought valiantly; some of the crews were firing at the German attackers while they were in the process of crashing and knew they could not survive.

According to the website of the 483rd Bombardment Group:

"…143 officers and [enlisted] men paid with their lives … yet the damage to the enemy morally and physically in losing 101 fighter aircraft destroyed or damaged, a sizeable portion of their already hard-pressed Air Force, is irreparable.... Rarely, if ever, in this war has an air attack been carried out against such overwhelming odds, estimated at 17 to 1 [enemy to Allied aircraft] ... individual gunners shot down three and four enemy planes...."[17]

Much of what the airmen had experienced in war would be reserved for an inner circle. It was why crews would often be in touch for 60 years or more. We might imagine a Memmingen mission, but we cannot touch the sights, sounds, the smells and emotions. The bomb group gatherings had meaning and purpose, bordering on the reverent.

Nat Bailen's crew flew some of the toughest bombing missions in Europe, including the bombing of the Ploesti oilfields in Romania on August 1, 1943. The run was from an altitude of 500 feet—about the height of a mid-sized Manhattan building.

Flight engineers such as Isadore Kozatch, Frederick Bartfeld, or Sol Shafner always impressed me with their knowledge of the most precise details of their bombers. Kozatch made it clear that a World War II heavy bomber had no business trying to bomb from a height of 500 feet. The results of the Ploesti mission, labeled "Operation Tidal Wave," were catastrophic.

"The first low level bombing run on the Ploesti oilfields was the worst thing that ever happened to the Air Force," said Kozatch. "They were coming in at 500 feet. They were going into each other. It was the worst planned deal ... they were blowing up. They didn't figure out what the flak would be like. And they lost probably half the people, and planes were going down all over the place. Then they decided they can't do that anymore, and they started high level bombing where you were flying 20,000 feet to 23,000 feet."

Bailen's calculations remarkably reflect the statement of Kozatch that at least 50 percent of the bombers on that mission were destroyed; 10 bombers from Bailen's group *alone* were lost, no fewer than 100 airmen from his group were killed.[18]

Bailen's B-24 Bomber, named *The Pin-down Girl*, complete with racy nose-art, flew to the right of the lead plane; had they been to the left, they would have been gone. Not only were there losses due to flak and enemy fighter aircraft, but the skies were so thick with smoke from burning oil that at an altitude of 500 feet, there was virtually no way for the bombers to escape their own carnage. The bombers crashed into each other, into factory smoke-stacks and buildings and unavoidably, the ground.

Like so many other aircrew who flew in the skies over Europe, Bailen said:

"We ended up flying 47 missions instead of 50. They let us go before 50. We lost so many planes from our group that's why we left there early. We lost a lot.

"When we first started out in Cerignola, Italy each squadron had 21 airplanes and there were four squadrons. Well, I'll tell you this, after two years we were lucky to have two squadrons left—that's the story. But we were grateful for them letting us go early, we were scared to death, you know, that we would get killed on one of the last three missions.

"The day we flew to Ploesti on that bombing run, we got hit with flak, but we were able to land the airplane where we were based. After we landed, we pulled over to where we parked our plane. We all got out of the airplane and we were just sitting there [in shock] on the ground.

"All of a sudden there was a truck that pulled up to us, and it's our boss, our commander. And he said, 'Fellas, you're going to go home now.' Well, we sat there and we cried like babies."

Bailen snuck into the Army Air Corps when he was barely older than a boy. He was a teenager when he left Italy to go back to the States for another duty station. He had used his navigational skills to help his crew stay alive during combat and they, in turn, would help him grow into manhood.

Unintended Heroes

Staff Sergeant Allen Sabol was a tail gunner on a B-24 Bomber. He was with the 8th Air Force, 492nd Bombardment Group. Sabol's quiet, humble and spiritual personality was always so impressive to me, perhaps due to his gratitude for simply being alive.

"[On this mission] we got hit pretty early on. I think one engine was out almost right away, and then another and I could see this black smoke coming back from the tail gun section where I was at. I knew we were in trouble—I could feel it."

As Sabol was scrambling to abandon the bomber, someone hollered over the intercom that he'd been hit.

"So when I got out of my position in the tail, and got into the waist gun area, Ted T—was sitting down, leaning up against the side of the ship with a pretty big wound on his thigh. He had lost a lot of blood and flesh from shrapnel. The other gunner had just walked away and left him there! I'm looking for an oxygen tank and a first-aid kit. Finally I found a tank and put him on oxygen then I gave him two curettes of morphine and put some powder over the wounds, bandaged them up as best I could.

"The flak hit our gas lines, and gasoline was pouring inside the ship. The pilot was beside himself because a little spark would've turned us into an inferno. I helped Ted into the back of the ship. He had passed out by then.

We opened the bottom hatch. I helped get him [on a static line]. There was a problem when we opened up that hatch. We were over water, and we signaled back we couldn't jump then, you know. Shortly after that, we made land. That's when I got Ted out.[19]

"I hung on to the plane with my right hand jumping out, and I got caught in the slipstream. It tore all the skin off my hand, and I lost use of my right hand. I'll tell you something—God told me what to do. He says open up that little patch right in front and pull out that pilot 'chute, and that's exactly what I did. There was a very famous fighter pilot who wrote a book called 'God is my Copilot.' If I'm going to write a book, it's going to say, 'God is my Pilot.' He's not the copilot, He's the pilot."

It was one thing to experience combat in a fighter plane or in a bomber, but quite another to be a liaison pilot in a canvas covered Cessna with a top speed of 65 miles per hour. Captain Robert Teitelbaum was with the 5th Army, 985th Battalion. His mission was to spot enemy positions and then to direct artillery fire to the target while dodging ground fire. He carried out this assignment in both the Second World War and the Korean conflict.[20]

"I reported to the front near to a small town north of Florence, Italy [early December 1944]. Harley H—[a superior officer] took me up on a first flight to show me around, and we were flying above the Mountains at about 10,000 feet. I looked down, and there was another spotter plane below.... I looked down again, and I saw what looked like somebody shaking a pepper shaker over the plane below and then all of a sudden Harley was flying (wildly) all over the sky. I said, 'Will you settle down a little bit? I want to see what's going on down there!' He said, 'Never mind, take

Staff Sergeant Allen Sabol in training (courtesy Allen Sabol).

a look at your tail.' I turned around and saw these German 88s [artillery] bursts behind us, and he's trying to avoid them. Fortunately he did. I started flying combat missions the very next day.... I flew well over 70 combat missions.

"We were about 10,000 feet in altitude most of the time, because we were flying above the mountains. The German 88s were shooting at us a lot of the times. I never flew in a straight line more than a few seconds at a time. I was always changing altitude and direction. The only time I settled down for a few seconds was when we had directed an artillery shell to a target and we observed the shell was on its way and communicated with the battery. Normally the shell would take maybe 10 to 15 to 20 seconds to get to the target area.

"So about a few seconds before it's supposed to hit the target area, I'd level off and fly in a straight line so that the observer and I can both look out at about a 45-degree angle and pick up the burst. As soon as we picked it up, he would note it, and if it was short, long, the right or left or whatever. I immediately changed course and started my evasive maneuvers again. This was going on all the time.

"Our airspeed was about 65 or 70 miles per hour. We were high enough, so that we were not in range of rifle fire. However, we were in the range of artillery, anti-aircraft guns and possibly larger things such as maybe 40 millimeters, 20 millimeters, etc. We tried to avoid them, which we did, fortunately—at least I did—but not everybody did. I flew mainly in Italy and the war ended when I was in Austria.

"Once I lost three feet off of one wing. I lost my landing gear twice. I lost the propellers twice. I had patches on top of patches. I've landed on ski jumps, I landed in a rice paddy, I landed in elephant grass, and one time in a potato patch.

"When I was flying, I saw quite a bit of the

Captain Robert J. Teitelbaum (courtesy Robert J. Teitelbaum).

devastation down below and I created some of it myself. All I wanted to do was annihilate as many of the enemy as possible, and if they had a Swastika, even more so."

Alvin Sherman's Final Run

First Lieutenant Alvin Sherman was a B-17 pilot with the 8th Air Force, 96th Bomb Group and 337th Squadron stationed in Snetterton Heath, England. As New Year's Eve 1944 was approaching, his crew would make their final bombing run and then they would get shipped home.

"We had a lot of rough missions, but oddly our last mission might have been our worst. Typically, the last mission was supposed to be the easiest for the crew. This was our 35th mission. We thought it was going to be an easy run, a milk run, over an easy target and in fact our bomber had a couple guns that were out, including the top turret.

"It was New Year's Eve, 1944. At 0300 or 0400 hours in the morning, the target was changed. We were going to Hamburg, to bomb the Blom and Vos

First Lieutenant Alvin Sherman (2nd from right) and crew fitting through hole shot out by flak (courtesy Alvin Sherman).

Shipyards. Hamburg was always a rough run. We were supposed to initially have fighter cover, but our bomb group was 32 minutes late in joining the main formation and so our fighter escorts never joined up with us.

"Over the target, we were hit by severe flak from German 88 mm anti-aircraft guns and it blew a huge hole in our right horizontal stabilizer. This made controlling the plane extremely difficult. We had to drop out of formation and then we were attacked by German Bf-109 fighter planes. At this point, between the flak and the fighter planes, four of my crew got severely wounded.

"One of the 20 mm shells from the German fighter plane canons exploded in the nose compartment and it started a huge fire. It wiped out the oxygen system and the nose [chin] turret. The bombardier was ready to bail out. I grabbed him and stopped him. As the fire raged throughout the nose of the plane, my navigator single-handedly fought the blaze to save the B-17.

"At the same time, the tail gunner and the ball turret gunner opened fire on the fighter planes. The tracers from their guns held the fighters at bay. The gunners didn't know the nose of the aircraft was engulfed in fire. They didn't confirm that they downed any enemy aircraft, but both gunners reported the fighters were spewing heavy black smoke.

"The only thing that saved us from more German fighter plane attacks is that a P-51 fighter passed us coming back from a mission and we fired a flare at it to show we were in trouble. It came to aid us and this finally chased away the German fighters.

"My plane, called *Ole Skatterflak*, became very difficult to fly. As we approached the North Sea, flying back to England, it took both me and my co-pilot using all our strength to keep the aircraft in a level position because the tail damage wanted to make the plane climb. We would go up a few hundred feet then down a few hundred feet. The question was if we could gain enough altitude to make it over the cliffs of England.

"Luckily we made it to the English coast and we came upon an English field, Woodbridge Air Base that had an extended runway. The plane was so damaged it never flew again. There was euphoria once it was all over, but I never saw the injured crewmembers again. They were rushed to a hospital. My knees were sore for many days afterward from trying to hold the wheel.

"On that last mission everyone on the crew was put in for the Distinguished Flying Cross [DFC]. My tail gunner, Jesse Reese, did not receive his DFC. Years later, I helped him put in for it and he finally received the commendation in 2014. Our navigator, the guy who fought the fire received the Silver Star. He decided to stay in the Air Force and made it to Colonel."

Sherman added:

"Not long before this mission, we went on a long bombing run into Berlin. My radio operator told me to tune into one of the channels. It was

Sophie Tucker singing, 'My Yiddishe Mama.' Imagine hearing that on a bombing run to Berlin!"

Revenge Over Europe

The accounts we have heard reflect the experiences of men and women in combat or the support of combat. On the surface, the stories could be the observations of the air war by men and women of most any nationality, race or religion. In one sense, that is a good thing; acts of courage and compassion were everywhere. These stories can stand as representative of the thousands of other stories that have now fallen to silence.

Nevertheless, Jews entering the armed forces perceived a much greater sense of urgency to destroy Hitler's machinery than did the population at large. Christians, Muslims or even atheists were not being made into scapegoats and exterminated by the Nazis, Jews were. Though some of the veterans claimed they didn't encounter anti–Semitism while in the military, they were aware of what Hitler was doing even if it was only a general feeling that things weren't going well for European Jewry. To quote navigator Nat Bailen:

"I had a university scholarship before I even went to the Air Force. The University of Louisville offered me a free deal because they wanted me to play football for them. I just didn't want to do it—I wanted to go into the service. You know what? I was looking to see if I could just find Hitler. I wanted get him and just tear him apart—that's how I felt."

Staff Sergeant Irwin Roth in training (courtesy Irwin Roth).

Thoughts of revenge were not uncommon among Jewish personnel and in many cases it was much more specific than the fact that Hitler hated Jews. For Staff Sergeant Irwin Roth, a flight engineer with the 15th Air Force, the motivation for payback was very personal and very specific.

"Towards the end of the war, I got word that my grandmother, my father's mother, a woman that none of us have ever known, she stayed over there [in Poland] and she was taken because they owned a small family farm. They were taken behind the barn and machine-gunned. And that's when I asked the commander, the bombardment group commander, if I could release the bombs on Berlin or Munich. I told him why, and he gave me permission, and I held the release—the bombardier yelled at me when I was to press the button to release them. I went on two missions to Berlin and two from Munich, so I did my share of bombing and killing there. It was revenge."

Staff Sergeant Morton Israel was brutally honest in regard to his attitude toward the Nazi regime:

"When we bombed Berlin, it was around February 23 of 1945. We went over with the biggest bomber fleet you have ever seen, and they cordoned off areas.

"We went to the mission, and hundreds of anti-aircraft guns were firing at us, and they were all over the place. You know something? It didn't bother me one bit killing German civilians. When an anti-aircraft shell hit our plane and knocked hydraulics out, and so forth, and we were shot at, I said I don't care how many Germans I kill. They're anti–Jewish, and that's it.

"I used to put my name on the bombs. I was the armorer-gunner, and this little Jew boy. I used to write it on the bombs 'From the little Jew boy,' OK?

Staff Sergeant Irwin Roth (courtesy Irwin Roth).

Staff Sergeant Morton U. Israel (second row, second from left) (courtesy Morton U. Israel).

"I've been to Israel 15 times and I used to stay sometimes in a hotel where the Germans were staying. You know, they were coming and visiting Israel. I never met a German my age who was in the war—they were all sent to camps, to farms, none of them ever told me they were in the war."

Technical Sergeant Arthur Toppston was a gunner with the 8th Air Force, 93rd Bombardment Group in addition to being the radio operator for his bomber (B-24).

"I flew out of a place called RAF Hardwick-on-the-wash, and it was about 20 miles from the eastern coast of England. Germany was too far for us at that time. We mainly flew into France and the Netherlands, sometimes in Belgium.

"Our mission was to go after German Air Force targets, mostly airplane factories.... I shot down several enemy aircraft; they were mostly Messerschmitt's, the 109s. It wasn't a frightening time for me. I was pretty angry with the Germans. When they extended our range, we were able to reach Germany, and I was on one of the first two missions to Berlin.... I was the only Jew on the crew, and I was exhilarated to get back at the Germans."

The comments of fighter pilot Harold Steinberg reflected a story-line that ran through nearly every interview I conducted—the lack of forgiveness of the American-Jewish airmen had toward the Germans.

"We knew as Jews that we disliked the Germans, the Nazis that was for sure. Nothing about them was complimentary, no matter what those son-of-a-bitches would do, no matter what I have read about them."

First Lieutenant and navigator James Ruttenberg never considered himself as being devout, but culturally he has always identified strongly with his Jewish heritage.

"Yes, we eventually went into Germany. I bombed Munich, Regensburg,[21] Linz and several German targets. It felt very good. When we knew we were going to a German target, for instance, if it was Munich, I wasn't happy because that was going to be a very rough time due to anti-aircraft guns. We knew it was going to be a bad day. On the way home, I felt very good because I felt that I had done something to the perpetrators of atrocities against the Jews. And Adolph Hitler became the Anti-Christ or whatever you want to call him, the devil.

"As a Jewish boy, I was doing my part to get back at those who had persecuted the Jews so badly. Even though, as I said, I did not have a religious upbringing. If you're born a Jew, you're a Jew, and that doesn't matter whether you're a rabbi or a fish monger, you're a Jew, and you are treated all the same way."

Tzimmes

Tzimmes is a dish that is frequently served on Rosh Hashanah, the Jewish New Year. It is a mixture of vegetables, fruits and nuts and can even contain meats. Tzimmes may be thought of as any grandma's secret stew or chowder recipe, handed down from generation to generation. The mixture of stories in this section are a stew of missed opportunities, or of sudden changes in orders, of irony or sadness or missions outside the norm. Like a family recipe, it was important to preserve these oddball stories.

There was a fine line between those who made it into a theater of combat as part of an air crew after training or those who went through training then served in support or those who had complete changes in orders.

Leon "Lee" Tulper went through basic training as an infantry soldier and then was able to transfer to the Army Air Corps. He became a cadet, soloed in a Piper Cub as a prospective pilot, but they had enough pilots, so then he was informed he would be switched to navigator or bombardier school.

"Everything was fine and I was supposed to go down to San Antonio for additional training, so comes the deal from President Roosevelt who says we've got too many pilots, bombardiers and navigators, and you were being sent back to your old outfit. I go down to Camp Shelby, Mississippi where they're forming a new division, the 65th Division mostly people who were transferred out of the [air corps] program to their original outfits."

Tulper's odyssey took him from training as a navigator or bombardier to becoming a radio operator in Patton's 3rd Army, 260th Infantry. He saw terrible combat across Europe, and. received the Purple Heart after a German S-mine or "Bouncing Betty" exploded near to his position injuring him and leaving him partially deaf for life.

The 260th Infantry was the first to liberate the Ohrdruf sub-camp of Dachau. Finding the camp was completely by chance; no one knew it was there. They first discovered manicured lawns, ornate gates and bloated Australian POWs who had been living on potatoes and water in the "front part" of the camp. Beyond the camp for soldiers, they saw strange buildings looming in the distance. The POWs warned them not to go back there.

"You didn't tell a G.I. he couldn't do something," said Tulper.

On April 6, 1945, Tulper rode on the second jeep into the camp, with its crematoria and nearby bins filled with shoes, clothing and bones. The camp's discovery was so shocking that their initial reaction to the piles of bones was that the Germans must have done a lot of deer hunting to feed the prisoners.

"I got to tell you a little Jewish kid comes up to me and tugs at my leg asking for food. I didn't have any. It killed me when he tugged at my leg. Ohrdruf was the place where Eisenhower went when he first saw the camps. Ohrdruf made me almost change my religion. I couldn't believe there was this fantastic God who could do something like that."

Staff Sergeant Leon S. Tulper in training (courtesy Leon S. Tulper).

Every April 6th, Lee Tulper goes into seclusion. Seventy years later, he is still unable to convey what he had experienced.

War could be as fickle as tragic. Even if a crewmember made it into the air and flew long distances, the missions might not necessarily involve combat.

Navy Aviation Radio Man (ARM) Daniel Eininger, was assigned to the Patuxent River Naval Station in Maryland on a Martin PBM Mariner "Flying Boat" seaplane. His crew flew a route that took them from Maryland to the Caribbean, then to Bermuda, on to Puerto Rico then to Trinidad, then British Guyana to Belen and Natal in Brazil and back again. They were a cargo transport squadron carrying freight, mail and passengers.

They almost made it to a combat area when his squadron was ordered to deliver a PBM to Saipan. They flew as far as the Marshall Islands when the "Flying Boat" broke down and the trip was terminated. Ironically, the closest they came to a wartime catastrophe was on a flight to Bermuda when both wings took a lightning strike that popped out dozens of rivets on both wingtips.

Sometimes men would stay in the Army Air Corps but would bounce from one assignment to another. Sergeant Albert Fuenfer was allocated to the 8th Air Force, 490th Bombardment Group.

"There was an [Army Air Force] school that they just finished putting into action up in Sioux Falls, South Dakota. So I went up there. The winter of 1942 I think, I finished at Sioux Falls being a radio operator. Then I went with a small group down to Boca Raton, Florida, for the summer and I was taught radar to be a radar operator.

"While we were there, we did scouting missions on older big bombers that they didn't use for bombing anymore. We flew from Boca Raton, Florida to Cuba with special equipment to detect whether there were German submarines in the area of South Florida.[22]

"They asked a group of us who had been trained to use the radar bomb site to train on the Bombing Through the Overcast [BTO] technology that they had perfected; it was very new. This was much more advanced radar than the original radar, which was like an oscilloscope.

"After we were trained on that, the command got a group of us together and they asked us 'Who wants flying duty?' and I said 'Me,' and I raised my hand. They asked us if we had medical problems. I said, 'Well, I have hay fever,' so they told me I couldn't fly. I had [also] previously trained in air-to-air gunnery with .50 caliber machine guns.

"While we were in Fort Meyers is when the Schweinfurt raids[23] were on. They lost a lot of guys over Schweinfurt. They doubled the number of guys that were training to be gunners and they suspended flying until they got the

P-51 Mustangs to accompany the B-17s and B-24s all the way to the target and back, and then the losses were much less.

"So they told us to be instructors—teach the optic bombardiers how to use the radar bomb site, I did that for a while. Then word came out, they were sending guys to England to maintain the radar sets—they didn't need us anymore for flying duty, just to maintain the BTO radar.

"About Christmas of 1944 we went by transport ship to Liverpool, England…. I was sent to an Army Air Force base called Eye, Station 134 in Suffolk in East Anglia, England, the 490th Bomb Group [Heavy]."

Radar was in its infancy and men such as Fuenfer were at its cutting edge, but as much as the Norden bombsite was deified, sometimes the technology could be more detrimental than helpful. First Lieutenant Robert Cohn was a pilot with the 8th Air Force, 452nd Bombardment Group.

"You know the Norden Bombsight?[24] It was only carried by two planes in a formation, the lead plane and the one on his right. The reason for that was, in case one went out, malfunctioned in the lead plane—they would

First Lieutenant Robert S. Cohn (front row, left) (courtesy Robert S. Cohn).

switch with the plane on the right—got it? Well, I was flying on the left of the lead plane that day, so when the thing went out in the lead plane they started to switch, and they collided. Yeah, right in front of me. Yep, sure did. There were airplane parts and bodies flying everywhere. That was kind of shaky—shook me up. No, I don't think about it unless I'm talking about it. It's not a subject you want to keep harping on."

There were several stories I recorded where the crews saw horrific collisions take place in formation especially when pilots were hastily shifted from one type of heavy bomber to another.

There were also times when the heavy bombers were called upon to do maneuvers they should not have been asked to do. The Ploesti oil refinery missions described earlier were devastating low level runs, but there were many other types of low level runs all but lost to history. Tail gunner Murray Codman of the 447th Bombardment Group recalled supplying the French Marquis resistance fighters:

"On two missions we didn't carry bombs, we carried canisters six to seven feet long and about three feet around. The canisters carried guns, ammo and other supplies deep into France near to the Swiss border. We dropped down to 300 to 500 feet. It was the only time we could actually see people. The first time we got away with it. The second time we went over a hill and all hell broke loose. The Germans were firing at us and we fired back with every gun we had. There were 17 guns on the plane and every gun was just firing. The plane just vibrated."

First Lieutenant Alfred Benjamin was a navigator on a B-17 bomber with the 8th Air Force assigned to the 384th Bombardment Group recalled a somewhat similar event:

Technical Sergeant Murray Codman being awarded French Medal of Honor in 2014 (courtesy Murray Codman).

"When the British were trapped in Arnhem, the Netherlands, we did a relief mission for them.[25] We were trying to take pressure off the British troops, and we flew in low altitude in groups of three. This was a very strange mission because we weren't used to flying that way, we weren't trained to fly that way. We were looking for little targets, small little targets. And they assigned us a bridge, for instance, and three planes would go try to get that bridge out, or a roadway or a crossing or a railroad track or something. I think we bombed from 1,000 to 1,200 feet, which was something we never did.

"But I'll tell you about one other mission, a mission deep into Germany, I think the town began with an 'M.'[26] The weather was not too good and we were flying along and we were into Germany already.

"We got a radio call saying that we couldn't bomb that particular site because it was not visual, and that there was an Allied POW camp nearby. They didn't want to take a chance having our bombs miss the target and hit the POW camp. So they asked us to go to an alternate target. And there we are, we're flying along looking for this secondary target. We couldn't find the secondary target because it was socked in.

"So the third thing you get is the target of opportunity. Now you can't bring your bombs back because you can't land with them. If you land with bombs, you're going to blow up the airport. So you have to either dump them in the ocean—and we didn't want to dump our bombs in the ocean at all. So we got to drop them somewhere in the enemy land—I mean that's what you're there for.

"Ahead of us, we see there's a break in the clouds and there's smoke coming out of a factory. So we thought that's our target of opportunity—it's a factory, it's working, it's got smoke. We set up and we bomb this thing with the three divisions; we obliterate this factory.

"Well, by the time we got back home, they had already sent a 'hot camera ship' back. The pictures that the hot camera ship takes get back before us. And what do you know; we bombed a shoe factory! OK, a shoe factory! But if you want to look at the news reels that they had in those days, you will find that after we bombed that shoe factory, the Germans had no more shoes for their soldiers. They had rags on their shoes instead. So that's the day our group won the war!"

A quick story from the Pacific theater illustrated another unusual assignment for heavy bombers. Sergeant Sidney Tendler was assigned to the 7th Emergency Rescue Squadron (ERS) in Okinawa. ERS used B-17s as rescue planes. They carried a boat called a "Flying Dutchman" that was attached to the bomb bay and was dropped with three parachutes. The boat contained equipment, a sail, radio, and a 30-day supply of food and water.

"We were on patrol every day and we were always on stand-by in case of an emergency. We would be ready to rescue B-29 crews that had flown out of Guam. In the time I was with the ERS we did about three or four rescues. We were very lucky."

Pvt. Leonard "Jerry" King, with the 316th Troop Carrier Group, 37th Troop Carrier Squadron, started his combat service from Egypt in 1943 where the group was transporting the 101st Airborne and British Air Devils into campaigns in North Africa to the last days of the war where they were transporting German POWs from Linz, Austria.

The history of troop carrier squadrons followed the arc of World War II itself. King went from North Africa to Sicily to England, France and Germany.

King was a Crew Chief/Mechanic working on aircraft and gliders. He dispelled another myth heard from time to time that Jews were not mechanically inclined enough to work around aircraft.

"Sure I was mechanically inclined. Not only that, after the war I was a contractor for 50 years. We were assigned to one plane and made sure the plane was flyable and to make sure the pilot was not endangered by any mechanical failures. I was responsible for all maintenance and repairs on the C-47. In Egypt we worked all night checking the lines, fuselage, instruments, brakes and so forth, because it was so hot during the day. We also worked on C-46s and later on, the C-53. I was also transferred to Heliopolis [Egypt] where I assembled AT-6s and gliders."

Gliders, as King explained were basically canvas, wood and pipe, made by the Heinz Pickle Company. There was no

Sergeant Sidney Tendler in 2014 (courtesy Sidney J. Tendler).

armor and no armaments. They were towed by the C-47s of his squadron. including the plane that King had maintained. On June 8, 1944 [D–Day + 2], the squadron was assigned the mission to drop gliders over Normandy; his pilot was killed in that action.

First Lieutenant Irvin Harris was a pilot with the 9th Air Force, 441st Troop Carrier Group, and 302nd Troop Carrier Squadron. The 302nd was also active in dropping paratroopers on D–Day.

"The final combat missions I flew were in transporting gasoline in five-gallon cans to General Patton's tanks. He was the initiator of what we used to call 'Spearheads,' which was a narrow corridor that went up through the frontlines. He would capture an airfield or a field that was capable of landing our aircraft. He would protect that spearhead long enough for us to pick up his wounded and for us to drop off the gasoline that he needed for his next advance.

"We would get out of there, because it would probably be overrun again by the Germans. So that was his plan, and we helped him with it, and it worked quite successfully. That's what spearheads were all about."

Leonard Luck, the navigator who described his D–Day experiences earlier in this chapter, flew with the 9th Air Force, 15th Troop Carrier Group. His group was also involved with the transport of fuel.

"One of the big things that we did, which I felt was even more important than dropping the paratroopers, was when Patton was making his move from the south and he needed gasoline. Patton's tanks would only get two and one-half miles to a gallon, and somebody from his office would call us at night, and tell us where they were going to be the next day and we would go there.

"He would have facilities for us to land. They put down wire or mesh or something. He would establish runways and we used to make two trips a day carrying gasoline for him. As I said, there was no armament on this plane at all. If we'd have encountered flak, even into our own gas tank it would have gotten the plane."

General Patton, it would seem, was virtually everywhere in Europe. Staff Sergeant Paul Luterman was assigned to the 8th Air Force, 301st Bombardment Group. He would eventually become an Army Air Corps safety instructor, but initially he was working to distribute supplies to the various air fields.

"When I was still in England, at the beginning of my tour, I was put in charge of a convoy of supplies that we were bringing down through Stratford-On-Avon. Stopped by an MP, I was told that General Patton was commandeering the convoy, and I was to turn it over. I said I'd be damned if I was handing it over to some MP on his word alone since we were carrying beef, liquor and penicillin for the troops and these items were scarce like gold. I told him I would not give it to anyone but Patton himself.

"We got on the road again and traveled for a while when I spotted a jeep with an American flag waving. It was coming towards me with none other than George S. Patton himself, mad as hell. He told me in no uncertain terms that when he ordered someone to take what he needed, he sure as hell better get it, and with that the convoy was his."

It was also Luterman who recalled: "On one Rosh Hashanah or Yom Kippur we had no Jewish chaplain. Cardinal Spellman happened to be visiting our troops and did our High Holiday services in both English and Hebrew."

Not to be outdone, navigator Nat Bailen, had one of the more memorable encounters involving clergy:

"When we completed the first 25 missions, we were given a week's trip to Capri for 'R&R.' Our crew first traveled to Rome, where we had a chance to see the Pope. Once we were in the church, they would carry the Pope the length of the floor. People were waiting and the Pope would be touching people's hands as they carried him down in front of everybody. That was St. Peter's Cathedral. I was standing there next to a wall that was about five feet high, with my group and the Pope came by and he touched my hand! Well, when I turned around to my crew, I said, 'Fellas, we're going to win this thing, we're going to come home,' and we did.

"I was very lucky. He passed very close and touched my right hand, and I didn't wash that hand until we got to Capri. I told my men that the Pope could fly on our airplane if he wanted to!"

Final Flights

First Lieutenant Stanley Newman was a fighter pilot assigned to the 10th Photo Reconnaissance Group, 162nd Tactical Reconnaissance Squadron.

"My squadron, the 162nd Tactical Reconnaissance squadron was flying combat missions from an airstrip near Nancy, France where I joined them in the spring of 1945. We were billeted in German quarters we had taken over. We drove 10 miles to get to the airstrip which was in Toul, France. We flew out of there until the Rhine River crossing and then we moved up close behind the front lines.

"Most of my missions were flying ground support and tactical reconnaissance. We had our guns, but a camera had been placed in the fuselage of the fighter plane. We often sought targets of opportunity. If it were something really small such as trucks or guns, we'd take care of it ourselves. We didn't want to waste P-47s. We'd come in on a pass and the P-47s would sometimes follow us and complete the attack. We would take pictures of the damage.

"I flew 57 missions in Europe. The war ended before I finished what would have been my tour. My missions could last anywhere from two to three hours; we couldn't stay up for too long because the fuselage fuel tank had been replaced by a camera. As our airfields were close to the battle lines, sometimes we would sometimes fly two or three missions in a day.

"At that stage in the war there was a lot of ground opposition but the Luftwaffe was either tied up with the Russians on the Eastern Front or going after Allied bombers.

"I saw German fighters twice. In the middle of April we engaged German jets. I learned several years after the war that the jets we engaged were flown by elite high scoring Aces commanded by Adolph Galland.[27]

"On V-E Day [May 8, 1945] we were on an early mission. We didn't expect opposition that day as the war was over. I was a wingman and we saw two German fighter planes. I got on the tail of an FW-190 and I really didn't want to shoot him down because we had been briefed the night before that it was the last day of the war. Then I saw a bunch of tracers being fired from where the other fighter was fighting with my leader. I fired a short burst over the top of his canopy but wasn't trying to hit him. He descended as I followed him down and bellied in. I could have easily killed him but I'm glad I didn't, because later events that day suggested to me they were just trying to give up. My leader took their approach to be a hostile pass.

"On the same day we had another mission. This time I was the leader. We took off from our base outside of Nuremburg. I saw a Bf-109 and I quickly got into shooting position on his tail. He immediately rocked his wings and put down his landing gear which was a sign of surrender. I wanted him to land at our nearby airstrip. I flew up beside him pointed back to my airfield and he nodded his head and proceeded to land on our grass strip. I had wanted his pistol as a souvenir but as I later found out his plane was rushed and surrounded by airmen. They stripped him of all his possessions right down to his underwear.

"Then later in the day they asked for volunteers to fly into Czechoslovakia. We ran across a German twin engine light transport plane, a Siebel Fh-104 or Siebel Si 204, which was headed in the direction of Switzerland. I pulled up alongside him and pointed west and he kept flying. I fired tracer bullets across his nose and then I flew alongside him again. Enroute to our airfield, we approached an Allied airfield and for which he started to let down and I got him back to our base by flying under him and zooming up.

"The passengers and crew were escorted to headquarters. This time I wanted to make sure I got his side-arm. I knocked on the door and a lieutenant colonel opened the door and said, 'What do you want?' I told him I would like a pistol. I was invited into the room where there were a high rank-ing German officer, his wife and daughter, his aide, his German shepherd and the two pilots. I got the pistol, saluted smartly and left. So on the last day of the war, I forced down two planes and forced another down that crash-landed."

Stanley Newman briefly returned to civilian life where he finished his aeronautical engineering studies. He reactivated and remained in service through the Korean conflict and then the Vietnam War. He would rise to the rank of Major General, and in 2008 was inducted into the Oklahoma Military Hall of Fame.

Reflections

Alfred Benjamin began his missions in Dungy, France on August 7, 1944, where his bombardment group bombed an oil depot; they finished their mis-sions over Mannheim, Germany in January 1945. On September 19, 1944, Rosh Hashanah (See Chapter 4), his bomber was shot down while on a bomb-ing run to the rail yards in Hamm, Germany. He and the rest of his crew safely bailed out over Biche, Belgium.

"When I came home from my missions, it was January 1945. I think I did my last mission on January 20, 1945. I came home, and I had a friend who was home on leave. It was the only friend I had left at home—everybody else was in service.

So he says, 'Let's go out and have a drink.' And we went down to a local bar, and he ordered a drink—he was younger than I was—and they served him. I was all dressed in my uniform with my wings and my battle stars and everything. And the bartender looked at me and says, 'You're not 21—I can't give you a drink.' Isn't that something?"

I imagine he and his buddy found a booth and talked. Maybe he sipped a soft drink. I picture a juke box and music, dimly-lit neon signs, the smell of cigarettes and stale beer. It is just as likely they talked about girls or baseball as more weighty matters. Underneath it all, the friends knew that something had changed, something that could never be shared except with those who had been there.

•• 4 ••

The Stars on My Wings—
the Pacific and CBI

From the 360 people who went overseas in the air crews [of my group], only 165 came home. It really bothered me when I first got back from the service.

—Staff Sergeant Mark Greenburg

Flak and Fighters—Death from Above and Below

The airmen I interviewed who served in the Pacific felt they had it easier than the Allied airmen in Europe. Such assessments were just a bit too self-deprecating; given the dangers they faced, no crew had it especially easy in either theater of combat.

Bombing runs over Japan involved fewer aircraft flying longer distances—and they usually flew lower. Many did not make it back. Cargo planes flying at tree-top level in the China-Burma-India Theater were decimated. Flak, of course was not limited to the skies over Europe. As the war was reaching its conclusion, aircraft could also be subjected to air to air *Kamikaze* attacks.

Second Lieutenant Louis Wirtzer was a navigator with the 10th Air Force, 7th Bombardment Group based in Kolkata (Calcutta), which was part of the CBI Theater of Operations.

"The Japanese occupied a lot of the eastern part of India and Burma. Stillwell, the Army general in that area, was fighting the Japanese in Burma and the eastern part of India.[1] In Burma we bombed bridges and fuel depots. In India, I think we mostly helped the ground troops, you know with bombing bridges and stuff like that to hamper the Japanese from getting reinforcements or from receiving their supplies. In India, we didn't have much problem with flak, but in Burma we did. In Burma, I think it was on my first mission that we were under fire from flak and also from Japanese fighter planes. The Japanese took a heavy toll on us.

73

"Flak is bigger than machine gun bullets. The artillery zeroes in on the planes flying above, and it comes up like a fire. You could see the shell coming up, and it's very scary. We flew, I would say, between 12,000 feet and 18,000 feet. My plane was hit with a little flak and we had some holes in the fuselage. But none of my crew sustained any injuries."

Wirtzer also recounted a story of a crewmember who quickly lost his cockiness under pressure:

"We had a bombardier from Texas, and he was like a little peacock, you know, small. The first mission we were on, we got jumped by Japanese fighters, and they shot down, I think, two or three planes right to the side of us. In order to protect yourself against fighters, you used to fly in a very close formation. Because we were flying so close, when the first bomber got hit, he turned into the other guy, and the both of them went down. And after that mission, the bombardier said he quit, and he would never fly again. They assigned another guy—I mean they had plenty of bombardiers. It was absolutely frightening, but as I said, being 19 years old, it happens to somebody else, not to you."

First Lieutenant Bernard Greene was a navigator-bombardier on a B-29 with the 20th Air Force, 49th Bombardment Group. His crew was sent on missions over Saipan Island in the Northern Marianas chain in May or June 1944. He likened the flak barrages to "Russian Roulette," then compared flak barrages in Europe versus the Pacific:

"I was more afraid of flak than I was of the fighters, believe it or not; the flak barrages were maddening. German flak I think was probably more accurate than the Japanese flak. But the guys of the 8th Air Force flew much higher altitude than we did. They were all the way up and once they started to bomb they were flying at 30,000 feet, causing the pursuing fighters to expend more gas as they were climbing up beneath the B-17s. The B-17s were shot down like flies for a while."

Technical Sergeant Marvin Leventon was a radio operator/gunner on a B-25 Mitchell medium bomber. He was with the 5th Air Force, 345th Bombardment Group that was initially based in New Guinea and then the Philippines. Many of Sergeant Leventon's missions were low level missions to Japanese Occupied Formosa (Taiwan).

"The Zeroes didn't even touch us until we went up into Formosa, and then they had some there. The missions were miserable due to flak. The ground fire is what really got us. When we lost airplanes, that's basically what we lost them to. As we moved up a little farther into Formosa, everything we did was always treetop level, and if we were going after shipping, we'd be right on the deck. They called it 'skip bombing.' There were factories on Formosa where the Japanese were making war materiel. We got hit a few times, but nothing that would bring us down. We lost an engine once and came back on one engine, but we were lucky."

Captain Robert "Bob" Friedman was a pilot with the U.S. Marine Corps in the Pacific. He flew the North American PBJ-1 Mitchell twin engine bomber.[2] He described a mission that was not so lucky:

"We did our final training on Espiritu Santo and then we went up to the active front to the provinces of New Guinea.[3] We flew medium altitude bombing missions and our target was Rabaul, which was Japanese held, along with Rabaul Harbor, and the five or six Japanese airfields that surrounded Rabaul.[4] Our job was to keep these targets from being fortified and re-supplied and to keep them neutralized.

"Every once in a while we would have a low level air raid against specific targets around Rabaul where the Japanese had stored ammunitions and airplanes. We didn't have any problems with Japanese fighters. They were limited by our pressure; they could hardly get off the ground, so we had them fenced in.

"We never got shot down, we got shot up. One mission we were on a medium altitude bombing raid over Rabaul and the anti-aircraft fire was very intense and we got hit. My tail gunner got killed immediately because we got it through the tail section. It also got my co-pilot, in the side of the head, but it wasn't anything too serious on the front of the plane, it was the back. We were half-way crippled and we got out of formation, we got back to our base which was about 150 miles from Rabaul."

Flight Officer Leon Rosen was a B-29 navigator with the 20th Air Force, 29th Bombardment Group.[5]

"When I was 18, I enlisted. We were called in February of 1943. My dad went with me to the subway station, and on the way we picked up a friend of ours who was going in the same day. Larry got shot down in a B-17 and was never recovered. We played football on the same team. Larry, too, was Jewish.

"I flew 18 missions. We bombed, amongst others, Tokyo, Nagoya, Osaka, Yokohama and Tachikawa. The biggest danger was anti-aircraft fire. When you saw a puff of smoke, you know it was geared for you and that it didn't make it [to your position].

"About 10 years ago, when we were still having reunions, Bill C—, who was my pilot, attended. I hadn't seen him in 50 years. At the banquet, the M.C. invited anybody who wanted to say anything to come and say it. I said, 'I want to pay tribute tonight to a gentleman to whom I owe everything....'

I tell about a mission over Tokyo when the floodlights picked us up. And that was the scariest because if one battery of floodlights got you, they all concentrated on you, and then all the anti-aircraft fire. I thought we had had it. Then Bill just did some remarkable piloting skills. He dipped 100 feet, he banked to the right, he went up 100 feet, and he lost them. If it weren't for that, we would've been gone.

"Most of the time, you would drop your bombs, and then somebody, usually me, would say the 'traditional words'—'Bombs away, let's get the fuck out of here.' And we would go back."

Unintended Heroes

Staff Sergeant Mark Greenburg was a radio operator assigned to the 5th Air Force, 375th Troop Carrier Group stationed at Port Moresby, New Guinea.

"Our job was to fly supplies over the jungles and drop them from our planes to the troops below. Sometimes we pushed the supplies out of the planes ourselves or we would have a couple of 'Aussies,' Australian soldiers we would take along and have them push supplies out. On occasion we would also carry paratroopers. When we first went into the Philippine Islands, they dropped paratroopers on Mindanao which was the southern island on the Philippines.

"Then there were missions where they would clear an area where we could land, and the 'medics would load any stretcher cases that we could pick up and we would take them back to Port Moresby [Papua New Guinea].

"We flew over hostile territory all the time. Our plane was the military version of the DC-3, which the Army labeled a C-47. It was strictly transport with no armor on it, and nothing at all, and we flew like that. In some areas we would have fighter cover over the top of us. The crew consisted of a pilot, co-pilot, radio-navigator and engineer. We would sometimes have a nurse and a combat medic.

"We were shot down once in hostile waters about 172 miles from Rabaul. Rabaul was the largest Japanese held position in the South Pacific. At the time we were shot down, we had two stretcher cases in the plane. The Zeros [Mitsubishi A6M Zero] got us, got our tail, so that we couldn't climb anymore, so we were flying about 10 feet over the top of the ocean and the pilot bellyflopped the plane into the water. We had about five to eight minutes to get the two stretcher cases out of the airplane and into the two life rafts. The medic went into one life raft with one patient, and the nurse into the other one with the other patient. The pilot then got into one, the co-pilot into the other one. The engineer and I had to hang on the side in water up to our neck.

"We were there for about six and a half hours before a Navy PBY 'Flying Boat' picked us up. I hung over the side for six and a half hours. The engineer was on the other life raft. After the rescue, it sort of played on my mind. I dreamt about it for many months … the life raft would have only fit so many you see. I spent a month in the hospital.

"Our crew flew 81 missions altogether. I consider all of us on that plane lucky. It was a kind of heavy duty. We brought back people who didn't make it. There were guys who were friends of mine in my Troop Carrier Group who were shot right out of the air.

"From the 360 people who went overseas in the air crews, only 165 came home. It really bothered me when I first got back from the service. After a while you get used to it, you get back into civilization, it goes away, but there are times you lay in bed at night and it comes back.

"Among my commendations, I have what is known as the Soldiers Medal which was given to me because I saved the lives of a pilot and the co-pilot who were in a plane accident on the ground.[6]

"When we first got overseas, we used to land in a place called Tatura (Australia), and our landing strip was grass, not metal or cement. So when the planes would take off, sometimes they would hit a hole so this one pilot was taking off, he hit this hole, and he lost control and he went into the other plane, and then the planes caught on fire.

"The cockpits where the two pilots were sitting came tearing down on the ground and were on fire. And I happened to be off that day, doing some work on my equipment, so I ran over there and I pulled the two of them by the back of their collar, away from the fire. I burned my hands but I didn't think anything more about. Finally, I don't know, 5th Air Force headquarters made a big thing about it, and then the general came and pinned the medal on me.

"I was just there. I was there at the time … it just so happened that it was right in front of me. I had to get these guys out of there, that's all. There were no pre-thoughts of anything. I didn't think about anything."

Lieutenant Junior Grade Lester Levitt was a fighter pilot assigned to the USS *Wasp*.[7] His act of bravery might sound somewhat routine if it wasn't noted that he was in enemy territory near an enemy fighter airbase that had just been strafed. He had no ammunition and he was nearly out of fuel.

"We were ordered to hit Clark field in the Philippines. Our assignment was strafing the planes on the ground. The Japanese had captured the Philippines and this was just before the Battle of Luzon.[8] So the four of us went up to 10,000 feet, and two of us go down and strafe—the other two stayed up at a higher elevation. When we finished strafing, we came back up and they go down and finish off whatever they could.[9] So my leader and I go down and strafed the shit out of them. And they're left burning, like three, four, or five airplanes. We pull out, go back up.

"Then after these guys went down, I said, 'Let's do it again.' So down we go again, but this time, as we're pulling out, the engine of my commander's plane is smoking—his engine is not on fire, but he's got smoke coming out. I pulled out underneath him, I looked, and he's losing all his oil. I said, 'Bud, you're going to have to ditch it, but not here.' He still had enough momentum. I said, 'Go out over the Lingayen Gulf.'[10]

"We got as far as we could, but we were still about 175 miles from our ship—and his motor started to conk out, and then he started to glide down, and I was telling him to keep the wheels up, don't leave the wheels down— I'm telling him—he knows more than I did! We go all the way down together—he makes a water landing beautifully, gets out on the wing, waves to me—but I wasn't going to leave him.

"So I already told the other two to go on back, we're running out of time due to fuel levels. I kept on circling while all these little fishing boats—they didn't know what the hell to do. He was sitting on a little tiny lifeboat. I circled him for about 40 minutes, and I was running out of time to get back. Finally, a Filipino fishing boat goes over to him, picks him up, he gets up on the deck and waves to me to go on home.

"I turned around and went back home, and there's a destroyer about 50 miles from the center of the group. You're supposed to circle them from the left to show that you're one of the good guys.

"I'm coming in, and I take a look at that Task-force and every one of these ships has to turn into the wind to take me, other-wise they'll run into each other. They all have to be going the same direction. So when they turned into the wind for me, I felt like I was King of the World.

Lieutenant Junior Grade Les Levitt (courtesy Les Levitt).

"After I landed, they started interrogating me, I told them, 'We can get him—I know exactly where he's at. I marked it on my map. Just get us a float plane, and I know exactly.' The admiral says, 'Sonny, you fly the plane—we'll fight the war.'

"I was put up for the Distinguished Flying Cross, but I never received it, because the skipper who put it up got killed. This was when I saved my buddy—they recognized that it was heroism, I guess. But I couldn't have done anything anyhow, because I finished strafing, I used up all my ammunition. I could have thrown a boot at them or something!"

Thinking about what might have happened had the Japanese picked up his buddy or if he, himself, had to make a crash landing, Levitt continued:

"There was a book that came out maybe six years ago. It was all about Chichi-jima Island and what they did to the flyers that they had captured.[11] They treated them well in the beginning until they saw that the war was going to be over, and then they executed them and cut their heads off. I didn't know about that at that time. All I knew was that I was ordered to strafe them, and they're going to kill me when they reached me with their flak."

Levitt also remembered another unusual mission he flew, this time to China:

"Our whole air group was going to hit Canton, China.[12] So we took off in the dark, and immediately I'm lost because it's so damn black there, I couldn't see anything. Finally, it got light and I've got two planes following me—they don't know where they're going either! So we head out, and I'm trying to look at my map, and I see we have to go real close to Hong Kong.

"Pretty soon we come over the mountains, very high, and poof-poof-poof, they start shooting flak at us. [Chuckle] I didn't do anything to them, what are they shooting at me for? So of course, I veered away, I went around the long way, and I missed the river going to Canton.

"And I said to the guys, 'Back—I think we missed it.' We each had a 500-pound bomb. The Japanese had occupied Canton and everywhere they were shooting up flak at us. By the way, what they did to the Chinese was terrible. I dropped my bomb on a building next to a runway and fired my rockets and got the hell out of there.

"Each one of us got interrogated after each mission [by Naval Intelligence]. I showed them what I hit and he said, 'You hit a Jap officer cavalry school!' I'll tell you something. I wasn't going to take the bomb back with me."

Navy Lieutenant Leon Frankel was the pilot of a TBM torpedo bomber; the Grumman Avenger. He was assigned to Air Group 9 and he flew 25 combined missions from the USS *Lexington* and the USS *Yorktown*.

THE SECRETARY OF THE NAVY
WASHINGTON

The President of the United States takes pleasure in presenting the NAVY CROSS to

LIEUTENANT, JUNIOR GRADE, LEON FRANKEL
UNITED STATES NAVAL RESERVE

for service as set forth in the following

CITATION:

"For extraordinary heroism as Pilot of a Torpedo Bomber in Torpedo Squadron NINE, attached to the U.S.S. YORKTOWN, in action against major units of the Japanese Fleet off Kyushu, Japan, April 7, 1945. Flying by instruments through a heavy overcast in a daring attack against an enemy light cruiser and a screening destroyer, Lieutenant, Junior Grade, Frankel broke through the clouds and pressed home his attack to point-blank range in the face of intense antiaircraft fire to score a direct hit and contribute materially to the sinking of the hostile cruiser a minute later. Subjected to a cross-fire of intense antiaircraft fire from the cruiser and destroyer during his retirement from the strike, he brought his plane and crew through unscathed. By his superior airmanship and gallant fighting spirit, Lieutenant, Junior Grade, Frankel upheld the highest traditions of the United States Naval Service."

For the President,

James Forrestal

Secretary of the Navy

Award of the Navy Cross to Leon Frankel (courtesy Leon Frankel).

"On February 16, 1945, Air Group 9 was ordered to take part in an attack on the Japanese aircraft infrastructure. This was the first attack on Tokyo since the Doolittle raid of 1942.[13] The Lexington was part of a huge task force, Task Force 58. There were 19 carriers involved in the operation plus battleships, destroyers and submarines. The purpose of the raid was to knock out Japanese aircraft factories, airfields and of course, any aircraft on the ground or in the air.

"The attack was timed to precede the full-scale battle for Iwo Jima on February 19, 1945. The resistance to the attack on Tokyo was intense, both from anti-aircraft fire and enemy aircraft. There were hundreds of Japanese aircraft defending their homeland. I don't know all of the planes the Japanese had in the air; it was mostly Zeros but also Oscars [Nakajima Ki-43 Hayabusa] and other aircraft.

"During air-to-air combat, the wing of a Japanese fighter plane hit the propeller of my commander's plane. The Japanese fighter spun into the ground and crashed.

"When I saw this happening I slowed down and pulled alongside the skipper. Another aircraft in the formation had been struck by anti-aircraft fire and was also barely able to maintain air speed, so a number of us in the formation defended the crippled aircraft from about 50 Japanese fighters. We battled the fighters for more than 85 miles across the mainland of Japan. Both my skipper and the other aircraft landed safely. For that I was awarded the Distinguished Flying Cross."

More than 1,000 American planes participated in the attack; 60 were lost and an additional 28 were forced to ditch.[14]

On April 7, 1945, Frankel had another opportunity to exhibit heroism under fire. Air Group 9 was ordered to join more than 400 aircraft for the purpose of intercepting the Japanese task force led by the *Yamato*.[15]

"The *Yamato* and its sister ship, *Musashi*, were the largest and most powerful battleships ever built. While we did not know the exact location of the *Yamato*, military intelligence had given us an accurate picture of where the Japanese cruiser *Yahagi* was located."

As his TBM broke through the clouds, he went after the *Yahagi*. Even though the *Yahagi* was putting up a massive amount of anti-aircraft fire, Frankel continued to bear down on the ship. He dropped his torpedo and scored a direct hit. Simultaneous to the attack on the *Yahagi*, he stated that six aircraft in his formation saw that the *Yamato* had been hit and they broke off their attack on the *Yahagi* and went after the Yamato and helped to destroy that vessel.

For his actions during this significant operation, Frankel was awarded the Navy Cross.[16] The Navy Cross is awarded only for heroism in combat and is the second highest award given to Navy personnel; only the Medal of Honor is higher.

Frankel's commendation, signed by James Forrestal, Secretary of the Navy, reads in part:

"For extraordinary heroism as Pilot of a Torpedo Bomber.... Lieutenant, Junior Grade Leon Frankel broke through the clouds and pressed home his attack at point blank range in the face of intense anti-aircraft fire to score a direct hit and contribute materially to the sinking of the hostile cruiser a minute later. Subjected to a cross fire of intense anti-aircraft fire from the cruiser and destroyer during his retirement from the strike, he brought his plane and crew through unscathed."

First Lieutenant and fighter pilot Gideon Lichtman, through his affiliation with the Newark Jewish community and his father's involvement with Judaic studies programs, was well aware of what was happening to European Jewry. In a sense, his knowledge of the dire situation in Europe added an extra dimension of stress to his wanting to exact the payment he was not able to fulfill.

"There was a comic strip called *Terry and the Pirates*[17] at that time … in these comics, they talked about the 'The 1st Air Commando Group,' which was a volunteer group and so forth and it stuck in the back of my mind. In any case, when I became a fighter pilot, somebody came in to headquarters at Clark Field in the Philippines and I heard about the fact that there was an air commando group that was requesting volunteers to join the 3rd Air Commando group. So I spoke to a couple of friends of mine, and three or four of us joined the 3rd Air Commando group.[18] This was about the end of 1943 or early in 1944.

"Once I was in the 3rd Air Command Group, I was doing some instructing and so forth. They always put me on some other duty. I kept trying to get out of being an instructor and test pilot. Whenever they assigned me those duties, I was furious because I wanted to get in to combat."

Though he got his wish to fly into combat, it was a bittersweet victory. Lichtman's father was the principal of a Hebrew school in Newark, New Jersey; through contacts his family was aware of what was happening to European Jewry.

"At Clark Field, we mainly flew missions escorting B-29s as they wreaked havoc over Japan. Oh, I would've given anything to get over to Germany. That was what I really wanted. That was probably the biggest disappointment of my whole life, that I couldn't kill some of those bastards."

Corporal Manfred Loeb was with the 14th Air Force, 27th Troop Carrier Squadron. The 27th flew most of its missions over Japanese-held positions, usually flying from the City of Sylhet, which was then in India (now Bangladesh). This was in the China-Burma-India theater, a critical front in the war against Japan.

"I was what they called a 'kicker.' My job was to see that the plane was properly loaded with whatever we had to drop. Everything had a parachute tied onto the loads before we took off. When we got a signal from the pilot, we pushed everything out.

"Once you got over the target, you were in much more danger than even when you were flying to the target. We had to get out of there quickly. We were in the Salween River campaign.[19] It was on the China-Burma border, over the Burma Road. We were dropping supplies supporting Chinese troops with American cadre.

"There were Japanese fighter planes in the area. These troops down there were fighting on the Burma Road trying to open the road, so that they could bring in supplies from India. China was completely cut off in those days.

"We had no armaments. We had a Thompson submachine gun sitting in the back, and each of us carried a pistol and that was it. We were subject to ground fire, especially over the targets—sometimes we had to call off the mission because of ground fire. It was very seldom that we had fighter escorts.

"Our crew was lucky, we never took any hits ourselves but our squadron did lose a lot of planes. When we dropped, we were only 300 feet above the target and we were subject to anything that was fired at us, I mean even rifle fire."

The Diary of a Pacific Gunner

Sherwin Goodman was an Aviation Ordinance Mate Second Class (AOM/2C) aboard the aircraft carrier USS Independence. He was a rear turret gunner on an Avenger TBM torpedo bomber and was involved in numerous sea and air battles in the Pacific.

In the late 1990s, Goodman realized that the detailed diary he kept of his war years was important enough for him to compile as memoirs. The following incidents are taken from his memoirs, as well as from interviews he gave for this book.

"We were sent to participate in the raid against Rabaul on November 11, 1943 … while we were taxiing up the flight deck to the catapult; I was sitting in the turret. As I looked up through the Plexiglas, I saw many Japanese planes attacking and the anti-aircraft fire from the ships dotting the sky. My pilot stopped

Aviation Ordinance Mate Second Class Sherwin H. Goodman (courtesy Sherwin H. Goodman).

the engine and we all jumped out of the plane to get a better look at the action. The sky was filled with the black smoke from the anti-aircraft fire; planes were falling in flames all around the task force. I watched in fascination as a Japanese torpedo bomber approached our side. It kept coming through the fire until it was hit and exploded less than a hundred yards from us … in twenty minutes it was all over.[20] There were 64 enemy planes in the water, and not one ship was damaged. What a way to celebrate Armistice Day!

"The first day of our assault on the Philippines we hit Mindanao and on the second day, Negros Island. There had been no Allied troop landings on the Philippines at the time. We were going up and down the Philippines to soften them up a little before MacArthur took over. It was intense action and the Air Force lost over a third of their people.

"The ship itself was not attacked during the day; most of the action was at night. When we were in the Straights of Formosa we were under attack for six straight nights.

"On September 13, [1944] we attacked Negros Island.[21] As we approached our target, we were jumped by six Japanese fighters. One of them started after our plane, opening fire at 2,500 feet. Just as I opened fire, one of our (aircraft carrier's 'Hellcats') hit him with a deflection shot and blew part of his port wing off. We began our glide down, and one of the enemy got on our tail. I opened fire and the gun jammed immediately. For some unknown reason he pulled away, and we continued on our bomb run. One of our Avengers was shot down by 'AAA' (anti-aircraft) fire, but the rest of us returned safely. One of our fighters was lost also. Our raids continued each day until the landings at Palau and Halmahera and then the fighters took over and provided support [for the troops].[22]

"On September 21, [1944] we attacked Manila for the first time. When we arrived over the city, I observed at least 50 Japanese ships of various sizes in the harbor. Some were afire and the smoke was rising to 5,000 feet. The anti-aircraft fire was very heavy and very accurate. All the way down our glide-bombing path the anti-aircraft bursts were bracketing our plane. I couldn't hear the bursts, but the thick, greasy smoke was everywhere. It was coming from the anti-aircraft batteries stationed all over the cities. Our bombs were planted smack into a large tool and machine plant at the shore, and it went up in a big flash. Then we attacked the ships in the harbor, strafing them as we passed. Our group rendezvoused over Corregidor Island and started home. We were able to watch other air groups attacking and saw two of them shot down. I thought, 'There but for the grace of God….'

"October 12 [1944] was strike day at Formosa. Our fighters went in first to sweep the area. They ran into a flight of Zeroes and in the ensuing fight, two of our fighter group were shot down along with a few of the enemy. We arrived on target shortly after and dropped our bombs along the runway at

Reigaryo Airfield, encountering medium anti-aircraft during the run … we got back to the USS *Cowpens* [Goodman's carrier] and re-fueled and re-armed in an hour and were back in the air for a second strike.

"Our target was Takao Harbor and before we got to our dive point their anti-aircraft fire blanketed the area.[23] As we dove, the enemy fire descended with us, tracking our path. Lt. M—, the pilot, spotted one of the anti-aircraft batteries firing at us and we changed course to drop the bombs dead center, blowing the guns and the men high into the air. The [Navy] plane directly behind us hit an ammo dump and the sheet of flame rose up 2,000 feet, higher than we were at that time. As we circled, we watched some of the dive bombers dropping bombs on a freighter, and saw one of our planes take a hit and dive into the water."

The Battle of Leyte Gulf could very well be one of the most pivotal sea battles for victory in the Pacific. The following mention in Goodman's diary illustrates the immensity of the operation:

"October 26 [1944].… The master-at-arms awakened the flight crews at 0500 and they fed us steak and eggs for the first time. Are they trying to be nice to us for a reason, I wondered? Take off was at 0600 and we had five Avengers and 12 fighters. We were joined by planes from the other two carriers.… [We] headed to the last reported position of the enemy fleet. When we arrived, there was only one cruiser. She began firing at us from a distance of three miles … some of our dive bombers began attacking, but the rest of the force kept searching.…

"Thirty minutes later, we heard the radio crackle, 'Tally Ho.' Fleet at northwest corner of Panay Island.[24] All groups report here. We turned to a new heading and in 15 minutes, were on station. Below us was a sight I'll never forget … there were four battleships, four cruisers and 10 destroyers. One of the battleships was the Yamato, a 60,000 ton monster but from our height they looked like models on a large map.

"At a range of five miles the Japanese ships began shooting at us with their large guns. The ships began turning away from us as we came roaring down out of the sun headed for the water with our torpedoes. I recited a quick prayer and hung on for dear life.

"We headed for the largest ship, but a cruiser and two destroyers got between us. The flak was the heaviest I had ever experienced; there were black bursts in the air, splashes in the water and the noise was deafening. The cruiser made the fatal mistake of turning back, exposing her starboard [right] side. All I could see were gun flashes along the ship. It looked ablaze … it seemed as if we were in a tunnel with tracer bullets passing by on both sides of us … finally our radioman, Ed 'Lefty' C—, watching his radar called out 'One thousand yards!' Lt. M—, our pilot continued on and dropped the 'fish' at 900 yards and began his turn … we were 600 yards from the target when I began to strafe all along the ship's side where I could see the gun crews.

"Flying away from the drop point, the anti-aircraft fire was 'walking' their shells closer in the water directly behind our plane. This continued for what seemed minutes, with us hugging the wave tops until they stopped shooting. I saw a tremendous water spout arise from the cruiser as one of our group's torpedoes found its mark. I yelled, 'It's a hit!' and then another water-spout appeared, then another…. It was reported to us later that day that the ship we hit was the cruiser Noshira and she sank soon after we left the scene.

"My pilot was Protestant and my radioman was Catholic. Whenever we took off on a mission my pilot would say, 'Well, we've got all of the religions covered.' The three of us painted our nick-names on the side of the plane where we sat. I painted, 'Abie's Baby' on the plane and underneath that, a flying Mogen David.

"Whenever we went on a mission, I said the *Shema Yisrael*. I carried a small prayer book with me that was protected by metal.

"My radioman is still alive and we talk about once a week. My pilot died about a year ago. I visited him one last time in the nursing home. We reminisced for about two hours. As I was leaving he said, 'This has been the best day of my life.'"

Kamikaze

In terms of combat experiences, the most emotional responses to questions during the interviews involved flyers and anti-aircraft gunners recalling Japanese *Kamikaze* attacks. Toward the end of the war in the Pacific, the desperation of the Japanese forces to achieve any type of military victory led to the use of their airmen and planes as human guided missiles to attack Allied aircraft. One of the reasons the fighter pilots so frequently strafed Japanese airfields or patrolled the skies around their fleets was to help prevent such attacks.

The Mitsubishi A6M "Zero" was 30 feet long, with a wingspan of 40 feet and it was 10 feet high. It had a speed in excess of 300 miles per hour and when fully loaded with explosives, it weighed 5,300 pounds. When it was aimed at a Navy vessel it was terrifying. What made it even scarier was the knowledge that the pilot did not care one bit about dying.

Lt. (JG) Maury Dubinsky, a fighter pilot assigned to the USS Intrepid[25]:

"In combat, we were primarily flying 'CAP,' which is combat air patrol over the fleet. We were specifically looking for the *Yamato*.[26] As a bomber-fighter

Lieutenant Junior Grade Maurice "Maury" Dubinsky, USS *Intrepid* Ready Room (at table, center, facing camera) (courtesy Maurice Dubinsky).

squadron, we were also knocking out aircraft on the ground in hangars, revetments and buildings. We weren't looking for planes in the air, that assignment was left to the fighter squadron.[27] So the fighter squadrons got all the credit for all the planes that they knocked down, and we were shooting planes on the ground which we got no credit for at all!

"I mean you shoot one plane out of the sky, and you're a hero, but if you shoot 25 on the ground, even though the strafes are dangerous you don't get credit. The bullets were coming past you and the anti-aircraft was thick, that didn't make you a hero by knocking out planes on the ground. But that was our job. It was terribly frightening.

"We called them sweeps, we didn't call them missions like the Army did. We did sweeps over Okinawa, Kyushu, and Shikoku, too. These are all Japanese islands. One of the raids was on a city called Usa. Before the war, everything [exported to the United States] that ... was made in Japan [came from] Usa.[28] That was one of our targets.

"We were hitting mostly ground targets. Of course, some of our guys shot down a few planes. The *Kamikazes* were thick in those days. *Kamikazes* could be anything they could fly, anything. There was no certain plane that was a *Kamikaze*. Any Japanese aircraft was a *Kamikaze*; it was a one-way trip.

They still had a lot of planes left, the Japanese did. When we dropped the first atomic bomb, the Japanese still had thousands of planes left. A *Kamikaze* was usually a single-engine plane like a fighter or a training plane."

However, despite all of the effort, a Japanese airman unable to accept his nation's inevitable defeat, and intent on dying for his country, could find a way to break through all of the defenses of a U.S. Navy vessel. On this particular day, Dubinsky was on the deck of his aircraft carrier.

"We were in what we called a 'Condition 13.' You're wearing a helmet, ready to get in your plane and fly if you have to. My wingman and I were on the railing on the side of the ship, when this *Kamikaze* started coming down at us. The only safe place for the officers was to go back into the ward room as it was armor plated. We knew something was going to hit, there were *Kamikazes* all over the area. The Yorktown was next to us and it shot down a couple planes. The battleship Missouri was with us all the time. One *Kamikaze* took a hit on the Missouri and just bounced off! They had 15-inch armor on the Missouri—it didn't bother her at all.

"The hangar deck on our carrier was wooden so they could make repairs real easy if something happened. We couldn't take off anymore because one of the *Kamikaze* planes was strafing the deck.

"Then we saw this plane coming down at us. Our anti-aircraft guns were firing. When the five-inch guns were firing, we knew we were OK—that was farther away. Then the 40-millimeters fired and that was bad—when the 20-millimeters started firing, we knew they were getting damn close. We tried to get back to the ready room underneath the deck. By that time, the *Kamikaze* went off [the explosives in the nose] and knocked out all the planes in the hangar and killed everybody on the hangar deck.

"My wingman caught a little piece of shrapnel in his leg. The sprinkler system went off on the hangar deck and doused the fires, but the *Kamikaze* did major damage. It bent the number three elevator—we couldn't operate without an elevator.

"Luckily we had good gunnery crews. In fact, one of the gunnery crews close to the end of the war was black. They never had black crews. Blacks were doing insignificant jobs, waiting on us and stuff like that. Finally they gave them some guns, 20 millimeters—there might have been some 40s there too. And they did a real good job of shooting down planes. In fact, the highest ranking black man on the gunnery crew got a Navy Cross, he did a terrific job to earn that. I'd hate to be standing there—you're not moving—you're in your guns. At least in an airplane you can move a little bit.

"When this *Kamikaze* hit, it hit the middle of the deck and didn't hit one of the gun mounts. Had that happened, he would've killed everybody in the gun mount in addition to killing the people on the inside hangar bay.

"About 22 people died. We watched the priests administering last rights and stuff; it was really bad. I can't get the dead out of my mind. I still think about it all the time. It was terrible, yeah."

Lester Levitt was on similar patrols to those of Maury Dubinsky.

"We were doing combat air patrol. The first airplane I shot down—I snuck away from my group so I could be the first one to get to him. I saw him, he was just a dot. I pulled away from the group, and then I gave them a tally-ho, and they followed me. I saw that dot, and I knew it had to be an enemy. But I withheld fire until I got close enough. He was low on the water. And I started to strafe … and he's smoking. I got right on his tail, shot him down and he went right in the water and exploded. I never felt any remorse for him, not the slightest—like shooting a pheasant. You know, you were just geared to this.

"We heard stories about how the Japanese would shoot the pilots who were in a parachute, and all that kind of stuff. I would never do that—I don't think so. In other words, if a pilot that I'm shooting jumped out of the airplane, I don't think I could've gone after him. There were two others I shot down. It was part of our duty."

First Lieutenant Leo Rose was with the 20th Air Force in the Pacific.

"Our missions from Saipan to Japan were long as hell, our average mission was 15 hours. The B-29 was the first pressurized plane. We were comfortable as long as we didn't get holes shot in the plane.

"When General LeMay later took charge of the 20th Air Force he started low altitude missions that were really, really scary. We went in on the firebomb raids, my crew was in that first mission, we went in at 3,000 feet at night and we 'knew' that we were not going to come home, we decided it would be impossible.

"We dropped radar rope when we opened our bomb bay doors and the searchlights would follow the radar rope to the ground.[29] They were shooting at the radar rope instead of shooting at the planes, and they didn't knock many of us down. But obviously, we couldn't go in formation, you can't fly formation at night so we were individually dropping firebombs.

"Luckily, we did not lose a lot of planes on those low altitude missions. Something ironic: I remember one of our first missions, we were flying at 30,000 feet and the Commanding officer that was briefing us said, 'Well, you won't have a problem with Jap Zero's because they're not maneuverable at 30,000 feet. I'm not even sure they can get up that high.' Well, we got to our mission and the Japs were out off of our wings doing barrel rolls. They were thumbing their nose at us.

"The *Kamikaze* pilots would fly at our formations, and they would try to just ram our planes. Those Jap Zeros were pretty damn good airplanes and they had damn good pilots; kids who knew how to fly. They'd give up their life for flying as a *Kamikaze* because they would try to ram us and knock us down.

"I shot a plane down one day. I had control of the forward turrets as the bombardier and we had upper and lower turrets, and if the planes were coming in from the front, I could control them both. If not, I would take the top one, and the waist gunner would take the middle one. I actually knocked down a plane, a Zero that was coming at us on one of the missions."

Fire Bombs and Atomic Bombs

The firebomb attacks on Japan prior to the use of atomic weapons were devastating. The Japanese population was repeatedly warned and bomber crews routinely dropped cautionary pamphlets on towns and cities. Warnings were also broadcast by radio in an effort to inject at least some humanity into the ugliness of what was happening.

First Lieutenant Bernard Greene was a navigator-bombardier with the 20th Air Force, 39th Bombardment Group, and 61st Bombardment Squadron.

"I did a lot of bomb dropping. We dropped demolition, fire producing incendiary bombs that weighed 500 pounds and napalm. The napalm had a rubbery petroleum base that stuck to buildings. We also dropped bombs with proximity fuses that would detonate about 100 feet above the ground. I do remember seeing some pamphlets in Japanese telling them to surrender. It was common knowledge that they were going to surrender.

"I remember being present at a meeting conducted by General Carl 'Tooey' Spaatz, who would later become the first Chief of Staff of the Air Force. He was in the meeting along with many senior aircraft commanders. In the meeting he told his officers that he was going to broadcast in Japanese telling them ahead of time the targets we were going to bomb. The broadcasts would say, 'We will bomb you, we will burn you down.' The idea was to actually bomb seven of nine towns. He asked us to speak up if there were any objections. Some asked, 'Won't it endanger some of the crews?' He ordered us to do it anyhow.

"Most of our major targets were in the Tokyo-Yokohama area, Kobe-Osaka, Nagoya and Nagasaki. The majority of our targets were made of wood. The Japanese de-centralized their armament manufacturing and it was done in homes and garages.

"Neither I nor any of my associates [crewmembers] had any inkling that there was an atomic weapon. Even before dropping the bomb, we flew over Tokyo and other cities and there was already a lot of devastation."

First Lieutenant Stuart Reichart was also a navigator-bombardier with the 20th Air Force. He was assigned to the 497th Bombardment Group, 870th Bombardment Squadron.

"When I started flying missions in January 1945 we were bombing from an altitude of 35,000 feet with poor results.

"General Curtis LeMay took over as Commander of the 20th Air Force in early 1945. On March 9, 1945, he directed a change in tactics from bombing Japan on daytime missions at 35,000 feet to nighttime incendiary bombing runs at 5,000 feet.

"Our group was told by the briefing officer that we would bomb the targets on an individual basis rather than in formations. When he made that announcement the mood in the room became very somber. Up until that time we did about two missions a month. But after the change in tactic, we flew five missions in nine days. Each bombing mission to the mainland took between 15 and 16 hours from Saipan.

"I was one of those who did fly on all five missions. On our second mission to Nagoya, Japan, we flew over the huge, roaring fire that had been created by our firebombs. I have never, ever experienced turbulence like that before or since. The plane was so damaged by the turbulence that it loosened all of the rivets in the plane and we could never fly it again.

"The five firebomb missions included two to Nagoya, one to Tokyo, one to Osaka and one to Kobe. Soon after those fire missions, General LeMay had us drop leaflets to warn the Japanese citizens. We told them where the next 16 targets would be. We dropped the leaflets all over Japan.

"Significant losses occurred on April 7, 1945, when General LeMay ordered us to fly a daytime mission over Tokyo at 15,000 feet. He was told that we stood a very good chance of losing 75 percent of the planes. His response was they will have to send more replacement crews and aircraft from the States.

"On that mission our bomber was badly hit by anti-aircraft. I found myself wiping away a lot of blood but fortunately it was mostly superficial. I would later receive the Purple Heart for those injuries. We were able to crash land on Iwo Jima.

"I went overseas with 20 crews and only two came back intact. In the early days before we conquered Iwo Jima our losses were significant."

Leo Rose, who also flew fire bomb missions, added:

"When we returned from our first firebomb mission, our tail gunner could see the fires from 150 to 200 miles out at sea. That was the turning point in the war with Japan; the culmination, of course, was the atomic bomb, but our firebombs were what really brought them to their knees.

"We just burnt things to the ground everywhere, it was just awful. But we didn't feel bad, because they were doing the same to us. That was the most dramatic part of flying missions, when we started dropping those firebombs."

There was planning for the invasion of Japan and several of the men interviewed were being prepared for, or had been shifted to, positions closer to Japan. For example, Sergeant Norman Kailo was a crew chief on a bomber with the 20th Air Force, 462nd Bombardment Group. His group had been transferred to Tinian Island in April 1945 from their duty station in the CBI Theater.

Staff Sergeant Sol Shafner was a crew chief with the 20th Air Force, 346th Bombardment Group.

"We picked up a new airplane in Renton, Washington and we flew to Quadraline Island [Kwajalein Atoll], refueled again and then flew on to Guam. The Air Force decided that they wanted to get closer to Japan. And we then flew to Tinian Island.

"I didn't know until after the war that the atomic bomb was brought to Tinian Island by a destroyer, the USS *Indianapolis*. They unloaded the bomb, and they assembled it on the *Enola Gay*, which dropped the bomb."

The Air Force then directed Shafner's B-29 to Okinawa. However, a few days later, the atomic bombs had been dropped and the war was over.

Corporal Barton Greenburg was preparing for overseas duty as a meteorologist.

"I did weather observer status and I was stationed at Platte, Kansas Air Force Base. Then I was transferred to an overseas training camp in Greensboro, North Carolina, preparing for a Japanese invasion when the war ended."

Technical Sergeant and flight engineer Isadore Kozatch stated that as he was about to leave the service they tried to ship him to Japan. He and many other veterans had been through hell in Europe and the last thing they wanted was to go off to another front. However, a major shift was in the offing.

There were many airmen who were caught in transition—they had gone into training rather late in the game and though prepared for combat in either theater, the European and the Pacific conflicts were concluding as they had joined units. Had an invasion occurred these airmen would have seen combat.

P-38 pilot Saul Nova joined the 80th Fighter Squadron as the unit was moving from the Philippines to New Guinea, and shortly after to an island called Ie Shima,[30] which was about 400 miles from the southern tip of Japan.

"We knew the invasion of Japan was coming, because all the time that I spent in the air was over enemy territory in Japan. My perception was that the invasion of Japan was planned for November of 1945. It was planned to land at three points: the very southern tip of Kyushu, there would be another group coming from the straits of the East China Sea and another point of attack from the straits of the Sea of Japan. It would have been very bloody. They would never have quit. You know, to this day, I would believe there are Japanese somewhere in the Pacific in some jungle still at war.

"But the mission that the 80th Fighter Squadron had was bridges. All the bridges in Japan are built on foundations. There are no suspension bridges, they're all foundations. So if you want to destroy a bridge like that, you can't do it from the air by dive-bombing or bombing. The only way you can do that is what's known as 'Skip Bombing.' It's like throwing a rock across the water. So on the P-38 you could carry two 500-pound bombs, one under each wing. We never carried any of those missiles.

"The reason they were doing that was to knock out the bridges and all the railroads to keep the Japanese from sending reinforcements from the north. There was an airbase on the very southern tip of Kyushu, and once that base was captured, we knew that we would be transferred from where we were to there. Of course, in August we dropped two bombs....

"You wouldn't have found anybody in my squadron that didn't think Harry Truman was a hero. They [the Japanese] would not have quit. As a matter of fact, we shot down three planes on the very day after the A-bombs were dropped.

"I did see Nagasaki, the second atom bomb site, 24 hours after the bombing. It was pretty devastated. But the only difference was, this was from one bomb, and other raids were 500 [fire bomb] raids.

"The atomic bomb was absolutely the right thing to do. The alternative would've been sacrificing hundreds of thousands of troops. Remember when we invaded Normandy beach, there were at least allies to team up with— there were the free French, there were other Dutch troops and we could make contact with them. In Japan, there was no one. If we invaded Japan, the catastrophe would've been enormous. We would've been the invaders. Should we have done it [dropped the atomic bomb]? Absolutely.

"When the Japanese surrendered, they sent a plane full of dignitaries from Japan to meet with General MacArthur in Manila. Our squadron was elected to ferry them and to give them protection. We escorted them to Ie Shima, where they landed, and refueled, and then went on to Manila."

Sometimes it seems that major news stories come to the most unlikely of people in the most unlikely of places, far ahead of the major news outlets or big time commentators. Dick Bosley was a truck driver assigned to the Base Services Squadron, 358th Air Service Group Headquarters, on Tinian Island.[31] He landed on Tinian in November of 1944.

"When we landed, there was still a little fighting going on and a lot of snipers. The Seabees were building these two tremendous airstrips on the north end of the island … the mission of the bombers was to fly up to Japan and mine the whole area, mine all the islands of Japan. They didn't start that mining until after Iwo Jima was captured.

"I was in about three air raids where the Japanese planes came in from Iwo Jima. They'd fly over the canal between Saipan and Tinian, and attack both islands with a few bombs, but they didn't get anything. About three months after we landed there, that's when the big fight was.

"I never met the pilot of the *Enola Gay*. They came over in [summer] 1945. There was about 15 bombers in that group. When we drove them from their ship to their barracks, one guy from the crew said, 'We're going to end the war.' Well, we thought that they were crazy. They were going to end the war in 30 days!

"We were on Tinian the day that the *Enola Gay* took off but we didn't know; they were taking off all the time, these bombers. They never hit the first target, you know, Hiroshima was a secondary target. It was too dark or something—raining or something—and they couldn't see it. And then three days later, Nagasaki was the city—I'm trying to remember the second plane's name....[32]

"They just dropped it and they flew away, because you saw how that bomb goes up. You know, they could have been caught in the smoke and everything, so they came right home. But when they got back to the base, who was there but General Arnold, commanding officer of the Air Force, and he decorated the whole crew right there when they landed.

"Well, it saved millions of American lives, I'll tell you that. The Japanese, their Air Force is practically shot because these guys were doing these *Kamikaze* missions. They'd kill themselves and bomb something."

First Lieutenant Marshall Keller was a bombardier with the 7th Air Force, 494th Bombardment Group, 867th Squadron.

"Yes, we did drop pamphlets toward the end of the war to warn people. I believe we dropped them over Kyushu and Nagasaki. They were in Japanese, so I couldn't understand them. I didn't know what they said.

"The mission I remember the best was my last mission, the 41st. I had flown with the same crew for 40 missions, but I filled in on one last mission for another other crew. The 41st mission was the day we were going to Nagasaki to firebomb.

"We saw a radiation cloud over Nagasaki and we didn't know what it was so we skirted it. We were afraid of the turbulence. It looked like a towering Cumulus cloud."

The story did not quite end there. This was another one of those "milk run" stories. Keller and his crew made it through 40 missions with his original crew and without his bomber suffering any damage. The 41st mission was with a different crew in a different aircraft. After the bomber skirted the radiation cloud, they were set upon by Japanese fighter planes. They had one engine shot away and they were hit by flak. Luckily they were able to make it back to base without crash landing.

Navy radioman 2nd Class Albert Kleeman was a crewmember on a PBM patrol bomber that was specially fitted with a radar dome. His squadron typically flew over Japanese-held territory from the dangerous height of 3,000 feet to 4,000 feet.

It was Kleeman's job to call out the positions of potential targets for future bombing runs. They flew over Hiroshima in September of 1945 after the treaty had been signed.

"To see it from the air is really the way to see what we did to that country, we flattened that country. Well, to me, the greatest president was Harry Truman who said, 'Let's drop it,' you know? I mean when you're out there, you don't think you're ever coming home—yeah, I had that feeling.

"Oh, an invasion of Japan would have been hell. When I was in Saipan, we were bringing in the casualties from Iwo Jima and it was terrible, it was horrible to see the wounded guys. Some of the planes in our squadron, I think two were in on Iwo Jima, but it wasn't me, thank God. History proves that it was horrible, it really was, but somebody had to fight it. I was happy I was up in the air."

Technical Sergeant Marvin Leventon, the B-25 radio operator, saw the destruction after the atomic bomb was dropped on Nagasaki.

"We were stationed on Ie Shima Airfield when the bombs were dropped on Nagasaki and Hiroshima. There was a reporter there from the *Chicago Sun*; I still have a copy of the article. We took him on a low-level tour over Nagasaki right after the bomb was dropped. The reporter sent each of us in the crew a copy of it, and I still have it. It was amazing, really, what that bomb did. So I guess I'm one

Second Lieutenant Marshall L. Keller (courtesy Marshall L. Keller).

of the few people who ever saw that. There was like a river or something running down the middle, and all one side was flat, and then the other side seemed as if it hadn't been hit."

Final Flights

The following accounts are from two airmen who by chance were called upon to fly final missions after the unofficial cessation of hostilities.

There were many fly-overs as the treaty marking the end of the war in the Pacific was being signed. However, for Radioman 1st Class Sol Schwartz, the mission in his Kingfisher seaplane was done for security purposes and not out of bravado.

"In May 1945, we sailed through the Panama Canal to meet up with the Naval Pacific Fleet in the Marianas Islands. From there we were part of the fleet and we were getting ready to invade Okinawa. After Okinawa we dropped the atomic bomb and Japanese surrendered.

"On V-J Day, I was assigned to a spotting mission along the coast of Japan. I remember we were flying over bases and prisoner of war camps. American POWs who had been released from the war camps were waving to us from the prison yards.

"We flew along the shore to make sure that all of the Japanese artillery was covered and could not fire prior to the treaty being signed. This might have been the last official mission of the war."

Saul Nova was a kid from The Bronx whose father sold from a pushcart. Nova was able to attain the achievement of becoming a P-38 fighter pilot.

"As the war was ending, we flew to Shanghai ... the Mayor of Shanghai said that when they saw the P-38s come over Shanghai—they'd heard rumors that the war was over—but when he saw the P-38s there, and there were no Japanese planes intercepting them, they knew that it was true, the war was over."[33]

Reflections

As the war was winding down in the Pacific, F/O Rosen had the opportunity to hear the stories of others who had been in combat.

"The U.S. Navy hospital ship would take those who needed immediate medical attention by ship to Guam. I would requisition a jeep every night and go down to that Naval hospital and sit and talk to these people about their fantastic stories.

"I remember one of the people I found was a member of a crew we went through training with. He told about how he parachuted out and was trapped in a tree. A mob came and they were going to soak him in oil and burn him. Then some military people came and said something in Japanese and stopped it. Then he [the crew man] went into interrogation, which was brutal. In the 90 days he was there, he lost 60 pounds. The guy told me that when he was in interrogation, the interrogator who was bilingual said—and think of these words, how haunting they are—'You Air Force personnel are not prisoners of war. You are not entitled to the Geneva Convention. You are enemy combatants.' How shocked I was—how shocked was anyone I told that to.

"And then I met a guy who showed me his stomach had button holes and buttons in it. He had an attack of appendicitis, and the Japanese wouldn't give him any medical care. There was a British surgeon there who operated without anesthesia and sewed him up.

"We were coming in for a landing—I think it was Iwo Jima—and I had the headset on, and I heard the most stirring words I ever heard in my life— it was, 'Gentlemen, prepare for your first peace time landing—the war is over' I don't know how to describe that. We didn't know if were we going out again tomorrow or the next day, and when it was going to happen."

•• 5 ••

"H" Stands for Hebrew

"We were animals. We were lower than animals."
—Allen Sabol, Stalag Luft IV

Soldiers are required to wear "dog tags" that are used for identification purposes. The need is obvious—sometimes, as we shall see, only the dog tag survives. If one is lucky, the tag can give surgeons vital information such a blood type; the tag can buy life itself.

Among other pieces of information stamped into the metal during WW II was the person's religion. Most Jewish personnel had the letter "H" on their dog tags for "Hebrew."[1] The dog tags would find their way to grieving families back through official channels, sometimes not; sometimes not for many years.

Shortly after Staff Sergeant Allen Sabol had been reported as missing in action, the following letter, signed by a Chaplain Harold R. Gietz, arrived at the Sabol's St. Louis home on August 10, 1944:

"Please accept my deepest sympathy on the recent loss of your son…. There are many things we would like to say, but for military and security reasons it is necessary that they be left unsaid. I'm sure that you will understand when we ask that you keep your faith in the Protective Mercy of God and do not give up your hopes of his safe return.

"There is every possibility that Sergeant Sabol landed safely in enemy territory…. With every good wish, hope and prayer that you will receive good news concerning your son."

It is perhaps comforting to imagine a Jewish chaplain rushing to the side of an injured Jewish airman. We might imagine a gentle hand on a shoulder, a prayer of well-being and for healing, a few minutes of conversation or wisdom or humor. For the most part, it is fantasy. With only 311 Jewish chaplains to serve one-half million Jewish servicemen and women in World War II, and less than 100 of them in the European theater, the chances of an injured or dying Jewish airman being attended to by "one of their own" were slim.[2]

In regard to the letter above, though the sentiment was appreciated enough for Sabol to have kept it for more than 65 years, Chaplain Harold R. Gietz was Lutheran, not Jewish.

In war it was the duty of chaplains in combat areas to meet the spiritual needs of all faiths.

Staff Sergeant Homer Goodman was a Ball Turret Gunner on a B-17, 100th Bombardment Group, 418th Squadron, that flew out of RAF Thorpe Abbot, England.

"We had a rabbi that came by only once every three months. But every day before a mission, there was a priest there. I asked him one day, 'Father would you mind if I went in and said prayers with you?' He said, 'Son, we're all praying for the same thing. You're more than welcome.' I didn't kneel down like they kneel down or didn't give [the sign of the cross], you know. But we all prayed to come back."

Sergeant Marvin G. Freeman, a cryptographer with the 385th Bombardment Group in Great Ashfield, England added:

"...occasionally I would go to Jewish services ... run by the chaplain, who could be Protestant or Catholic, who did his best. Some of the Jewish guys who knew more than I did would help out. It would last maybe an hour. It was kind of nice of the Army doing that."

The experiences of Lieutenant JG Maurice Dubinsky, the Navy fighter pilot assigned to the aircraft carrier *Intrepid* in the Pacific were similar to the men in Europe.

"We had services every Friday night. The Protestant chaplain ran the service. A Jewish boy from Brooklyn did the Hebrew part of it. Once in a while I'd see people who didn't exactly look Jewish coming to services because they found out we were serving wine!

"I went to all the services in the Navy—I went to Catholic and Protestant services too—I wanted to cover all of the bases, so I went to all of them."

While it is unfair to give the impression that Jewish chaplains were completely absent from the lives of Jewish airmen, Jewish airmen who were religious or who needed spiritual support often had to rely on one another.

Jews have always found ways to join together in worship, with or without the presence of a rabbi or chaplain. The more learned in the religion help the less learned; it is not a burden, rather a good deed. The "H" became a symbol, a declaration, and an identity. To members of a religious minority, especially in the ugliness of wartime, to locate others of your faith was a joy and comfort. That was the blessing of the "H."

In Judaism, you cannot conduct a full service to include the reading of the Torah, unless you have a *Minyan* or ten Jews brought together in prayer.[3] The tenth person who makes up the *Minyan* blesses the service.

Lieutenant Bernard Eder was a B-17 pilot with the 15th Air Force, 483rd Bombardment Group. He recalled the following:

"We get to Gander [Newfoundland], and out comes the jeep with the little flag.[4] We follow them in to where the airplanes are parked … this guy comes over to me and salutes, I salute back, and he says, 'Are there any Jewish crewmembers on your crew?' I said, 'Yeah, why?' He said, 'Well there's a Jewish holiday going on in the mess hall, and they need to know if there's any Jews on your plane, because they want you to join the ceremony.' That was Yom Kippur, September 1944.

"I went. They were looking for a Minyan and I said, 'Look, I've been flying for 7½ hours, I'm tired. You go pray—I'm going to lie down on one of these tables and go to sleep.' And that's what I did.

"There was no rabbi or anything but this was a group of Jewish men, airmen, who wanted to celebrate Yom Kippur, and I was the [tenth man] Minyan."

Sergeant Milton Fields who was assigned to Persian Gulf Command, recalled a story of his brother-in-law and another Jewish soldier who had come across a bombed out synagogue in a small French town. It was Rosh Hashanah 1944, and they gained permission to hold services in the space. Truckloads of Jewish infantrymen were brought in from the field.

Neither man was a rabbi, but they felt that they were performing a good deed by allowing Jewish soldiers to pray together.

The Curse

The curse for the Jewish airmen who flew over German-held territory, was the uneasy, gut-wrenching feeling that sooner or later, the "H" might get him killed.[5]

Staff Sergeant Morton Israel was a ball turret gunner on a B-24 bomber, assigned to the 446th Bombardment Group, and as many airmen did, he kept a diary. The following is from a 1943 briefing he attended:

"At a briefing, Intelligence [said] lately a few Air Force prisoners now were escaping back to Allied lines but *no* Jewish Air Force men were returning. Intelligence advised us Jewish fliers to hide our Jewish identity and dog tags because 'H' was on them, and the inference was Jewish prisoners of war were being treated differently."

A very small percentage of Jewish airmen claimed a different religious affiliation upon entering the service or left the religious designation blank as they were fearful of being captured. However, I never personally encountered an airman who admitted to this practice.

First Lieutenant George Lichter, remembered volunteering to work at his duty station as the Officer of the Day on Christmas (1944) so his fellow airmen could celebrate their holiday:

"I said, 'I'm Jewish, so I can be Officer of the Day and relieve somebody.' I wanted them to know I was Jewish, and I had 'H' for Hebrew on my dog tags. This guy comes to me, that nobody in the squadron liked, and he said, 'I want you to know I'm Jewish.' So I said, 'What do you want me to do? Make a party for you?' He said, 'No, no, no. I wanted you to know I'm Jewish, but I have 'B' for Baptist on my dog tag.[6] He told me this to say because if he got shot down or killed, he wanted a Jewish burial.' I was so glad they didn't know he was Jewish [because I couldn't stand him], I can't tell you."

Robert Teitelbaum was a liaison pilot who spotted and directed artillery fire. He was with the 5th Army, 985th Battalion and flew missions throughout Italy.

"I had heard about throwing away your dog tags. I didn't. I was a very good shot, and I carried a .45 on my hip. If they were going to kill me, I figured they were going with me."[7]

Every airman I interviewed knew that Hitler was making it bad for the Jews. At the time, no one could fathom how bad it was, but the issue of the "H" was a real and honest fear for the Jewish airmen. The following are the first-person recollections of ten Jewish airmen, a *Minyan*, who fell, or thought they were falling, to Nazi-held earth.

Falling from the Sky

First Lieutenant Alfred Benjamin flew out of RAF Grafton Underwood in England with the 8th Air Force. One mission in particular stands out in his memory:

"The mission was to either Hamm or Osnabrück Germany. This was my 13th mission. Incidentally, the mission was on September 19, 1944, and that mission was [fell on]Rosh Hashanah.

"Now I had the opportunity that day, if I wanted to, to say I won't fly on Rosh Hashanah. But I didn't want to change my luck in any way—I didn't want to shift anything around—so I flew that day."

As Benjamin explained, it was also a matter of loyalty; he would not abandon his crew.

"Over the target, we were hit by flak, and we lost oil in one of the engines. So we had to drop out of the formation and limp home on our own.

"Now we passed the Rhine River, and the Germans used flak barges—they would float these barges up and down, so we didn't know where they were. When we crossed over the Rhine, one of the flak barges was right under us, and they let go with us, and we lost two [more] engines.

"We started to drop everything out of the plane. We loosened everything we could and tried to get as far into friendly territory as we could. We kept losing altitude. We got down to about—I would say 12,000 feet to 13,000 feet, and this poor little engine was struggling along. My pilot said, 'I can't hold this thing much longer—we're going to have to go out.' His navigator, who was me, said, 'We can't go yet. Because I'm Jewish, and if I go now, I'm going to die.' I knew that if I went down I'd be dead.

"The crew knew it too. I had this map that showed where the German lines were in the morning, as far as intelligence could give us. I just told the pilot to head for this particular spot, and we'd just go as long as we could. We jumped, and we were about 10,000 feet. I landed on this soft spot on the ground and looked around, and I was surrounded by these people with submachine guns holding me prisoner. I thought, 'Oh, I'm gone.' But as it turned out, these were Belgian Free Forces. The Germans had pulled out that morning...."

"Rosh Hashanah has a special memory for me now, especially if it happens to fall on September 19th."

Ira Weinstein

First Lieutenant Ira Weinstein flew with the 8th Air Force out of RAF Tibenham, England, as part of the 445th Bombardment Group. Weinstein was raised in a Chicago suburb, in an Orthodox household with religious roots that went back to the Russian pale.

The date was September 27, 1944, and Weinstein knew he was tempting fate. Not only was it Yom Kippur but it also coincided with a rest day for his regular crew. Nevertheless, he attended a bombardment group briefing. He was motivated to look for an easy last mission; he had only one more mission in order to complete his 25th and final bomb run. He could return to stateside duty and his newly-wed life.

The mission was as safe as those types of missions could get; the bombers would have a fighter escort to the target. The objective was Kassel, a German town with numerous weapons factories.

First Lieutenant Ira P. Weinstein (standing, left) (courtesy Ira P. Weinstein).

"I went to the colonel and I said, 'Let me fly today. See if there's an opening on a crew.' He said, 'What are you, stupid? You don't volunteer, it's a Jewish holiday. You've got a three-day pass. Go to London. Have some fun. You know you never volunteer in the Army!' I remember that so clearly."[8]

"The Colonel wasn't Jewish but he was a straightforward guy. He was compassionate. I had a reputation. I am only five feet tall. So everybody knew me. If I went up to the bar, I had to look over the bar to order a drink! Everybody knew the little guy that was flying."

Even more to the point, Weinstein was a navigator-bombardier and an officer, but he volunteered to be a gunner in the nose of the lead plane of the squadron with a crew he had never flown with before. As happens in life, it is those times when we take something or someone for granted and mishandle that situation, that we pay the dearest price.

The Kassel Mission was among the most devastating air battles of the Second World War. As the 445th Bombardment Group approached its intended target, the lead bomber veered significantly off course. The rest of the 445th Bombardment Group followed. The theory that had originally been developed was that there was a significant navigation error that caused the 445th Bombardment Group to break from the bomber "stream" of 1,200 aircraft.

However, some historians speculate that the rocket research laboratories in Gottingen, Germany were the real target of the 445th, and the rest of the formation was diversionary. Whatever the reason, the bombers of the 445th lost their fighter escort and between 125 and 150 German fighter planes came out of the clouds to attack them.

Of the 35 bombers that made up the 445th Bombardment Group on that mission, only four returned to the base. In what has been described as "history's most concentrated air battle," within minutes, 28 bombers and 29 fighter planes were destroyed.[9] Within minutes, 118 Americans were killed and 121 were taken prisoner. Said Weinstein:

"God punished me by getting me shot down. He saved my life because I didn't get killed, OK? Only three of us got out of my airplane alive.

"The day I went on the mission, I went to get my parachute. The guy in the parachute room said, 'Sorry, lieutenant, your parachute is being re-packed.' I always wore a chest chute. As a bombardier, I always took the [chest] chute off and laid it by my side."

Had he followed the same procedure on this flight, he would have never found his chute in time. On this particular flight he continued to wear his main parachute on his back.

The nose turret gun was the forward-most position on the B-24 bomber. To get to the position, the airman crawled through a short tunnel, and then shut a door behind him. Weinstein was so busy defending the plane he didn't comprehend how badly the plane was damaged. When the realization hit, there was sheer panic as the door behind him was locked tight. The navigator pulled Weinstein out backwards.

"I owe five people my life, and he was one of them. Then I go to bail out, and my parachute gets caught on the bomb sight. I'm dangling out of the airplane, and the airplane is in a spin with terrific centrifugal force.[10] I chinned myself back up into the airplane, unhooked my strap, and got out again. All I can tell you, it's God's will."

The issue of the SS killing captured air corps personnel, and Jews in particular, may have been true, but the risk was compounded by a larger reality: Hitler said that it was a *civilian duty* to kill the *Terrorflieger* (terror flyers) who were presumably responsible for bombing their villages.[11]

Weinstein related the following to historian Aaron Elson of the Kassel Mission Historical Society of what had occurred prior to his capture.[12]

"I landed up in the hills, where a bunch of kids were picnicking. I got rid of my 'chute and ran up in the hills and I hid under some trees. My pilot, D–, must have bailed out of the top hatch. I'm presuming he must have hit his feet on the rudders. I saw him come down in the valley. He couldn't get up. Pretty soon some farmers came along and they pitch-forked him to death. When night came along, I went down and got his dog tags, and they had stripped him of everything but his underpants."

Weinstein evaded capture for more than a week by hiding in the forests and moving at night. He stole potatoes and other vegetables. As he couldn't swim, he was unable cross the lakes into Switzerland. He came upon a town named Nentershausen.

"There must have been twenty churches in the town. So I thought, 'If I'm ever going to get a fair shake, it'll be in a place where they had so many churches.'"

Filled with terror, Weinstein walked from the dense woods into the center of town.

"This kid walks alongside of me and says, 'You must be one of the Americans they're looking for.' I said, 'Yeah, what's going to happen to me?' He said, 'Well, I'm going to take you to the Burgermeister [Mayor].' I said to him, 'How come you speak such good English?' He said, "Well, I went to school in Milwaukee.' He took me to the Burgermeister—I must have looked like death warmed over, because remember the airplane was on fire, lots of grit, lots of soot, lots of stuff, burning oil. I hadn't shaved probably for two weeks."

The *Burgermeister* and his wife fed him soup and bread.

"The Burgermeister looked at my dog tags and said to me, 'If I turn you over to the military in this town that are the SS troops, they'll shoot you on sight. If you stay here, I will call the Air Force, the Luftwaffe, and they'll take care of you.' I have lived my whole life with Bashert.[13] What if he had said, 'Kill this Jewish son-of-a-bitch?'

"You know, at that time, I think the Burgermeister and his wife were so kind to me because there were a lot of Germans that began to realize that not only were they going to lose the war, but what was happening was wrong. I thought that anyplace where they have so many church steeples, there's got to be people with compassion."

Two hours later, guards from the *Luftwaffe* took him prisoner, drove him to a barracks, then threw him in with twenty other prisoners. Two of the enlisted men were badly injured and in dire need of medical attention. Weinstein realized that as he was the senior officer, it was his duty to request that the German commanding officer give the men medical attention.

"First I saluted him, and I gave him my name, rank, and serial number, and I said, 'Sir, according to the Geneva Convention, we have two badly wounded men, [and] they're entitled to medical care.' He came out from behind the desk with a riding crop, and hit me across the cheek and split my cheek open. 'I'll tell you about the Geneva Convention. You're bombing our schools and our churches and you're killing our people.'"

Shortly after, guards came into the cell and removed the prisoners for treatment. However, Weinstein and some other prisoners were forced to go to the American bombers that had been shot down. They were ordered to salvage the guns and bury the dead. He came upon *his* bomber, and had the task of burying the unrecognizable bodies of the men he had flown with only hours before.[14] He was then taken back for interrogation.

"The German intelligence was way above whatever we had. If you think you can outsmart them, or you're going to tell them some things so they'll be good to you, you could be there for weeks. Whatever he asked me, I said my name, rank, and serial number, and that's all he could get out of me. He [the interrogator] said to me, 'You're not an American—you're a spy—you were my neighbor in Frankfurt.' Well, you know, if you're a spy, you get shot.[15] You have to understand these guys were brilliant. They used all these little tricks. I didn't respond to that. I said my name, rank, and serial number, and that's all he ever got out of me. That's what we had been told to do.

"I was one of those guys that would not change my dog tags. The other thing is, they used to tell you, keep your dog tags, because if they find you without them, they're going to claim you're a spy and shoot you on the spot. So I know a lot of guys got rid of their dog tags—I didn't, and mine was stamped with an 'H.'"

Irwin Stovroff

Second Lieutenant Irwin Stovroff was brought down by flak near Caen, France on August 13, 1944. A bombardier assigned to the 8th Air Force, 44th Bombardment Group, 506th Bombardment Squadron. It was to be his 35th and final mission.[16]

Stovroff realized he was going to bail out into the German front lines. While he still had altitude, he threw away his dog tags. On the ground, the crew was immediately rounded up and marched to a cemetery for execution. An officer stepped in and wouldn't allow it. Stovroff still does not understand why.

The POWs were loaded on a truck and during the ride, Stovroff's pilot rolled over the side, through the canvas cover of the truck, and managed to escape back to friendly lines. The rest were transported by truck and train to a Dulag Luft, or interrogation center, in Wetzlar, Germany, where they were placed in solitary.

"My interrogator asked me questions I could not and would not answer. I gave him the usual name, rank and serial number, and told him that was all I had to give, and knew very little else.

"On my third trip to interrogation, he said, 'I know who you are and what you are [meaning Jewish].' He told me he could save my life, then proceeded to name my father, mother, brother, sister, the grammar school I had attended, even the name of a former girlfriend! He then said he lived on Ashland Avenue, next to the girl I was dating pre-war. He had lived on the next street, in Buffalo, New York! He said he remembered being in class with my older sister, and then he informed me that I had been his newspaper boy!

"He had come to Germany to be with his grandmother, and stayed. He again said he would help me, and he put a question mark on my records next to religion. His father was a piano teacher, and sure enough, the girl I knew took piano lessons from him, from his father."

After solitary confinement and interrogation at the Dulag Luft, Stovroff was packed into a boxcar with fifty other prisoners for a three-day transport to Stalag Luft I located in Barth, Germany.[17] The train was strafed by Allied fighters because the Germans did not put POW markings on the train.

Paul Kaufman

Paul Kaufman, as with Irwin Stovroff, would wind up in Stalag Luft I. However, his story shows that prisoners were caught or captured in a variety of ways. Each capture could carry its own degree of terror or absurdity.

"My rank was that of Second Lieutenant and I was a crewmember on a B-17 bomber that flew out of RAF Knettishall, England. We were part of the 388th Bombardment Group, 560th Bombardment Squadron. We were a replacement crew. The aircraft we would be shot down in was named *The Millie—K.*

Second Lieutenant Irwin J. Stovroff (courtesy Irwin J. Stovroff).

"We were shot down due to flak over Merseburg, Germany, which was a heavily protected site due to the synthetic oil plants. Estimates were that there were anywhere from 1,200 to 2,200 anti-aircraft guns in the city.

"The bomber sustained damage to the number one and number four engines. We figured that sooner or later fire would go through the wall. I got hit above the left eye, the left shoulder and left leg. The pilot had his right hand shot off up to the knuckles. The engineer had head wounds and the radioman in both legs. We made it as far as Koblenz and decided to abandon ship. There were nine of us in the crew and we all managed to get out and about 15 to 20 seconds after we got out, the plane exploded.

"In jumping, I lost my boots, my .45 went flying too. It wasn't much of a trip to the ground. It was a clear day and there wasn't too much wind blowing. On the way down, I saw a lot of farmers running toward me.[18] I landed in a freshly plowed field and at first I thought I was in France as I landed not more than 30 feet away from a farmer wearing a smock and a beret.

"Farmers came after me and then I heard a couple of shots or I thought I did. There was a captain [Hauptmann] with 10 or 12 Hitler youth. Their only armament was the little daggers that kids carry but the Hauptmann had an automatic weapon.

"He was friendly enough and he said, 'Come, come,' and I was a little bit bloody especially around the head. Then I noticed the women were running after me screaming. They wanted my parachute. He [the Hauptmann] was going to take me into town. They brought in my navigator. He had broken his back and they were carrying him on a ladder.

"I got a ride in an early model Volkswagen and they drove us toward the town of Flammersfeld which was our destination and on the way we were going through a dense forest. We stopped and I was told to get out. I thought, 'This is it,' but they just changed drivers. They took us into the cellar of the city hall, a yellow wooden building. We had four or five changes of guards. Finally there was an older man, a corporal, and he spoke English. He said, 'Are you an Englishman?' I said, 'No, I'm an American.' He got so excited. He asked if I had ever been to New York. I told him I lived in New York and he went wild. He asked me if I had ever been to the Cotton Club! I asked him how he knew. He was a musician on the Steamship Bremen and he came to New York every three weeks. He gave me one cigarette and they even sent a doctor down who said I was fit. They brought in another one of my crew who had a shattered leg and they took away the navigator with the broken back.

"Four guards came to take me to an airfield about 10 miles away. We were marching through Germany. They put my crewmember on a bicycle but the pain in his leg was so great he kept passing out. Finally they put him in a wheelbarrow and I was pushing him. I had had nothing to eat or drink.

Whenever columns of German soldiers would pass us, once they got behind us they would stretch out their right arms and say, 'Heil Hitler!'

"On the way to the airfield we walked; me barefoot, to the town of Altenkirchen first. It was a medieval looking town. I went uphill with the wheelbarrow dodging horse manure. Old women were hitting me with their pocketbooks. There was a water fountain at the top of the hill and I was able to get water.

"An SS lieutenant colonel in a beautiful uniform went over to our guards and said that we were 'terror flyers' and that he'd take over. The older guard stood up to the SS and said that he was sorry but that he had orders from the commanding general. My guard wouldn't give me up and the SS knocked me down and gave me a good kick in the ribs and then walked away. The Luftwaffe guys at the airfield had a different attitude. We were airmen and they were airmen. I asked for food for six of our crew who were there.

"We got on a train that night to Frankfurt. The head guard said, 'No noise, don't speak, etc.' They put us in the last car and gave us a knife and some rye bread. The Frankfurt train station had been bombed and was still smoldering. There were two British airmen hanging from the rafters. A crazy old lady was yelling at us saying, 'Kill them, kill them!'

"They put me on a trolley car took me to Oberursel where I was interrogated. They put me in a solitary cell after we had all been briefed. All I gave them was my name, rank and serial number.

"After nine days of interrogation, I got put on a train where we went to Wetzlar, Germany where we were de-loused, given a chance to clean up and issued clothes. Two days later we were put on a boxcar to Stalag Luft I. On the way, we got strafed in a marshalling yard. We were cheering while the Germans were hiding under the train."

Allen Sabol

Staff Sergeant Allen Sabol was assigned to the 8th Air Force, 492nd Bombardment Group, 856th Bombardment Squadron as a tail gunner on a B-24. On August 4, 1944, he was on his sixth mission heading for the submarine pens at Kiel, Germany. At that point in the war, German submarines were wreaking havoc on shipping in the Atlantic.

Sabol's plane encountered flak almost from the start of the mission. The loss of Sabol's aircraft and his act of saving the life of a fellow crewmember was described in Chapter 4. However, there would be no leading actor-type escape for Sabol himself. With a badly injured right hand and strong winds almost blowing him into the sea, he was immediately captured.

"There was the local police and whoever with guns and everything. They took us to a town named Leck.[19] We were in solitary for a day or two. They hurried us out of the police station because the town folks found out about us and were going to hang us. They were getting a rope. The police got us out just in time.[20] They put us on a truck and then we went on the train to the Dulag Luft.

"Almost all Air Force, enlisted and officers, went through what's called a Dulag Luft, which was the interrogation center. You emptied your pockets. They cleaned you out. And they say, 'If you don't tell us everything, we won't tell the Red Cross that we got you.' Of course, you wanted your parents to know that you were safe.

"The Jewish boys were told, 'Throw your dog tags away immediately,' because on the dog tag it's got an 'H.' I kept my dog tags. The [U.S.] government issued Jews a prayer book. I kept my prayer book, because I always used to do a little praying. I couldn't read the Hebrew, but I could always pray in English, going over the target and coming back.

"I told the interrogator I'm Jewish—of course he sees my dog tags. He sees the prayer book. Oh man, it was scary. He's jumping up and down, he went crazy. He was calling me a Jew bastard, a dirty Jew.

"I really wanted to get that little prayer book back after being stripped, but I couldn't. The only thing I could get a hold of was a pair of my gunner wings. Fortunately, whatever happened, happened, I can't tell you. I kept asking for years, did I do the right thing [by keeping my dog tags]? I would ask religious people, knowledgeable people, and they didn't know what I was talking about.

"Until one day not too long ago, I found a passage—you know what the Chumash is?[21] I found a little passage that says, 'Don't look for miracles. They do happen.' That told me that I did the right thing. We were put on a train and sent to Stalag Luft IV, the camp in Poland."

Robert Lerner

Staff Sergeant Robert "Bob" Lerner was a gunner on a B-26 Martin "Marauder." The B-26 carried a crew of six. Lerner flew with the 9th Air Force, 386th Bombardment Group, and 555th Bombardment Squadron.

In the winter of 1943, V-2 rockets were pounding London and other targets. It fell on the 386th Bomb Group to locate and destroy rocket launchers in France, Holland and Belgium. While on their 16th mission to the French coast, Lerner's bomber was hit by intense anti-aircraft fire.

"We dropped from 12,000 feet to 3,000 feet. I sat on a bucket there [in the bomber] with my head down, knowing we were going to die. Somehow the copilot—he was half knocked out himself when the shell exploded—pulled the plane out of a steep dive.

"The pilot went to get out, but he took a shell right in his back, and it was wide open. He was dying. The copilot tried to ease him out of the chair, but he wouldn't go—he said, 'You better go ahead because I can't make it.'

"I and the other four bailed out. But everybody got out as far as I'm concerned, everybody but the pilot. Part of my parachute got caught in a tree, and I was half kind of dangling a couple feet off the ground. Then here comes a row of German soldiers about ten to twelve to fifteen coming toward me, and they took me prisoner."

Lerner was transported by train to the Dulag Luft interrogation center near Frankfurt, Germany.

"Well, the interrogator said to me, he says, 'What is your religion?' I was going to tell him Episcopalian or whatever because I threw away my dog tags because they got Hebrew on it, the 'H.' He says, 'What is your religion?' So as God was my witness—I said I'm a Hebrew. He said, 'You're a Hebrew? They haven't shot you yet?' So that turned my ears up. He was just trying to scare me.

"It just came out—I wasn't going to deny my religion, and that's the God's honest truth. When the interrogation was over, then they lined us all up and put us in cells. The next morning, they let me out [of my solitary cell]. The [other bunch of guys] were [already] going to a prisoner of war camp. I said, 'Oh my God, the bastard's [are] going to shoot me after all. But I just got a scare there, that's all. Why they called me out, I don't know, but they didn't talk to me or anything. That was it."

Yale Feingold

Staff Sergeant Yale Feingold was a gunner with the 8th Air Force, 95th Bombardment Group, 336th Bombardment Squadron. He said he felt somewhat lucky to have been taken a prisoner. Eighth Air Force bomber crews were told early on in the air war "if you make it to your 16th mission you're probably dead." The 8th Air Force suffered about 47 percent of all the casualties in the air war. Feingold had made it to his 24th mission.

"We flew 24 missions over Germany, and I got shot down on the 24th. On the last mission the name of the plane we were in was called the *Sack Robber*, because we never got enough sleep. We used to wake up early in the morning to go on a mission. I believe we flew our first missions in the latter part of 1943 through March of 1944. We were shot down before D–Day.

"We had one more mission to go, and we were scheduled to go back to the states on a bond tour. My bags were packed and everything—we were scheduled to go back. When we completed that mission, we had one more to go. At that time, we only had to fly 25 missions, and then you were done, you went back to the states. But we got shot down on the 24th—very unfortunate. It might have been a good thing, because even though I spent 14 or 15 months in Germany, I might have been sent somewhere else, and it could have been a worse ending.

"I got shot down over Augsburg, Germany, and I did parachute down. I was taken prisoner and interrogated and then I was sent off to Frankfurt, and interrogated in Frankfurt.

"I've heard stories over the years about the SS, although everybody that I know—and I had a couple friends that were prisoners also—we never heard of any of them that were actually captured and brutalized or killed—I don't know, I can't say. Although I was very lucky, because I never wore my dog tags around my neck—I just didn't like them dangling there. So I had my dog tags on an O-ring, and I had them attached to my shoes, a pair of shoes, in the plane. And I figured if I ever had to jump, I would just grab my shoes and click that O-ring. Because I wore a different kind of boot in the ball turret—I wore like a heated boot.

"Well, I jumped out of the plane, and I forgot to grab my shoes with my dog tags. When I got interrogated in Frankfurt, they obviously knew I was a Jew, and maybe I am a little Semitic looking. But I was interrogated with the Germans and the Red Cross there, and I was never threatened in any way. I expected to be shot as a Jew without a dog tag. Fortunately, I was sent off to a camp from there, and I never was threatened as a Jew in Germany as a prisoner. They asked me very little, my name and serial number, where I came from, what my position was. They kept me in a cell for about three days, and then I just got on one of those boxcars with a lot of other poor souls, and we were shipped all the way up into a camp in East Prussia.

"I was actually in about three or four different camps. I was originally way up in East Prussia up on the Baltic. When the Russians started to advance in that area, we were transported across the Baltic and went to a town called Stettin, Germany [Note: After the war, Szczcin, Poland] I remember, and marched to a camp there."

William "Bill" Wagner

Technical Sergeant Bill Wagner was a radioman and waist gunner on a B-17 that was assigned to the 8th Air Force, 457th Bombardment Group and 749th Bombardment Squadron. On March 21, 1945, the Bombardment Group was ordered to attack airfields around Hopsten, Germany where the Me-262 jets were based.

German jet aircraft were a frightening sight for the Allied bomber crews.[22] On a prior mission, Wagner's plane encountered gunfire from a German jet. He recalled scrambling from the radio compartment to the waist gun in an attempt to get off a shot. The jet fired off a few rounds and they went through the radio compartment where he had been sitting. Wagner's crew was credited with knocking down one of only four Me-262s in aerial combat during the Second World War. The jets were precious to the Germans and the airfields were heavily guarded.[23]

"We got clobbered by flak. The pilot had no control. We were given the order to evacuate. I didn't hit the ground right and I cracked my ankle. I took off my dog tags and hid them in my pocket. Five minutes or less after I hit the ground, we were set upon by German troops. We figured that this was the German home guard, consisting of soldiers as well as civilians. Had the SS, rather than the home guard, found us, I don't know how it would've turned out for me.

"Guys like me and other Jewish airmen would talk about, among other things, what about your dog tags if you ever get shot down over Germany? And guys told me they had a different set of dog tags made that revealed that they were Protestant or Catholic. They were the smart ones. I was the lucky one. I hid mine."

He was marched into the town of Schwelm.

"I remembered being by myself—not an official jail, but just like a beer hall, possibly, with a spare room. And that's where I remember being kept until other guys were captured. I don't remember really rubbing shoulders with them [the other prisoners] in Schwelm. I remember being marched with them on the way to the prison camp, but that was it."

While under guard, Wagner was visited by a young girl in traditional German garb. Her name was "Luz" or "Lucia." She spoke halting English, and seemed fascinated by the downed airman. The scene was bizarre.

"I imagine we talked about the usual subjects, but a specific subject, I couldn't tell you. I was absolutely dumbfounded by the scenario. I can recall how she was dressed; very small-townish, what you would expect a country girl to wear, including knit socks that came up to her knees. She wasn't angry. There wasn't any bitterness. It was like being on the moon because her words, or something to the equivalent were, 'I've never seen an American before, I never talked to one. I really wanted to experience.' I think something saved me that day. I spoke in front of a Catholic girl's school once and said that I thought that it might have been God. I'm not an atheist—I'm an agnostic."

Jack Sorkin

Second Lieutenant Jack Sorkin flew out of RAF Podington, England, assigned to the 8th Air Force, 92nd Bombardment Group, 325th Bombardment Squadron. He was a navigator on a B-17 named *Coker's Jokers*. The bomber formation was flying a mission over Cottbus, in eastern Germany, where they were met by anti-aircraft fire and fighter planes.

"We were attacked by fighters and in fact, that's what shot us down. But I think the flak was what probably got more of us. The flak hit the wing, and went through the nose. One of the shells blew up, and I got a piece in my leg. I heard somebody say, 'There goes the wing.' I hooked up my chest pack and went out the hatch. Three of us didn't make it."

He landed in a field by some woods. Any thought of making a heroic run toward the trees was quickly forgotten; the shrapnel in his leg forced him to crawl.

"Somebody came up behind me and said, 'Hände hoch! Hands up!' He was pointing a gun at me, and that was the end of my attempt to escape. This was a civilian."

The civilian was a member of the German Home Guard. They brought Sorkin to a jail.

"We got picked up by the armed forces and ended up at Stalag VII-A. When the interrogation took place, the interrogator said, 'I see by your dog tags you are Jewish.' I said yes. It didn't go much further than that. He knew what base I had come from. I figured they probably had [a record of] the insignia on the airplane. We had a triangle B on our tail—and I'm sure they must have had a list of all the groups that flew and what their insignias were."

Bernard Eder

It was Bernard Eder who volunteered to sleep on a table in the mess hall so his fellow Jews could conduct the full Yom Kippur service just a few feet away. Despite his good deed, Eder was shot down in enemy territory in November 1944 while he flying a civilian harassment mission.

"I would fly along with five other planes and on this mission we flew into Czechoslovakia, where they were making gun barrels for their big Howitzers and cannon. We dropped two preset bombs. The Germans didn't know who was coming, because we were all in the clouds. And we would throw chaff, little pieces of foil, out of the side windows and that chaff would be picked up the German radar, and they'd think there were a lot of planes coming. The people [laborers] had to go down into the shelters, and they lost a day's work trying to find and then defuse the bombs.

"I was shot down by anti-aircraft fire on my ninth mission. When we were first captured, it was in the Alps because we were trying to get to Switzerland on two engines. We just couldn't get high enough to get over some of the rocks. I had the crew bail out, and then I bailed out. I was captured by three ski troopers and they took me to a little town on a one-horse sleigh like you see with Santa Claus. The town had one major building, the town hall. They took me upstairs to a little jail where the town drunks stayed.

"They gave me an apple that first night. They were chopping kraut—everybody was chopping up cabbage, because that's about all they had to eat. Next day, they took me down to the mayor's office. There's a little girl—maybe she was 13, 14 years old, and the only telephone in the town. The mayor or whoever he was rang up someone, and the little girl talked to someone.

"She turned to me and she said, 'I speak softly in the name of the police—what is your name?' I gave her my name, and she gave it to the [listener]. Then she turned to me and asked, 'What is your rank?' And I say second lieutenant. She repeated that on the phone, and she says, 'What is your serial number?' She had trouble saying that. I gave her my number. Then she said, 'What was your base?' I said, 'Nichts, I cannot tell you any more—that's all I have to tell you, is my name, my rank, and my serial number.' She turned white, because I understood that she was going to tell these people on the telephone that I refused to answer any more questions.

"But she went back on the phone, and I could hear how her explanation went—I couldn't repeat it to you now, but she said, 'Convention cease.' Evidently they understood that I was invoking my rights under the Geneva Convention. They didn't bother me anymore, but she was scared silly. Every time she questioned me, all three times, she would say first, 'I speak softly in the name of the police.' Now she said to me 'police,' but it could have been Gestapo—it could have been anybody.

"I stayed there three days, and then the guards took me on a narrow gauge railroad down to this airbase, and that's where I met my crew. We took the trains to the interrogation center. I was questioned for two weeks.

"Our guards kept us pretty much alive. We were in the station [going to interrogation] and an old man came up and started shouting and cursing at us. The guards told him to move on, and he went away. He came back with about ten kids, and they started throwing rocks at us. That's when our guards really got upset and made them leave. The old man I can understand, but why would these kids come and throw rocks at other human beings?

"One of my crewmembers, an officer, was a Bostonian Catholic. He had a crucifix on and they tore it off of his neck, and they threw it in the fire. I said I'm next because my dog tags have an 'H' on them but they didn't. They knew I was the commander of the aircraft, and that I was in charge of these other eight men who were with me."

Imprisonment

In the European Theater in World War II, 12,000 Heavy bombers (B-17s and B-24s) were shot down, along with more than 6,000 fighter planes.[24] The crew on a B-17 bomber or B-24 bomber was normally 10. There were also Medium bombers, such as the B-26; the crew was six. More than 88,000 airmen died in World War II with another 3,600 who went missing in action.[25]

In regard to statistics, consider just one more: about 36,000 prisoners of the air war were captured by Germany and its European Allies.[26]

The Nazis set up a series of Stalag Lufts intended solely for POWS who were crewmembers of bombers or fighter planes.[27] The Nazi regime, and specifically Hermann Goering, considered aviators a step above the common infantryman. Goering, himself a World War I "Ace," created the Stalag Lufts specifically under the command of the Luftwaffe to house Allied pilots and crews. The camps were segregated by rank, either officers or enlisted.

Stalag Luft III

In regard to the Jewish airmen, the German Stalag system had an obvious incongruity. On one hand, the Nazis set the extermination of the Jews as one of its highest priorities, and on the other (at least in the first years of the war), camps such as Stalag Luft III allowed Jewish aviators to remain unharmed.

Bernard Eder, the pilot who was interrogated by the young girl, wound up in Stalag Luft III, a prison camp for officers. The camp was near Sagan, Germany.[28] Stalag Luft III was the camp on which the movie *The Great Escape* was based.

"Our camp had an auditorium. We had a music room, we had classrooms, and we had correspondence courses with the University of London. You could learn anything you wanted in that camp."

There was a system in place for bidding on Red Cross food packages, and every so often beer was made available.[29] There was a camp newspaper, camp radio station, sports, and occasional access to a "swimming pool" that was normally in use as a reservoir.

"I'll tell you what, Christmas we put on—and I was a trumpet player, so I know this intimately ... we put on the *Messiah*, the whole thing. The German officers, guards, and people came in and listened. Handel was German and they got a big kick out of it. We put on the play *The Boys from Syracuse*. We had musical instruments from the International YMCA."

However, appearances were deceiving. Six months prior to Eder's imprisonment in Stalag Luft III, 77 British officers had tunneled from the North compound. Of the 77 escapees, all but two were re-captured. On Hitler's command, 50 of the 75 were executed by the Gestapo. The bodies were cremated. Sometime later, 50 urns were returned to the camp.

Eder pointed out that as a "Kriege," or prisoner-of-war, they had very little day-to-day contact with their captors.[30] Guards were called "Goons," and they were not to be trusted, even those who could be bribed. The guards harassed, stole, spied and listened.

"Some officers and men of the camp's garrison were genuinely hated by the prisoners. Most of the others tried to be decent to the POWs, often under difficult circumstances and the threat of severe punishment if they were caught doing anything that could be considered contrary to Germany's war effort."[31]

Jack Sorkin was also a prisoner at Stalag Luft III. Over the course of several months, the flak that had embedded itself in his leg slowly worked its way out. In fact, many of the airmen I interviewed recalled pieces of metal or Plexiglas slowly coming to the surface—sometimes years after the injury. As opposed to Bernard Eder, Jack Sorkin recalled several anti–Semitic incidents among his fellow POW officers, but mostly it was talk. This is rather incredible; anti–Semitism was alive and well among fellow Allied airmen even inside POW camps!

"There was one guy from Chicago.... I don't remember his last name—but he was a big burly guy. He made some [remarks] ... and the other guys who were not Jewish sort of told me afterwards that he wasn't speaking for all of them at all, and that we were all together in this, and that kind of thing."

The Gauntlet

Allen Sabol never doubted that he was headed for trouble. After interrogation, he was packed on a rail car without food or water and sent to Stalag

Luft IV. The camp was located in Gross Tychow, Poland.[32] The cattle cars could be jammed with as many as 85 POWs, equaling the manner of transport of ghetto residents to the concentration camps.

The simple brick train station that stood in the small town of Keifeide, Germany, was about two and a half miles from the entrance to Stalag Luft IV. The POWs had to run a gauntlet between the train station and the prison.

Upon leaving the boxcars, the groups of prisoners, sometimes shackled, sometimes not, were run in formation. Most carried heavy backpacks. While running, the townspeople threw all kinds of objects at them; they were struck with rifle butts, kicked, and spit on. If a man slowed, he was bayoneted in the legs and buttocks. The stab wounds went in as deep as three inches. If a man fell, he was set upon by attack dogs. *If* a man had been able to unshackle himself and take off into the woods, he would have been met by guards who were hiding behind trees to shoot them as escapees.

Sabol recalled:

"I don't know exactly how far from the train station to the camp. Most of us were shackled, and we were walking up to the camp. And about halfway there, this German officer comes down and raises all kinds of—he really put on a big show, because the guards didn't run us. We were supposed to run from the train station, and here we're shackled together. When you have those—they're vicious dogs—terribly vicious—and those bayonets, you just took off and did exactly what they wanted. We made it; nobody was badly hurt. But previously there were some casualties."

Captain Henry J. Wynsen, was the Senior American Medical Officer at Stalag Luft IV. He gave testimony for the Judge Advocate General's Office, on July 20, 1945, and stated the following:

"[I] and Captain Wilber McKee treated injured American and British soldiers who had been bayoneted, clubbed, and bitten by dogs, while on route from the railroad station to Stalag Luft IV, a distance of approximately three kilometers. The number of wounds [per soldier] varied from one to as many as sixty...."[33]

Robert "Bob" Lerner, the airman whose B-26 was shot down over France while trying to destroy V-2 rocket launchers, was initially imprisoned at Stalag Luft VI, in Heydekrug, in eastern Germany. Heydekrug is a town located in a desolate, wind-blown area on the edge of the Baltic Sea in what was Memelland, now Lithuania. Yale Feingold was also part of the Stalag Luft VI prison population.

In mid–July 1944, the camp authorities rounded up the prisoners of Stalag Luft VI, had them quickly gather their possessions, and marched them to boxcars for relocation. The Russians were bearing down. Some called the POW relocation the "Heydekrug Run" while others remember it as a vision of hell.[34]

Bob Lerner, Yale Feingold and 1,000 other American airmen were transported to the sea port town of Memel. They were forced down a ladder at gunpoint into the darkened hull of a confiscated Russian rust-bucket of a ship, the *Masuren*. They were packed three men deep. The heat and stink was oppressive beyond imagination. In addition, the waters had been heavily mined by Allied bombers, and though the vessel had crude anti-mine protection, the prisoners knew the ship could strike a mine and explode at any moment. The first day, the men were briefly allowed on deck. Lerner said:

"Now there was one guy, I guess he was a little off his rocker by now, he wouldn't go [back] down in the hull, and he jumped overboard. The Germans tried to get him back, but he wouldn't come in, so they machine gunned him. Actually, it was the best thing that could have happened to him because otherwise he'd have drowned.

"We were in the hull … and we had nothing to eat or drink for three days. Now if you had to use the bathroom, there were none. They didn't let you. So we sat there like that because there was no room to move around."

The ship docked in the German port city of Swinemünde, where the already weakened and filthy prisoners were shackled, and loaded in boxcars for the trip to the Keifeide train station, where they were then forced to run the gauntlet into Stalag Luft IV. Bob Lerner's recollection of the run was similar to Sabol's:

"When they moved us to Stalag Luft IV, they ran us for about three miles up to where the camp was. The guys that couldn't keep up or fell—they let them have it with the bayonet in the legs."

If Stalag Luft III was a model camp for officers, Stalag Luft IV was notches below. Camp life was basic and harsh. According to Sabol:

"[The barracks] were … just put up wood sides, and the whole thing was wood all the way around. The bunks were—well we had straw for mattresses. [The bunks] were two high because there was probably 25 or more in a room, at least."

Stalag Luft IV was intended for NCOs, sergeants of all ranks. There were 40 wooden huts with each hut containing about 200 men. Each hut was further subdivided into rooms. The camp was twice as crowded as it should have been. In some compounds, men slept on the floor. There was no heat. The POWs learned to make crude stoves.

Jewish Prisoners in Stalag Luft IV

If there was no segregation of Jews in Stalag Luft IV, it was not for lack of trying. The following deposition was taken from William Krebs in June of 1947 by the Judge Advocate, War Crimes Investigation. Krebs was transferred from Stalag Luft VI in the same group as Bob Lerner and Yale Feingold. He became invaluable to the POW leadership as he spoke fluent German.

"Reinhard Fahnert had charge of the prison guard and supervised the distribution of food to the prisoners. Fahnert was a rough character, and was always after anyone of Jewish extraction. He wanted to segregate all Jewish prisoners from the others in order to give them all the hard work and menial tasks."

Lerner added:

"There were some rumors that the Germans were going to segregate the Jewish prisoners. But it never took place, so they let us alone. We stayed in our own barracks. But they [those in charge of the Stalag Luft] did put out Jewish propaganda and materials that were gathered up [by the prisoners] and burned.

"When we were on the march, one of the Germans said to me, 'What are you doing in this Army? Don't you know there's not one Jew in the American Air Force or Army?' That's the information he gave me—that was Hitler's propaganda. Strange, isn't it?"[35]

Following the war, a deposition was given by Frank Paules, Allied POW camp leader, in regard to Captain of the Guards, Walther Pickhardt.[36] The captain was placed under arrest for his brutality.

"It was reported by friendly German personnel that during his many speeches to guards, he [Pickhardt] stated it would be better if the POW's were all shot, then they would not have to feed them; that POW's were swine and not to be treated as men. Pickhardt was one of the most fanatical Nazis I ever encountered. He had the complete confidence of the camp commander, and the regime of terror seemed to be part of a plan carefully mapped out by both Bombach [the commander] and Pickhardt."

Given the mind-set of both Fahnert and Pickhardt, it is likely they would have isolated and then forced slave labor upon the Jewish personnel as happened in other camps.

Allen Sabol and Bob Lerner had never met prior to being POWs. Sabol was driven out of his room in the barracks and joined up with the men in Lerner's room.

"In Bob Lerner's room, there were several Jewish boys. It was fortunate for me, because the room that I was assigned to ... there were such anti–Semitic people there, that I just didn't spend hardly any time in that room. Anti-Semitism was running wild. [They said] 'Jews don't fight, and Jews don't do this, and this, and everything.' They had nobody else to hammer. That's why they'll always have us, because without us they'll start hammering on each other.

"Of course, there was no recourse you know, I just let it, just brushed it off, so I happened to go into Bob's room and just fell in with those guys."

If activities in Stalag Luft III and Stalag Luft IV suggested potential problems for Jewish personnel, Stalag Luft I, a camp for Allied air force officers, made little secret of its intentions.

Segregation

Stalag Luft I located in Barth, Germany, was isolated by the Baltic Sea, forests and marshes. Though a camp for officers like Stalag Luft III, there was little pretense at creating a "paradise." The Kommandant and his staff took Hitler's edict seriously—to segregate and ultimately to execute all of the Jewish prisoners.

Irwin Stovroff, the prisoner who was interrogated by the son of his sister's piano teacher, Paul Kaufman, the prisoner who transported a fallen crewmember in a wheelbarrow and Ira Weinstein, the airman who was shot down in the carnage of the Kassel Mission, were all sent to Stalag Luft I following their interrogations.

In February of 1945, guards pulled Stovroff out of formation and marched him to an assembly point in a remote part of the camp. He was put into an all Jewish barracks. Stovroff did dispel a rumor—Jewish airmen in Stalag Luft I were not required to wear a yellow star.

"There was no doubt about it, they knew I was Jewish. As we began to settle down in the [segregated barracks], it was very much—as far as getting food or getting coal for your furnace, or going out for inspection, I don't think there was very much difference. The real difference was in your mind.

"Let me put it this way—let's say you're in a whole group with a whole bunch of people—everybody was exactly the same. All of a sudden you are pulled out, and you are put into a special barracks. You are taken away from the whole group, and there you are as a single group standing out there in a place where you are really hated because of your religion. Now how would you think? It's not only isolating. You begin to feel that, you know, what is the future now?"

On September 8th, 2001, Stovroff was asked to make comments at a Stalag Luft I reunion in Barth, Germany. In order to write his speech, he reached out to other Jewish prisoners who were in the segregated barracks with him.[37]

"After being shot down, eventual capture, beatings, solitary confinement, and interrogations were our fate. While riding in the box cars we were strafed and bombed by the Allied forces and finally reached the relative safety of Stalag Luft I, except for about 250 Jewish Air Force officers who at a later date were segregated with a death sentence to follow.

"While we all shared the guard houses, the guards, the dogs, inspections, roll calls, the food or lack of it, nothing could compare to the feeling of helplessness that came over us when Hitler issued this order [to segregate and execute the Jewish prisoners]. In early February, 1945 the segregation began by using different methods in each compound.

"I was in Compound 2 when my name was called to remain in formation when others were dismissed. Major Cy Manierre, a brother to my co-pilot [who was in Stovroff's original barracks] was Adjutant in Compound 3 and had told his brother that Jewish personnel would be moved from the camp at some time on a death sentence because of being Jews.

"To this day, I believe that strength and sheer guts of our American POW leaders, Colonel Hubert Zemke and Colonel Spicer who we understood told the Kommandant that this was a violation of the Geneva Convention [and] that a protest would be filed and given to the International Inspectors were what saved us. In addition, the action by the Nazi's was a crime against American Officers; persecuted for their religious beliefs. The following is my story and [that of] other Jewish Officers:

"'I was marched out of my compound to the segregated barracks in North I, Block I, Room 13 which was next to a munitions dump. There was a minimum of fourteen Jewish men per room. We were allowed to eat in the central mess hall but most of our time was spent in a segregated area. The element of not knowing the next move placed a tremendous amount of pressure on all Jewish prisoners....'"

Ex-POW Max Kateff remembered:

"After being in camp for about four months, Hitler ordered all Jews to be killed. Other Jewish-American officers and I were forced from our barracks and separated from the camp in preparation for their final solution. A senior American officer was able to prevent this from happening. This is something I will never forget."

Similarly, Aaron Kuptsow volunteered:

"One morning, in early February, at roll call, they called out a bunch of our names and told us to remain after dismissal. After the others left, we were marched through the camp to another barracks and were told that was our new home. I was in a room with 13 others—and after talking for a few minutes, we realized that we were all Jewish. All other rooms were checked and they were also Jewish and realized that this was a Jewish barracks. Our barracks was in a distant corner of the camp surrounded by barbed wire and isolated. Rumors started to spread that, during one night, we would probably be marched out and sent to death camps and no one would know. A decision was made to notify the Geneva Convention of our situation through our camp American top officers.... The process could take months, but there was nothing else we could do."

The Paul Kaufman Story

If the stories Stovroff told of isolation, possible forced labor and execution were not alarming enough, the story of Paul Kaufman takes the first-hand accounts to another level.

"We arrived at the town of Barth and then into camp. The prison camp was crude with barbed wire, guard towers and Swastikas. There were rolls of barbed wire between barbed wire fences in the compounds.

"I again got interrogated and signed in. While on line to be processed, I remember that there was a guard who had once lived in Long Island City [New York] and he asked each prisoner his religion. When it got to me, I said 'Jewish.' He said, 'Oh, will you keep your beard?' [Note: he was clean-shaven.]

"Life in camp for the first couple of weeks was new and strange. We had roll call two times a day and the numbers had to match. I was assigned to a 16 man room. We had a secret radio somewhere in the camp and we were happy when we heard that the Russians and the Americans were doing well.

"At Christmas of 1944 we received Red Cross Parcels and a loaf of bread. We had home-made brew made from prunes and raisins. On that Christmas Eve we had an old wind-up Victrola and records and we played songs like, *I'll Be Home for Christmas*. Then the parcels stopped for two months and we started to lose a lot of weight. I would sometimes bend over to tie my shoes and I would faint.

"[When] the week the Battle of the Bulge was going on it became clear that the war was not going well for the Germans. Hitler issued an order to kill all the Jewish prisoners and we thought it was all a rumor. I saw Colonel Zemke, our Senior POW Officer. I walked up to him and saluted and I said, 'Colonel, there's a crazy rumor that they're going to kill all the Jews.' He said, 'I'm working on it,' and he kept walking. Three or four days later, the Germans came to get me. I waved good-bye to everybody [in my barracks] with a lot

Second Lieutenant Paul P. Kaufman, POW file taken from kommandant's office. Note "Jude!" written by guards (courtesy Andrew and Corinne Kaufman).

of bravado. They gave me chocolate and margarine and told me to make a run for it.

"I said to myself, 'Run where?'

"You think of crazy things. I wanted to be shot from the front and not from the back. What difference it would make, I don't know. They took me out of the main gate to an open field. I was freezing. I just had on an overcoat over my underwear and I had on boots but no socks. It was a miserable, freezing, cold night. The guards had a big fire going in an oil drum. I tried to get over to it and they told me to stand in front of a rock. So I did. Three of the guards picked up rifles and I said to myself, 'This is it.'

"I didn't think about mother or father or sister or family or friends. I just thought about how dumb this is and how am I going to stand? At first I thought I would salute, but then why would I salute them? I put my hands at 'Parade Rest,' and they leveled their rifles and I heard three clicks. They laughed like hell. They had no orders to shoot me. They wanted to see what kind of reaction they would get. Unfortunately, they didn't tell me that.

"Another group of guys soon arrived and by morning there were more than 200 and the next morning they marched us back into the compound. I went into Block 11. I had to find a bed; there was no one there that I knew.

"It was so damn embarrassing and I felt so betrayed. What was the worst wasn't the fear of death. What haunts me is the humiliation of not being considered an American soldier but of being singled out because I was a Jew.

"There were a lot of Jews in camp who didn't get taken. We knew or we suspected that our camp commander Zemke had the Germans round us up to get us together and sort of put us on ice. We knew that any day could be our last day, but the days went on. There was a deal made between Colonel Zemke with von Warren to offer him free conduct behind the American lines.[38]

"The Germans knew they were losing the war. The Bulge was over and they were down to their last bullets. It was a matter of who was going to get them, us or the Russians.

"Every guard was sure we'd make a separate peace and both of us would fight the Russians. They were convinced of that. They knew what they did to the Russians.

"In May 1945, there were no dogs, no guards in the tower. They had marched off into the night. I found out much later there was an agreement with Colonel Zemke and the Germans. They agreed not to take us hostages which they wanted to do. The POWs would fight to the last man if they had tried to take us hostage. We let them walk out without making any fuss.

"We know a Russian column caught up with the guards because the dogs came back. I doubt that any of the guards survived. Two days later the Russians came to the camp. They had no clue as to who we were. POWs took off and 'went home' on their own. I went into town and saw the cathedral. There was tremendous euphoria obviously. We stayed with the Russians 10 days before the Americans caught up. We were over 9,000 officers.

"They evacuated us to Camp Lucky Strike, a kind of depot.[39] They put us back into decent condition. I was sitting by myself in the mess hall and an officer came up to me and said, 'How're you doing son?' I looked up and it was General Eisenhower and an aide. Nothing came out of my mouth."

There is one last detail of the Paul Kaufman story. After the guards and their officers fled the camp, Kaufman found his way into the Kommandant's office. In their haste to retreat, the camp administration abandoned their files and Kaufman was able to find his records. Under religion, it was officially typed "jüdisch" (Jewish). However, over his POW pictures front and profile someone had written in a bold, blue script, "Jude!" It was an exercise in eugenics; there is little doubt at least some of the Jewish airmen were singled out.

Ira Weinstein, on the other hand, had a quite a different experience in the same camp.

"When I became a prisoner, the camp was not segregated. At one point, Hitler came to our camp—this was months after I was a POW, maybe three, four, five months, I don't remember. He left word that all the Jews were to be separated, taken out and shot. They went through every room. They took out all the Jews and put them in a separate camp. I was not put in that camp—they never took me out of my room.

"I went to the American Commanding Officer [Zemke] and I said, 'Colonel, I'm Jewish.' He said, 'Go back in your room, shut up and be quiet. You don't know how lucky you are.' So I never was in that camp with the other Jews, they just segregated them in another compound.[40]

"The American Commander of the camp was Hubert Zemke. He was an ace during the war. He had a German heritage, I think, and he spoke German. He went to the—this is a story I remember—he went to the German commander and said, 'There are only 100 of you, and 12,000 of us. You move one man out of this camp [to the concentration camps], we're going to riot. You'll kill a lot of us; we'll kill a lot of you. So I wouldn't plan on that if I were you.' I don't think that the German Commander of the camp would've done it anyhow."

Weinstein noted that some of the prisoners were unsympathetic to the plight of the Jewish airman:

"I don't think there was any special sympathy for us, no, not at all. This was after the Jews were moved, alright? I forget what this guy said—he was not a nice guy to begin with. As a matter of fact, we used to get a shower once a week or once a month—I don't remember what it was—and he never went. Well, there was a first lieutenant in our room who had been commissioned a couple months ahead of me, so he was the ranking officer in our room. He said to this guy, 'You know, if you don't take a shower, we're going to move your bed out into the hall.' We did, OK? This guy came into the room, sometime after the Jews were already marked, and he made some [anti–Semitic] remark. Because I was so little, I slept on the fourth level of the bunk. I jumped down off that bed on top of him, and we had a pretty good to-do until the guys separated us."

The story of Stalag Luft I is the story of righteousness; every Jewish airman who survived Stalag Luft I owes a debt of gratitude to Senior Allied Officer, Colonel Hubert "Hub" Zemke and Colonel Henry Russell Spicer. Indeed, Spicer gave such an impassioned speech against his captors, he was sent to solitary and sentenced to death. It was reported that Spicer missed the German firing squad by one day as the Russian advance caused the Germans to run away.

There is a touching story, one of many to emerge from Stalag Luft I, related by oral historian Aaron Elson of brothers and POWs Bernard and Bob Levine. Elson writes:

"'Bernie' took part in what likely was the only organized regular clandestine Jewish prayer service in a Nazi prison camp. His two sons are in possession of a wooden Star of David in two triangular parts that was used in the service."[41]

Forced Marches

If any sympathy could be mustered for Germany in the waning months of World War II, it was eradicated in the Malmedy massacre of December 1944. At Malmedy, and other towns near The Battle of the Bulge, SS troops executed hundreds of Americans they had taken prisoner.

Though badly beaten at "The Bulge" by the Allied forces, Hitler and his most ardent followers turned their attention toward the POWs in the camps as their last bargaining chip. All pretense of the Geneva Convention had been dropped. It is believed that Hitler would work to strike a deal for the lives of the POWs in exchange for a dignified armistice. Were the negotiations to fail, he would use the POWs as human shields, or execute them outright.[42]

In order for Hitler to implement his plan, it was necessary to move the POWs into Germany. However, there was one major obstacle: the Nazis were well aware that the advancing Soviet troops would show them no mercy. The Soviets sought revenge for the atrocities the Germans had committed. Beginning in late January 1945, many of the airmen held in captivity were ordered to collect their belongings and as much food as they had been able to hoard in preparation to vacate the camps.

The experiences of the men of Stalag Luft IV are among the worst encountered by any of the prisoners of war in the European or Pacific Theaters. Before addressing the forced march, it is necessary to first detail the conditions of the POWs prior to the order to vacate the camp.

The food ration in the Stalag POW camps was about 1,200 calories per day. A soldier normally needs about 3,500 calories per day.[43] Red Cross food packages supplemented prisoner diets. However, in Stalag Luft IV, the food packages as well as warm clothing were withheld, "lost," or delayed.

The prisoners of Stalag Luft IV were infested with lice and fleas, hence, dermatitis; many had severe infections resulting from unsanitary conditions and malnutrition. Some had not fully recovered from being beaten with rifle butts, the dog bites, or stabbing with bayonets. None had been seen by a dentist and almost none had access to medical treatment.[44] The camp also had its share of the emotionally ill; depression was part of the price of survival.

What the 9,500 or so men of Stalag Luft IV *did have* was each other, and on the march, four or five good friends would get together and form what they called "Combines." Allen Sabol and Robert Lerner became friends because of their religion. They became brothers-in-arms as the result of the need to survive. Sabol stated:

"We were told we were going to evacuate the camp. There was two feet of snow on the ground; it was a very cold, terrible weather, one of the coldest and snowiest on record.

"We heard it as a rumor a couple weeks before we left. We didn't know what to do, so we thought we better start sewing up things like facemasks— different things. February the 1st, I guess it was, some of us are called out on the road, and ordered to take what we could carry—a blanket, no extra clothes hardly; we left practically everything there and we started walking."[45]

The reader might wonder why the prisoners were not laden with every morsel of food they could grab, especially after the food stores were pointlessly opened to allow the starving prisoners extra rations. The POWs were told the march would last only three days. Besides, how much can a person on the edge of starvation carry in two feet of snow and in sub-zero weather?

Many of the POW camps were emptied at nearly the same time, and up to 90,000 Allied prisoners began their aimless wandering back to Germany. The prisoners were accompanied by a burned out collection of guards, some brutal, some humane, all of whom had seen too damn much. The mass of prisoners marched over three basic routes: Northern, Central, and Southern.

Bob Lerner added:

"When the Russians made their move, they [the Germans] had to get us out of there. They wanted to turn us over to the Americans so the Americans would go easy on the Germans.[46] They'd say, 'Look at your men—they're all well-fed.' And that's what they were hoping for. Because when the Russians caught any German soldier, they killed them, most of them. We went from

East Prussia—they tried to get us deep into Germany away from the Russians...."

The confusion of the rapid mass camp evacuations created opportunities for the POWs. Lerner related the following:

"Did I tell you I escaped? The first night out, me and two others decided we're going to escape and get back to camp. We asked Allen Sabol to come with us, but he didn't want to—he was a little scared.[47] When we'd get back to camp [we figured] the Russians would liberate us. The guards told us not to try to escape, because we didn't know who will catch us. If we get caught by some civilians, they may kill you, but we went anyway.

"When it started to get dark, the three of us took off. We ran all around all night trying to find a place—it was raining. And we did find a place—it was a farmhouse. We went in to a barn, and they had a hay loft with hay in there, so we took off our clothes and laid down in the hay and in the morning, this German comes in—he's a 75 year-old little German man—and he had a cat, and the cat came up where we were, and the cat's sitting on top of my friend who was underneath the hay. And this German kept calling for him, 'Here, kitty, kitty.' So my friend grabbed the cat and threw him over the railing!

"The farmer came up [to the loft] and started to use the pitchfork, digging into all this straw and hay. We jumped up and said, 'Krieges gefanger—prisoner of war.' He says, 'Why did you stay here? Why didn't you come into the house? It's much better and warmer.' So he took us in, he practically washed our feet, he fed us. He had two women there—one was a girl and the other was a woman—they were French.

"The Germans brought over a whole lot of French women to work the fields because the men were all in the war. After a while, the woman says, 'Look I'm going to go out and get you some real hot soup.' So she goes out and comes back with the police. She turned us in.[48]

"So she turned us into the police. The police turned us over [to the Kommandant]. He was a son-of-a-bitch. We called him the 'Beast of Berlin.' So the first thing he says, 'Rosenfeld'—that was what they called President Roosevelt, they called him Rosenfeld—'will not be able to help you now.'[49] So they put us in a truck—I thought they were going to shoot us, so we said our good-byes. We rode for about three-four-five hours, and lo and behold, there was our group sitting on the side of the road, and he dropped us off there. Thank God we were with our bunch again."

It wasn't a three day hike as they had been told; it would be 86 days and nearly 600 miles. The camp guards supplied no food, no potable water, and on most nights, no shelter. Medical care was non-existent. However, the men had an angel in the form of Captain Leslie Caplan, an American Flight Surgeon, also Jewish, who marched with the men and gave them whatever help he could.[50]

It wasn't long before dysentery, diphtheria, and typhus ripped through the POWs. Men grew weak, they crawled or were supported. The worst cases were transported in ox carts that were pulled by the prisoners. Some of the POWs collapsed in the snow. The columns marched on and the men were not seen again.

Sabol recalled:

"We remembered some of the towns and everything, but we had no maps, and we didn't know where we were. It was immaterial. It was so cold, we were so hungry, and the water was snow on the ground. They didn't follow us with any food. One time Bob [Lerner] and I asked each other, what do we eat? We don't know."

When Sabol and Lerner and their combine got lucky, they would find frozen potatoes or kohlrabi piled near a barn. There are stories of men eating grass, stealing pig feed, or eating rats. On occasion, they would find a dead horse that had been intentionally strafed by Allied fighter planes. A horse carcass was like manna. Allen Sabol remembered the guards taunting the prisoners with loaves of bread or sausages that they carried in their gun belts.

There is debate as to the number of prisoners who died on the Stalag Luft IV march. Captain (Dr.) Leslie Caplan, who was the Flight Surgeon for the 719th Squadron, 449 Bomb Group, testified that about 6,000 men were ordered to leave the camp on foot with very little notice.[51] Caplan stated:

"Of those who started on the march [from Stalag Luft IV], about 1,500 perished from disease, starvation, or at the hands of the German guards while attempting to escape. In terms of the percentage of mortality, it came very close to the Bataan Death March."

Others will claim the mortality numbers to be much less.[52] The question needs to be raised as to how many men succumbed to injuries caused by the beatings, frostbite or from diseases such as tuberculosis in the months and years following the march.

Yale Feingold recalled:

"We were on the road marching from February to May, with no camp. We were living on the highway and in barns and out in the open for months. It was a brutal march, terrible. My feet were very bad. We lived on a product that's grown there called kohlrabi—it's like a turnip. There were fields and fields of those, and we used to go into the fields and take these like turnips, and we would peel them and eat them raw. We had very little food—rations were very minimal. I weighed about 160 pounds when I went in the service, and I came home when I was liberated weighing about 120. The Germans marched us so much so that we wouldn't be captured by our friends. The only thing that they [the Germans] had going at the end of the war was the prisoners. I don't know why they really held us—it was ridiculous. They marched and marched us, any way and in any direction where there wasn't the war coming toward them.

"The German [guard] that was marching alongside of us was a [regular] soldier. I don't think many of them were really 'gung-ho Hitler.' They were soldiers, they were drafted, they were put into the service, and they were told to fight a war. They weren't part of the SS or the group of die-hard Germans. The ones that were assigned to marching us—they were just poor German slobs.

"At the very end, we could hear the artillery approaching for days and days before the final [liberation]—when we woke up one morning, and they [the guards] weren't there. The English liberated us. It was wonderful, yeah. We were told like, go in this direction—you're free—go! And we took off, and we slept—I was with a few fellas who I was friendly with along the way. And we just started marching away from the war...."

After months of crossing and crisscrossing the Northern German countryside, the prisoners were liberated in late April and early May 1945 by elements of the 104th Infantry. As with Feingold's recollection, Sabol and Lerner both reported that one evening the German guards just vanished. Soon after, the prisoners heard the clanking of Allied tanks. The men wept at the sight of their comrades-in-arms. However, their liberators had no food. The prisoners commandeered anything with wheels in order to find food.

Sabol would not be physically able to return to civilian life for more than a year after his liberation. He went through five hospitals before his infections had cleared.

Though these men had endured the most notorious march of the European theater, many POWs from other camps were on marches as well. Lerner observed:

"We were 3,000 sergeants, but others from other camps were marching as well—the officers, lieutenants and up (in rank) were all marching—we could see them on a different road or hill coming down. We saw three or four different groups of men marching into Germany."

March of the Officers

Jack Sorkin and Bernard Eder marched along with thousands of other officers. Sorkin and 2,500 other men were given the order to vacate Stalag

Luft III on January 27, 1945. They marched in the snow for three days until they reached a railhead. They were crammed fifty into a boxcar and were taken south to Moosburg, Bavaria which was Stalag VII-A. They reached their new camp on February 2, 1945.

Bernard Eder had followed a similar path. His group of 2,500 men was given two hours' notice to march on January 31, 1945. Not only was Eder sick from infection, he had taken a fall and tore up his knee. He told me the following story of an *almost* escape—and a slice of humanity in the middle of war:

"The next day [of the march] I couldn't walk. I was kind of delirious and they put me on a hay cart along with the other sick. There were eight or nine of us, and a Polish kid driving it, with two horses. A German guard, a Volkssturm, who was an old man with a gun, was walking behind.[53] He had one hand on the hay cart and that helped him. Well, we were at the end of the parade and at that point, the Polish driver kept getting farther and farther behind. We came to a fork in the road and he turned left. Pretty soon, they [the column] were out of sight, you know, maybe a hundred yards ahead. One of the fellows [POWs] who spoke Polish asked him, 'Where are you going?' He said, 'Well, this is a shortcut to the Russian lines which are coming across the Polish plain, and I'll take you to safety.' We were kind of elated, but we were still very sick.

"We rounded a bend, where there was a little grove of trees, and there was a German halftrack stuck in the mud, in a ditch. They waved us down. It was a German major. He said, 'Where are you going?' And the driver says, 'I'm taking these guys to the rail.' He said, 'Nichts, nichts, you're on the wrong road!' And he said, 'Bring the men down! Get them out here and help us pull this!' There was only the major and his driver—he said, 'Help us pull this halftrack out of the ditch.'

"This is something that I remember all of my life—I mean every day of my life—the Polish kid said, 'But these are sick men.' The major did not say a word—he just held out his hand, his driver unslung his machine gun, and handed it to him, and the major cocked it, and he pointed it at us. He said in German, get off, and help, and we did as best we could, and we got it back on the road. He accompanied us back to the fork and made sure we took the right fork and so forth. That's how we almost escaped to Poland. That's the closest I came to getting killed."

Stalag VII-A in Moosburg, Bavaria, swelled with officers and enlisted men from the various marches. Conditions were filthy; vermin overran the 85 acre site. The camp was originally designed to hold 10,000 men, but at war's end, more than 80,000 Allied troops were crammed into the space.[54] The Stalag was more like a lawless shanty town than an organized camp.

Reports of Hitler's plan to bring the prisoners to Bavaria seemed to have credibility. As the 14th Armored Division closed on Stalag VII-A the Germans mustered as many as 7,000 troops and an SS Division to defend the camp. At first, the Allied advance was surprised by the size of the German defense. However, the Allies had learned their lessons at The Battle of the Bulge. They remembered Malmedy and what the SS was capable of doing to Allied prisoners. They met the SS with a ferocious attack. The camp was liberated on April 29, 1945.

Stalag Luft I

The liberation of Stalag Luft I has been touched upon. There was no gunfire, but gunfire threatened. Colonel Zemke saved men like Ira Weinstein, Paul Kaufman, and Irwin Stovroff.

As Stovroff stated:

"Russian contact forces came in and liberated us. We didn't have to do anything. As a matter of fact, after the Russians began to settle in, we were advised not to leave the camp—that they might kill you because they wouldn't believe you were an American.[55] The Russians weren't playing anti–Semitism at that time. They had so much hatred for the Germans that they didn't worry about us being Jews. They really and truly hated the Germans beyond belief. They killed them indiscriminately, man, woman, and child, they didn't care."

By April and May 1945, Europe and Eastern Europe were already being carved up by the Soviets and the West. Stalag Luft I and the nearby town of Barth would ultimately become part of East Germany. There were more complex negotiations for the release and transport of Allied prisoners out of the camp and through Soviet-held territory than the negotiations between Zemke and his German captors. The liberation foretold the Cold War.

Harvey Horn's Strange Journey

Flight Officer Harvey Horn, was a navigator attached to the 772nd Bomber Squadron, 463rd Bomber Group of the 15th Air Force. His B-17, named *Pretty Baby's Boys*, was knocked down by flak on March 20, 1945, near to (then) Zagreb, Yugoslavia.

Horn was taken prisoner by the German Navy, as the bomber was forced to crash land in Kvarner Bay near the city of Fiume, Italy.[56] The Navy picked the crew up at gunpoint and turned them over to the Wehrmacht for interrogation and imprisonment.

Flight Officer Harvey Horn (front row, second from left) (courtesy Harvey S. Horn).

Horn and two other officers were first marched to an Italian manor that had been commandeered by the Germans, and then they were transported to an SS prison in Trieste that also held Italian partisans. The airmen were thrown into a 5' × 5', lice-infested cell and fed bread, cabbage soup and *ersatz* coffee. The next morning they were interrogated one at a time; Horn's crewmates each returned within a couple of hours. However, he was taken to another section of the prison and put in isolation into a 3' × 8' closet.

"I clutched my dog tag with the 'H' embossed on it. I don't know how long I lay there going over and over who I was, what I was. Finally, after much agonizing, I made a decision: I am Jewish, I will always be Jewish. Even though they must know I'm Jewish from my dog tags, I will tell them. A huge load was lifted from my chest."

Horn can't recall how long he was held in the closet. When the guards finally came to collect him, he was led to a well-appointed office with a polished wood desk and brass doorknobs.

"Sitting behind a large desk was a blond, Aryan-looking German. He was about thirty with the shoulder insignia of a captain. In a pleasant, calm, quiet voice he started to question me. He talked, I listened, and finally we got to the dreaded subject of the 'H' on my dog tag. Yes, I am Jewish. He went into a long story, saying American Jews were different than European Jews.

Years later my crew told me that they thought I was put into solitary because I was Jewish. I think that I survived because the Germans in Italy knew that the war was lost. I was very fortunate."

Horn was sent back to his cell with the other crew mates. For five days, they heard the screams of Italian partisans being tortured, some of whom, they would learn, were hung by meat hooks. The men were then trucked to a camp outside of Udine, Italy and to Verona, Italy to the Luftwasser Air Field. However, Horn's strange journey was only beginning.

Harvey Horn *never* made it to a permanent POW camp. At the air field, he and several other airmen were met by a squad of Wehrmacht guards who were in their 40s and 50s. Each POW was given a suitcase filled with 50 pounds of wheat. Every so often, they would scoop a handful of wheat which was to be their ration. They were told their final destination was Germany.

"We mostly walked and rode on the back of carts, or on trucks that burned wood for fuel."

Horn had lost his boots during the bomber's crash landing. He was forced to walk in the felt slippers that were worn by the airmen to protect them from the cold at high altitude. He developed blisters that became infected. Each step became more painful than the one before.

He could not have outrun the guards, and saw no reason to do so. His guards became his protectors. Most of the townspeople would have killed him without hesitation. The townspeople had helplessly watched as their families, friends, pets and all worldly possessions were blown to pieces in the steady bombing.

Horn said his guards

"...had been fighting on the Russian front and looked tired and defeated ... they protected us. We had a couple of incidents in Munich and they stood up for us."

One day, while riding on a wagon, and for no apparent reason, the prisoners and guards started singing the song *Lili Marlene*.[57]

At one point they rode a train through the Brenner Pass. The train was strafed by American fighter planes.[58] Prisoners and guards ran off the train and hid for cover. When on the march, the group avoided German artillery and small arms fire, and then the return volleys from the other side. The prisoners and guards were "between wars"; they viewed the craziness around them as visitors from another planet.

"As we walked along the road, we saw anti-aircraft batteries with young Germans and they were boasting and bragging and all that crap. They thought they could win the war … they never would have won, of course. They didn't believe the war was over."

The prisoners also realized that they had become excess baggage. Even the camps wanted no part of them. During an artillery attack, guards and prisoners attempted to gain access to a shelter with an International Red Cross insignia and were denied entry by SS guards.

"We were on the road going to Munich and then we go into the Nuremberg camp, Stalag 13-D. We were there awhile, and then we were on the road again."

In the Nuremberg camp, Horn was finally able to find a pair of boots. A man claiming to be a physician repaired his infected feet. At first the boots were too painful to wear, but there was no time to recuperate. The guards and POWs were caught in the siege of Nuremberg. The guards had initially been led by a colonel and a captain, but both German officers slipped away in the night.

In agony from his infected feet and swollen infected legs, Horn finally collapsed in the snow. The remaining German guards poked his legs with bayonets and yelled at him to get up. A French prisoner rose to Harvey's defense, and in German, told them that Horn was finished.

"Someone in the group started to talk to the [German] sergeant that the war was lost. He should give up. We would tell the Americans that the guards were only following orders. They would be fed and well taken care of, after a short pause, the sergeant agreed."

The group took refuge in a hayloft. All of them hid from the retreating Germans. The German soldiers would have killed the guards or the POWs with equal dispatch. After the German soldiers left, the area around the farmhouse started to get shelled from the 86th "Blackhawk" division of the Third Army.

Ex-guards, a German farmer and his family and the ex-POWs went to the basement of the farmhouse to protect themselves from the artillery. The artillery continued un-abated until the next morning.

When the Third Army approached, Harvey Horn and the other American prisoners waved white flags and yelled that they were Americans. As they had promised, they protected their guards and told the American troops that the Germans should be fed and treated fairly.

Judaism values the concept of *Tikkun Olam*; of repairing the world. Whether conscious of choosing to repair the world or not, Harvey Horn and the other ex-prisoners did what generations of Jewish sages would have expected of them by shielding their former guards from harm.

Wagner's Diet

Bill Wagner was the airman who was questioned by the young girl in German peasant garb. After interrogation, Wagner and a group of prisoners were marched to Stalag 11-B, a POW camp near Fallingbostel in northwestern Germany.

Wagner carried a sense of doom when being marched through wartime Poland and Germany. He and the other POWs had heard enough rumors through families and friends to suspect something awful was unfolding to the Jews of Europe.

He set a simple goal for himself: to be as inconspicuous as possible, to survive. Though he understood some German by knowledge of *Yiddish*, and even heard the guards talk of *Juden* (Jews), he kept his mouth shut and hoped for the best. He would go on to Stalag 11-B but only for a brief time.

"There was no secret the Russians were getting close—the guards told us that. We were led on another march, sleeping in barns, getting infected with a terrific case of lice. May 3, 1945, it snowed a little bit, as if we needed that. That's all I remember until getting up that morning without seeing any guards around, and seeing tanks in the distance that were lumbering up to this area. I don't know whether they were alerted to the fact there might be some POWs there, but they were American tanks."

They were liberated around May 8, 1945. To this day Mr. Wagner can't remember the act of eating or drinking for the 47 days of his capture. It is a medical impossibility, but such is the mind of a man fearing for his life.

One Who Made It

We will never really know how many downed Allied airmen were successful in making their escape from Nazi-held Europe back to freedom. The best estimate given was by Larry Grauerholz of the Air Forces Escape and Evasion Society (AFEES) at 2,800 men, though other sources will state it was as high as 5,000.[59] We do know this—every evasion story was also a story of providence.

It has been more than 70 years since Homer Goodman's escape. He remembers the basics of his survival but much is obliterated by time, trauma and post-traumatic stress.

"We were on a bombing mission to Regensburg where there was a Messerschmitt factory. I think it was sometime in late September 1944. It is hard to remember because it was so long ago. On our way back, we took a lot of flak. Our wing tip got shot up. Our plane was on fire, and we all bailed out. We were at 32,000 feet. Maybe ten seconds after I left the plane, it exploded. I fell about 25,000 feet before I pulled the ripcord, because I'm over an anti-aircraft battery. I thought if one of those things goes through my 'chute, I'd go straight down.

"The wind caught all the [other] guys and took them into Belgium, where they got in touch with the underground, and the underground took and flew them back to England. The wind blew me into a forest somewhere in Germany. I got the hell out of there and I kept going into the forest. I kept going farther and farther, just hiding out. I had a compass on my leg, so I knew which way I had to head.

"I was scared—especially with an 'H' on my dog tag for Hebrew. I traveled at night and slept during the day. I lay in a ditch one time—German soldiers marched right by me. I covered myself with leaves and bark. They weren't ten feet away from me. It took them over an hour to march [there were so many]. They were singing and yelling.

"I ate bugs, worms, leaves, bark on trees. I ate anything I could find. One time I come across a farmer's yard, caught a chicken, pulled it apart, and ate it raw. You do a lot of things when you're hungry, but I had to do it to survive. I had plenty of water—there were a lot of rivers running.

"I prayed; I really did. I prayed all the time in the forest. I prayed by myself—I mean there was no shul I could go to, no other Jew I could talk to. Oh, yeah, God was with me. I'll tell you something—I don't know what I done without it [God] to survive. He helped me survive, you know? Up there, and down there, He helped me survive.

"I was in the western part of Germany, about 80 miles from Belgium. It took me six weeks to walk that distance. When I made that jump, I weighed 182 pounds. When I reached the American lines six weeks later.... I weighed 95.

"I was crawling—I didn't know who had me. The Americans picked me up at the Battle of the Bulge. They saw I had on my American flying suit and my dog tags. The medics took me and put me in a truck. I didn't know where I was going. I spent a week in Brussels in a hospital, a week in Paris in a hospital, a week in London in a hospital, and they sent me home."

The Pieces

The stories of the Jewish POWs do not necessarily end on a high note. The memories of the camps and marches started to again enter their dreams and daydreams as they headed into retirement. The older they got, the harder it got; if 70 was bad, 80 was worse. It was especially bad if a spouse had gone before them, and particularly difficult for the Jewish airmen who suffered anti–Semitism, violence and sometimes segregation in the camps, and then unbelievable brutality on the marches outside the camps.

Post-traumatic stress will be briefly explored in Appendix II with Phillip Elbaum LCSW, one of America's leading experts on this condition in World War II veterans.

•• 6 ••

My Brother's Keeper

"I'm Jewish, and you're Jewish, and I didn't want one of these bas-tards to get hold of you and really work you over."
—Cadet Harold Steinberg's upperclassman

Many of the Jewish men and women who served together would remain friends for 50 years, or 60 years or more after the war. The memories of what they had shared in their youth were immovable, like bugs trapped in amber.

However, the experiences were seldom understood by those with no frame of reference. The Jewish veterans rarely talked of their service except to other veterans at meetings of the Jewish War Veterans, American Legion, and Veterans of Foreign Wars or at bomb group reunions. Families frequently didn't want to listen to "Grandpa's Stories," or the memories they tried to share could be drowned out by political correctness and other agendas. Their rabbis offered little solace. Many of the Jewish veterans carried their stories to their graves. I believe the American-Jewish community is the worse for this.

In this chapter I was able to capture stories, both good and bad, that became part of the fabric of the lives of men and women who appear in this book.

The Bond

Fighter pilot Harold Steinberg told a story of kinship and closure that swept from his first days as a young cadet through to walking the beaches at Normandy as an old man.

"Interestingly, when I first went into cadet school, I was, of course, an underclassman. The upperclassmen, of course, would work on the under-classmen, you know, and put them in 'braces,' with your back straight and your chin in and so forth.

"This one guy was pretty rough on me for the first day. Then after we broke up the formation, he came over to me and said, 'Look, I want you to know what happened. I'm Jewish, and you're Jewish, and I didn't want one of these bastards to get hold of you and really work you over.' So as a result, he was the upperclassman assigned to me. His name was Dave G—.

"Then sometime after that, there was a young Jewish pilot that came into training and his name was Wayne P—, a real nice young man. He just started to fly with us. He took up a P-47 fighter plane on a test flight and the engine quit on him. He brought it in dead-stick. That was a trick all of its own, because that plane didn't glide too good. So the next day, they asked him to fly it again—if he would fly it again because they told him they had fixed it. It stalled and he didn't make it.

"I would have [sought other Jews out], but it so happened that in our squadron, there were only a couple of Jewish guys and neither made it [they were killed in action]. One of the other guys in my squadron, and my closest friend in cadet school, was Don S—. He didn't come back from a mission. I asked one of the pilots who was on the mission as to what happened: 'Everybody is back except Don,' he said. 'What the hell happened to him?' I asked. He said, 'Don just went into a cloud bank, and nobody knows what the hell happened to him.' So I lost track of him after that.

"We went with a group of veterans to the 65th anniversary of the Greatest Generation, and we went into this huge cemetery in France. Each American veteran was assigned a young man and a young lady who were college students.[1] We were talking about things, and we were going through this cemetery, and as I was talking to the two students, I said, 'You know, I never knew what happened– there's a fellow by the name of Don S—who I flew with all the way from when we were cadets, all the way through combat until he disappeared. I never did find out what the hell ever happened with him.'

"Anyway, the young lady leaves and ten minutes or so goes by, and all at once here comes this little gal—comes up and says, 'Harold, you have to see this!' So of course, I went with her, and they had these granite tablets all along this entire wall. She said, 'Look here,' and there was his name, Don S—. And that was the only thing that I had [to remember him by]. Of course, I wanted to call his parents, but neither were alive by then. But it was interesting and this little girl, she just picked it up. She picked out that Don S—."

Sometimes it is difficult to ignore the possibility of Providence. Flight Officer Leon Rosen talked of his wartime friends and heroes, including a man he thought had died many years before. They found each other in a most unlikely place.

"I wasn't the only Jew in my crew. There was one other, the radar operator and for a little while we served together. Then he came down with cancer, and they took him back to the States, and we got a replacement. So for most of the missions we flew, I was the only Jew. Yeah, some made remarks some times. There were some farm boys in my squadron from Iowa. They never saw a Jew before, you know. They would make caustic and improper remarks.

"There were five officers and six enlisted men on the crew. The officers were the pilot, the copilot, bombardier, navigator and the radar operator. Then we had a flight engineer, two side gunners, a tail gunner, and a central fire control gunner and radio operator.

"The radar operator also lived in New York and I felt close to him because he was Jewish. When we were flying in combat, our mothers had periodic conversations. Our mothers got to know each other because of our thing.

"There were two heroes that I had in the years I was in the service. One was Carl S—. Carl was a typical Air Force guy that Clark Gable might play. He was commanding officer of the 29th Bombardment Group, our bomb group. You'd go on a briefing session before the mission—and the operations officer would talk, the munitions officer, the navigation officer, the chaplain, and then the commanding officer, Carl S—.

"I'll never forget that in the briefings Carl might just as soon turn to me and say, 'Bork [Rosen's nickname], make room for me, I'm coming,' and here I was an 18 year old kid, and what a confidence builder, that the old man, the top guy, he was coming along too.

"The other guy was somebody who's legendary. There was one and only one Jewish chaplain in the whole 20th Air Force.[2] David C—was a captain who conducted services in our area. Remember that the Marianas were composed of three major islands—Saipan, Tinian, and Guam. He was on Saipan on Friday night. Then they flew him to Guam, where I was, and he conducted a service on Saturday morning. Then they flew him to Tinian where he conducted a service on Saturday afternoon.

"If you had a particularly difficult mission that day, he would give you an *aliyah*.[3] Somewhere, somehow, in the archives, there's a picture of me with a *Talit* and a *Yarmulke* on and everything about the reasons why I was at the service. I went every Saturday, even though I did not come from a religious household. You knew your life was in danger and there was prayer. It also was an opportunity to get together with other Jewish personnel in the bomb group, in the wing and we regularly went. There weren't too many of us, but we went regularly.

"We always had a Minyan [10 men]. I remember when the war had ended, and we were waiting to get rotated back home, and there was a Rosh Hashanah service at the naval hangar for about 1,000 people. This was on Guam and there were people from all branches of armed services, including female nurses. I tried to locate Rabbi C—about 4 or 5 years ago. I did manage to locate his widow in Los Angeles. He had died some ten years earlier. I think she may have remarried but I'm not sure. But we talked about the rabbi.

"He was my hero due to the fact that he could minister to all of the Jewish personnel who wanted ministering to, in the entire 20th Air Force. Other religions had their clergy people for much smaller groups of people. There was only room for one Jewish chaplain.

"When we'd line up on the flight line before boarding a plane for a combat mission, I used to say my own little private prayer, that God, if you let me live for 24 more hours, I might make it to 80 years of age, and I did. I came close to dying a couple times.

"Paul K—was the name of the radar operator. As I mentioned, Paul, after several missions, got sick. The military hospital diagnosed it as serious. It was colon cancer. He was flown back to the States and treated at Walter Reed General Hospital. I never heard from him after that point. It made me feel guilty that I didn't follow-up on it. I know, I said to myself, how can I call his mother and say, 'Can I talk to Paul?' and have her say, 'He died.' I didn't know how to do that. So I guess I was a coward, and I didn't.

"Some eight to 10 years after the war, I'm in Miami Beach on a vacation. I was in a bachelor pad. We went to the Highlife Jai Alai Fronton, and I was down near where the betting windows were, and I hear somebody call out my name, and it's Paul! He underwent some six operations, and he was fine. He lived in Miami, so he was alive and well then."

Technical Sergeant and radio operator Marvin Leventon was in the 345th Bombardment Group, also known as the "Air Apaches." The 345th was one of the most decorated groups in the Pacific. They flew the B-25 "Mitchell" medium bomber. While in training, he related a highly improbable scenario:

"When we were training as a crew, it was a six-man crew, and three of us were Jewish—the pilot, the navigator, and me. And we used to talk Yiddish on the intercom just to get the other ones bugged out! But I never had any problems, as far as being Jewish is concerned, and anybody making cracks."

Captain David Dulberg was a training officer at Peterson Air Force Base in Colorado Springs, Colorado. Dulberg shared an experience common to many Jewish personnel who were assigned to bases around the country—the strong outreach of the Jewish townspeople to help the young Jewish recruits to feel more at home.

"The base provost marshall was Jewish. Marty D—had been with me in officer's training school. He was six foot three, and a bulky, big guy and very bright. He became the base Provost Marshall. One of my better friends was from Portland, Oregon, Jack T—, who was a Jewish guy in the adjutant general's office. The Jews were spread out throughout the base.

"A week or two or three after I got to my assignment, I went into town, because I heard some people had started a small Reform Jewish group and they were meeting at the Episcopalian Church or the Lutheran Church. I went there on a Sunday, and they were giving lox and bagels to the soldiers from Peterson Field.

"I met a family from Colorado Springs who had come from Brooklyn … he and his wife and I became very friendly and I had a place to be if I went into town. There were a number of congregations. There was a regular conservative group in town that I didn't go to, but some of the men did. A number of the merchants, a jewelry store and a Jewish-owned department store … reached out to the men. They didn't give dances and parties, but they reached out. They were available, and I knew there were Jewish people in town … over the years I became friendly with a couple of the families that were in town."

Peterson AFB was also used as a POW camp for German prisoners of war. For a brief time, Dulberg was put in charge of German POW work details.

Sergeant Marvin G. Freeman, the cryptographer assigned to the 385th Bombardment Group, which was part of the 8th Air Force, tells stories of what we might call Jewish pride:

"When I was in intelligence, we would get there early before the briefings. They would put up the flight pattern on a big map of Europe. I would watch. Then all the air crews would come in—pilots, gunners—and we would roll up the screen so they could see the map. And the looks on their faces—because they knew, these guys knew where they were going to go. So I knew they were going to Regensburg, Germany, I knew they were going to Ploesti, Romania beforehand.

"I really give a lot of credit to those guys. They lived almost in luxury, and then the next thing you know—they're over some city getting flak thrown at them or engaging in enemy airplanes diving at them.

"The first guy to finish his missions was a Major Franks from St. Louis who's this Jewish fellow, the first guy to finish the 25. No, I never really talked to Major Franks, just to say hello or nod, because I knew him from going into service with him. But the fact that he was a Jewish guy, and everybody knew it, kind of helped our airbase a bit perhaps. It made me feel good—here's a Jewish guy who's finishing his missions.

"One of the things about Franks—you know, these guys would go up, and if somebody had a hangnail, and they knew it was a real bad mission, they could abort. Or maybe [they could say] there's something wrong with their plane—abort means you could get out of it. You don't fly the mission, you just come back.

"When we first were there in 1943, maybe there were 50 to 75 to 100 planes per mission; two years later in 1945, they would always send 1,000 bombers. There would always be a few planes that would tag along maybe as far as the English coast to make sure that we had 18 per squadron. If a bomber crew would abort, these extra planes would take their place. Major Franks finished his 25 missions without ever having to abort, which showed to all on the base that the man had guts, which was something to be proud of."

Pilot Sidney Gasser tells an amusing story of discovery in regard to another member of the 302nd Troop Carrier squadron:

"I never asked anybody if they were Jewish, and nobody ever asked me. I served with a man and I didn't even know he was Jewish. We were in the same squadron. We flew together, I think, several times. We were together the whole time we were in Europe. After the war, there was a group of pilots meeting here [Atlanta, Georgia] and I invited him to come and stay with us. We were sitting around the house, and he started playing with a dreidel, and I said, 'How do you know about the dreidel?' and he said, 'I'm Jewish.'[4] And that was the first time we knew that about each other. So much for all of us Jews having radar, huh, that we automatically can find each other!

First Lieutenant Herbert Pearlman (courtesy Herbert Pearlman).

"Coming from Oklahoma, I had a lot of anti–Semitism—not really overt, but just not being able to join the groups of people that Protestants belonged to. But you know, they [Protestants] all look alike to me!"

Sometimes Jews could find each other in the most unexpected of places. One wonders if there weren't other forces at work besides random chance. The following incident is both amusing and just a touch disturbing.

First Lieutenant Herbert Pearlman described a scene in a cocktail lounge in Piccadilly Circus. He went into the lounge to wait for a navigator friend who was also from the 379th Bombardment Group. Like Pearlman, the navigator was from Brooklyn and was also Jewish.

As he was waiting, he spotted

a sloppy drunk American soldier approach a table where two attractive, young blond women were sitting. Though they were trying to ignore the drunk, he was insistent. Pearlman, as an officer, felt it his duty to send the soldier away, and he did so without incident.

"The young ladies thanked me politely and resumed their conversation between themselves. I could not help but hear some of it, and was surprised when one of them said the soldier was a 'Shika' [Yiddish for drunk]. I told them I did not understand much Yiddish, but that I knew what Shika meant. When they asked me how I knew what it meant, it was their turn to be surprised when I told them I was Jewish.

"They got all excited and told me they were Jewish too … they could not believe there was a Jewish pilot in the U.S. Air Corps. They did not think there were any Jewish soldiers in the U.S. forces. I wished my navigator friend could come along soon so that I could show them that I was not the only one."

Family Bonds

The bonds shared by families followed them into combat. Brothers, sisters, mothers and fathers shared what they could over improbably vast distances. There is no end to the stories of Jewish sons and mothers. The anecdotes often drip with so much nostalgia that they become parody. However, the events that led to these bonds in wartime are hardly trivial.

First Lieutenant Bernard Greene was a B-29 bombardier with the 61st Bombardment Squadron, 39th Bombardment Group. He and his mother shared a beautiful bond that stemmed from traditional candle lighting.

"Right before I shipped out to Guam, I saw my mother lighting candles before the first Seder in the spring of 1945. President Roosevelt had just died and it was a sad time for our family. As my mother was lighting the Passover candles, she said, 'I will be praying for you every Shabbat[5] until you come home.'

"I got hold of a candle lighting table, and I calculated the time difference between Guam and my mother's home in Brooklyn. Whenever I was on the plane, flying to or from a mission, I would meditate, almost like I was in a trace, thinking about my mother lighting candles at the same time. My crewmembers thought I was dozing off, but I wasn't."

On May 11, 1945, a Friday, Greene's B-29 bomber was on a mission to strike the Kawasaki Aircraft factory in Kobe, Japan. As bombardier, Lieutenant Greene took the plane over the target and dropped a partial bomb load even though the plane took a direct hit from flak. The flak knocked out an engine along with the hydraulic system causing the bomb bay doors to remain open. A crippled aircraft that was forced to drop out of formation was often a "dead" aircraft.

As the bomber began to lose altitude, they were subjected to 45 Japanese fighter plane attacks. The elevator trim tabs in the tail section were shot away.[6] Nonetheless, the bomber was successfully able to land on Iwo Jima and the crew was subsequently awarded the Distinguished Flying Cross. As they returned to base the next day (Saturday on Guam), Greene was thinking about his mother lighting candles and "prayed with her."

Samuel Nilva was an investigator assigned to the Provost Marshall's Office at Greensboro Air Force Base, North Carolina and later to Bolling Air Force Base, Washington, D.C., handling criminal cases involving desertion and murder.

"I had two brothers and two sisters. All three of the brothers were in the service. My brother, Allen, was staffed as Judge Advocate to General Wheeler in Southeast Asia.[7] Allen was stationed in Ceylon which is now Sri Lanka.

"My brother Jake was in the Navy Air Corps, and he was an aviation machinist's mate on a PBY [Catalina Flying Boat] which was stationed in Australia.

"On their 25th mission, he got very sick with stomach trouble. They were going on a mission to bomb the Japanese base at Tindari in Southeast Asia prior to the invasion of the Philippines.[8] They had just dropped a bomb on a fuel dump when they were shot down. The PBY had a very slow rate of climb and rifle fire hit a cable with a lucky shot. They were captured by the Japanese and Jake was beheaded on Thanksgiving Day 1944.

"The reason we knew all this happened is because one of the pharmacist mates from Stillwater, Minnesota, was a friend of Jake's. Prior to the mission when he was captured, Jake was very sick due to severe stomach trouble. When the pharmacist mate came back from the service, he told us the whole story.

"Jake's commanding officer said, 'Jake, you're sick, you don't have to go on this mission.' But Jake said, 'No, I've got to go, because if something happens, they'll say the Jew got out of it.' He was very defensive if anybody made remarks about the Jews.

"We knew that my brother Jake was missing in action, so I asked my commanding officer's permission if I could go over to the Navy department and find out if there was any news. He said, 'No, you can't go. You're on duty, and you can't get time out for that.' This was when I was at Bolling [AFB] and it was 1945 already.

"So I walked out of his office in dismay and I was sad. The secretary, who was a civilian girl, said to me, 'That goddamn Jew.' And I looked at her, and I said, 'What do you mean?' She says, 'He's a Jew.' I said, 'My dear, so am

I.' She says, 'Well, I'm sorry. You go and take care and find about your brother, and I'll cover for you.' That was an interesting experience in my life.

"There was a strange additional event. There was a family from St. Paul, Minnesota called S—. One of their children was named Kenneth S—and he was a lawyer. He was attached to the prosecutor's office after the war. He actually prosecuted the two Japanese ensigns that beheaded my brother and they were given very light sentences. They had been held prisoner for about two to three years and they let them go.

"My wife and I, when we were living in Des Moines after the war, picked up the newspaper one day, and I see an article in the paper that the Army had court-martialed a soldier named Willie J—, a black soldier who had killed a Japanese woman. I investigated it a little bit, and I found out that she was a Geisha girl.

"When I saw that, I wrote to Eisenhower. General Eisenhower was at that time already the chief of staff, and he was stationed in Washington, D.C. I wrote a letter right to him directly, and I said, 'Please explain the death penalty of an American soldier for killing a Japanese Geisha girl, when the Japanese officers that beheaded my brother were given light prison sentences.' I got a letter from Eisenhower's chief of staff, explaining to me that my letter was received, and it was given attention immediately. About three or four months later, there appeared an article in the Des Moines paper that the soldier was given a life sentence—they changed it from the death penalty to a life sentence. I still have that letter."

In terms of brotherly love, it is difficult to match the experiences of identical twins Courtney and Earl Shanken.

"When I ended my tour of combat duty, I was a First Lieutenant. I was with the 15th Air Force, 450th Bombardment Group, 722nd Bomb Squadron. Our B-24s [tails] were painted white for identification purposes and Axis Sally [German propagandist], kept referring to us as 'those white-tailed B-24s.' We eventually called ourselves 'The Cottontails.'[9]

"I was born in St. Louis, Missouri and there were four children. My twin brother Earl and I were the two youngest.

"At the beginning of the war a college education was one of the requirements for getting into the Army Air Corps cadet program. They put both my brother and I into navigation. All cadets wanted to be pilots of course, but they put us where they needed us.

"It is said that those of us who scored the highest on their entrance examinations went into navigation school. A lot of the Jewish guys were in college all ready. A lot of the navigators were like aerial bookkeepers but today we are dinosaurs, they don't even use navigation, they use GPS and computer systems.

"However, I've been very active in our bombardment group association and I've talked to a lot of the guys in my association who were former instructors. They were told to wash out the Jewish guys from pilot school.

"Earl and I wound up in the same squadron. At that time, brothers could request to stay together. This was before the Sullivan case.[10] In addition, the Sullivan case specified all brothers serving aboard the same ship or in the same unit—if another member of the family was serving in another unit, and you could still serve with a brother. In our case, we had an older brother who was in the medical corps.

"We would often fly in the same formation and we were both very aware of each other. There was one mission where his crew was in the lead and we were far back. Our plane had developed engine trouble early into the mission and we had to turn around and go home. On the return, my brother's plane got low on fuel and had to land for refueling at Corsica. He didn't return to base until three hours later. He didn't see my plane on the way back and I didn't see his plane return. We both thought that each other's bomber had been shot down.

"There was a mission where he was not on his bomber on a particular day, and I saw his bomber get shot down right off my wing, and I thought, 'Thank God he's not on it.'

"The navigator on a B-24 didn't have a gun position, but when we were under attack we put our heads up the dome and we called out attacking planes by the clock.[11] In the case of German fighter plane attacks, we would call out fighter plane positions to the gunners. On this particular day I was so intent on Earl's bomber, I almost called out attacking fighters for his plane rather than mine which would have been dangerous for my crew.

"One incident that was funny was a situation where both my brother and I were on the same plane one day and I was the pilotage navigator in the nose.[12] This voice came over the intercom and it asked, 'How many minutes to the enemy territory?' and I said, 'Ten minutes, sir.' And he said, 'You don't have to call me sir, I'm your brother.'

"Both my brother and I recently received the French Legion of Honor, France's highest military award, for missions we flew two weeks before prior to D–Day. Our squadron was assigned the job of wiping out railroad centers at Marseilles, the submarine repair facilities at Toulon, and the railroad center in Nice. By the time of D–Day itself, I had already finished my missions on May 27, 1944."

Belief Among Brothers

Milton Fields was a man who deeply cared about his fellow Jewish soldiers. He volunteered for duties that were descriptive of a para-chaplain. His military service was peppered with anecdotes such as the experience that follows:

"Relationships between Muslims and Jews were excellent in those days; no problems. The Jewish communities were well established and they were very prominent. I had contact with the Jewish community in Teheran as I was an understudy to the chaplain. We had one Jewish chaplain in Iran for the entire Persian Gulf Command and I worked with him.

"In 1943, I had a fascinating experience in Iran. The Jewish chaplain said that he had five or six different bases where he had to go to arrange for Passover Seder. He said, 'Milton, you take over and plan a Seder. And I'll be back in time to conduct services for the Seder.' We ended up serving a kosher meal to 150 Jewish soldiers at the barracks outside of Teheran. The soldiers that came to the service were from many places around the area.

"The chaplain pulled out a fantastic PR coup. The Jewish welfare board informed us that our Pesach [Passover] supplies were on the boat, but they wouldn't get to Iran until July. He had the Quartermaster bakers make Matzo under his supervision and it was beautiful. When the pictures of the Matzo baking came out in the Stars and Stripes newspaper, the Quartermaster bakers were all black. How do you like that? They were respectful of the process, that's right."

While serving in Iran and Iraq, Fields had another experience that foreshadowed the unfolding Holocaust.

"In Tehran [1943], I attended a service for orphaned kids and what an impression that left on me. The chaplain had heard about a group of orphaned Jewish children from Warsaw, Poland and Russia that were being moved by Hadassah to Palestine.[13] We went there. [The service] wasn't in a synagogue but an auditorium; we went to Friday night services, just the chaplain and me as guests. We brought along candy bars that we had bought at the army post exchange and we passed those out.

"The service was a traditional Orthodox service, and I was very, very much moved, with the kids all getting up, or most of them getting up, and saying *Kaddish* [the Jewish prayer for the dead, for their parents and relatives], and singing some Yiddish songs. The songs were very plaintive. They weren't 'Second Avenue Yiddish Theater' [comedy] songs, these were songs like, 'Please Give Me a Bagel and Butter' type songs. My guess is that there were about 100 children altogether."

Shortly after, and on behalf of the Jewish chaplain, Fields traveled to Palestine to secure candles and prayer books for High Holiday services. While in Palestine he briefly met with Henrietta Szold. Szold is considered one of the greatest Jewish women of the previous century. She was directly responsible for the transport and for saving the orphaned children that Fields encountered. Fields talked to her about the service he had witnessed. She was by then in her mid–80s. She passed away shortly after the war ended.

Norm Kailo was a crew chief and Technical Sergeant with the 20th Air Force, 462nd Bombardment Group, in the CBI Theater.

"In order to get to China, you had to get 'over the hump' [the Himalayas]. The reason for having a base in China was that the base was where the B-29 bombers took off to bomb Japan. You couldn't do it from India, it was too far.

"I spent most of my time in India. It was quite unique to be there. We took over an old British air base with our B-29s.[14] We had different barracks for the enlisted men and for the flight crews, who were generally officers.

"As a mechanic, I was generally assigned to one plane. On the B-29s, I was crew chief, and I was in charge of a couple of ground crewmen. I was responsible for signing off on the B-29 before each flight. If I didn't sign off on it, they couldn't use it. We had quite a responsibility.

"Over in India, there were several Jewish fellows in each barracks. There were probably about 20 in total. By the way, our barracks had thatch roofs—they weren't wooden barracks, because that's what you had in India. You couldn't have a solid roof—it'd be too damn hot.

"You didn't have any anti–Semitism in the Far East. They had Chinese Jews, Japanese Jews—I never knew that until I got there. There were Jews in China, Japan and Burma.

"The first Passover I ever attended was in India. The chaplain in our base asked if any of us would like to attend a Seder. I never attended a Seder in my life as I was brought up as an agnostic, so my first real Jewish experience was in India. None of us were too excited or interested, until they told us that there would be Jewish food from the states. Then they got a good crowd.

"We attended the Seder, about a dozen of us, including one of the Jewish fellows in my barracks, Arnold G—. Arnold became a lifelong friend of mine. Just prior to going overseas, there was another coincidence. We got on the boat in the Los Angeles area. Everybody was writing letters before we took off, to mail to our families. I wrote my letters and Arnold wrote his. I just knew him offhandedly at that point.

"He was mailing his letter next to the building that Marilyn, my future wife, lived in. Arnold's envelope was addressed to 1643 Andrews Street, and Marilyn's address was 1641 Andrews Street. So his wife and my future wife were in buildings right next to each other. They never knew each other before Arnold and I met, but they did after that. We became very close friends after the war. We went out together, and we followed each other up until just a few months ago when he passed away."

It was not uncommon for crews in the European Theater to name and decorate their aircraft. The names of the aircraft and the nose artwork frequently conveyed messages and images that were patriotic, or war-like or reflected popular culture (*Heaven Can Wait*, *Hell in Heaven*, *The 8 Ball*, or *Ameri-can*). Contrary to belief, sexualized images or pin-up art, were not the norm.

In the case of Staff Sergeant Morton Israel, you might describe his bomber as being a "Jewish" bomber. Incredibly, three of the crewmembers were Jews and even the aircraft's name reflected a Jewish tradition.

"I really had very, very little anti–Semitism. In fact our crew ate in Kosher restaurants all the time. You didn't ask me the name of our plane— our plane was the *Mammala and the Ten Little Kitsels!*"

Israel's pilot was a gentile, but felt a kinship to all aspects of Jewish culture.

"He came up with it himself. He thought of it. I mean he came out with it and that was the name of the plane. Our pilot was a swell guy and he came to my house after the war. They [the crew] all loved Kosher food and we ate in a Kosher restaurant in London all the time. Every time we ate there, there was a bottle of the best liquor brought to the table that you could get and everything else."

Corporal Harold Newmark was assigned to the 13th Air Force as an engine mechanic to an Air-Sea rescue group.

"As the war was ending, I wound up in the Philippines at Clark Field. I spent about six to eight months in the Philippines where I was involved in engine operations. I was with a group that did air rescue work, both amphibious and air surveillance. I stayed in the Philippines until 1946.

"I didn't encounter any anti–Semitism while in the military and in fact I had an opposite experience. I was in the Philippines in a bar which was the company recreation room. I was with this guy from Buffalo, New York; a Catholic guy and a lot of fun. We got along very well. There was a guy at the end of the bar who was a drunk and he's making derogatory comments about the Jews. So we're listening to this loudmouth and this Catholic guy gets up, walks over to the loudmouth and gives him one strong hit to the stomach. It knocks the drunk off the stool and sends him to the hospital. My friend comes back over to where he was sitting and he said, 'I can't stand arrogant, prejudiced bastards. Now what were we talking about?'"

First Lieutenant Arthur Sherman, a bombardier with the 464th Bombardment Group for the first 11 missions of his service, recalled the following story of someone doing the right thing because it was simply the right thing:

"As you know, everything in the Army is alphabetical. My best friend in the service was Archie S—, a Lutheran from Aiken, Minnesota [who had a very Jewish sounding name]. I was close to him in bomber school and we went overseas together. Since Archie's last name was S—, everyone took him for being Jewish. Because he was so tough, Archie wouldn't take much from people so he was constantly fighting. One day he says to me, 'Sherman, you Jews are always fighting!' I couldn't help but start laughing. I lost track of Archie after I was wounded and I did not find out until later that he died in combat in August 1944. I miss him every time I hear 'Taps.'"

Cain and Abel

It is Genesis 4:9 that contains among the most well-known questions of the Bible. God asks: "Where is your brother Abel?" along with Cain's response: "I don't know. Am I my brother's keeper?" Rabbis explain that the exchange is not positive. In World War II Jews would reach out to one another, but they could also harass and reject one another.

First Lieutenant Maurice Ashkinaz was a bombardier with the 448th Bombardment Group of the 8th Air Force. The Group flew B-24 "Liberator" bombers and hit targets such as ball bearing plants, synthetic oil refineries and aircraft engine factories. He originally wanted to be a pilot, but when he failed training, he did what many other impetuous young people might do and reacted with anger instead of reason. It was when he had a change of heart that he discovered an unexpected obstacle.

"When I washed out of pilot training, they said to me, 'What do you want to do? You are also qualified to be a navigator and a bombardier.' I said, 'No, forget it. I'm just going to become a private. I don't want to be an officer, I just want to be a private.' The personnel guy said to me, 'If you want to do that, you can go into the ranks. You've got a college education. You'll probably get an office job.' And I said, 'OK, that's what I want to do.' So I became a private.

"I went by train for two days and two nights to a place in Arkansas. The field was an advanced glider training station.[15] I got there in the middle of the night and I was still wearing [my cadet officers' uniform]. And the only difference anybody could tell was, instead of a spread eagle on the hat, it was a big propeller with wings.

"They found a place for me to sleep overnight, and they told me the next morning to get up and report to an office, so that's what I did. I went to that office the next morning, unshaven, with my officer's uniform on. They told me to wait a minute, and then they ushered me into this office. I walked into the desk, stood at attention, and the person sitting behind the desk didn't even look up at me. He was a captain.

"I was standing at attention for around five minutes or so. I went into an 'at-ease,' and he looked up and screamed, 'You can't stand there at-ease—attention!' He started to bawl the hell out of me, how come I was so unshaven, and how come I was still wearing an officer's uniform, and screaming at me.

"His name was Captain L—, something like that—I can't think of his first name. Anyway, he was a lawyer from Brooklyn and naturally a Jew. So after bawling me out, he told me to report to the payroll office the next day. Who was in charge of the payroll office? Captain L—.

"I reported to the payroll office the next morning, and there were close to 40 people working in the office. I proceeded to light up a cigarette and everyone yelled, 'Don't light that cigarette! Captain L—is liable to come in, and he'll tear everybody's hair out!' OK, so I sat down. Well, he walked in, and it was like a prison. Nobody could talk—nobody did nothing. He used to call morning alerts, like at 6:00 a.m. in the morning. All the employees of the payroll office gathered at attention outside. He used to walk out and look at everybody and say, 'OK, go back!' period. As it turned out, I was there about three months, I think. We'd light up a cigarette, and we'd have a guy watching in the back door for Captain L—, so everybody could douse their cigarettes.

"He was the worst son-of-a-bitch you ever saw in your life. I didn't care for where I was—it was a bad setup. So I came to him one morning, and I said to him, 'Sir, I want to reapply to the cadets.' He said, 'You can't do that.' I said, 'What do you mean, I can't do it?' He said, 'You can't do it—I won't recommend you.' I guess I mouthed off to him and said that if he could show me an army regulation that he can refuse to recommend me, then I'll follow through. Well, there was no such regulation. So after spouting off and spitting at me, he said, 'Well, there's going to be a cadet board coming through here in a few weeks. And I'll put your name in, and you can meet the board.' So that's what I did.

"When I met the board, I guess there was about three or four high-ranking officers—the ranking officer of the board was a full bird colonel—and also Captain L—.

"The board started to question me, and I answered all their questions. Every time they asked me something, he [Captain L—] would say he didn't recommend me—he would come in and interrupt me all the time.

"Finally the colonel looked at L—and said, 'What have you got against this guy? Why are you doing this?' Then the colonel asked me, 'OK, what school do you want to go to?' And I said I wanted to go to bombardier school, and the colonel says, 'You got it.'

"Oh, yeah, sure. Captain L—knew I was Jewish, so anyway, I left there and I went to bombardier school.

"I became a bombardier and navigator and I was commissioned as a second lieutenant. Now I'm passing up many months in between now. I went to bombardier school [then] I was sent to El Paso, Texas, to Biggs Army Airfield to meet nine other men to be a member of the crew to make up ten people. That is where I met the crew, nine others. That was the first time, of course, that any one of us ten men met each other.

"The ten of us were training together for combat. The pilot was married, and the copilot was married, and I was married, and those were only people that were married—everybody else was younger. So we trained together.

"We were able to be sociable together. Everybody liked each other—that was the time you'd say to yourself, 'Yeah, I can get along with this guy and that guy.' Because let me tell you something—you get ten men in a bomber, and every man is breathing on the other guy, and every guy is counting on the other guy to keep them alive. You've got ten people that are pretty close—it's not like a battalion of soldiers.

"Yes, the other guys knew I was Jewish, but we never discussed anything—nobody discussed a thing. So we're flying our missions and we're in combat, OK? One night, or one afternoon, I walked into the barbershop, and who is sitting in the barber's chair? It was Major L—. He had gotten promoted. I don't say a goddamn thing—I don't say anything to him. He doesn't recognize me, naturally, I'm just one of thousands of faces to him. But to me he is one face.

"I tell one of the guys in the Quonset hut about this L—, and he said he played poker with L— all the time. I said, 'Next time you play poker with him, ask him if he remembers a guy, Ashkinaz.'

"One evening, I think it was after the 22nd or 23rd mission that we had flown, we're in the officer's club getting toasted. I look over, and I see this Major L— talking to a bunch of guys, you know, sitting down. I'm dead-drunk, and I say I got to go over there and talk to that son-of-a-bitch. And they're saying, 'Maury, don't do it, don't start.'

"Well, I went over there, and I tore into that guy. I really just called him every name under the sun. Basically my problem with him was that we Jews had worked so many, many years to become persons to be recognized, and persons to be talked to, and I said to him, 'You son-of-a-bitch, in five minutes, you ruined hundreds of years of Jews trying to become assimilated.' I really gave it to him.

"Well, he threatened to court-martial me and the whole bit. I said, 'Yeah, go ahead, I don't give a goddamn.' Because if I don't fly, my crew won't fly, because when you flew, flying was not something that you were ordered to do.

"He was angry because I was giving him all kinds of hell. I have no idea if other people knew he was Jewish. All I said was, 'You screwed it up the for all the Jewish [servicemen]—everybody! You are the worst person to represent the Jews.' Everything I said to him was pointed, that he as a Jew had ruined hundreds of years that Jews were trying to become assimilated. Anyway, the night was over. The next morning, I went to the mess hall, and guys came up to me and were shaking my hand. And then of course, I don't know that this was because of me, but he was transferred out of that base, and that's the last I ever heard of him. I'll never forget him, and I'll never forget my copilot trying to stop me from doing it."

Staff Sergeant Ira Greinsky was a gunnery instructor with the Western Technical Training Command. He trained personnel mainly for the B-29 bomber. Most of his students would be assigned to the Pacific Theater.

"We got a new company commander who was Jewish, and he had the mistaken idea that he didn't want to show favoritism to Jewish instructors. So he put all of us on a transfer list to be shipped overseas. We made a complaint through the chaplain about his action, and the next day he was gone."

George Shafer was a corporal assigned to the 6th Service Command where he was shuttled from one domestic assignment to the next. It was personally frustrating for him as he desperately wanted to get into a combat assignment.

"All I did was travel around the country. They just kept shipping me out. I spent a couple or three months here and there, to places like Ft. Sumner in New Mexico and then to Mountain Home, Idaho, and I was sent to places like that were a little bit forlorn, you know, and I didn't feel that I contributed anything to the war effort because I could do anything.[16]

"There was a First Lieutenant in personnel that I approached for an overseas assignment ... I thought if I could go overseas I'd get [more points and get] out sooner and he said, 'When I need you, I'll call for you, and don't bother me.' The next time I saw him, he was a Captain and he was stationed where I was stationed, in Rapid City, South Dakota. I went to see him. He was Jewish too. I told him I would like to go overseas ... because I felt that I wasn't doing anything to help just being in the States. So he said, 'The next time you come around here, I'll court martial you. Don't be so anxious to go.' So I never went back to see him again."

In closing my interview with Sergeant Sidney Tendler, who was with the 7th Emergency Rescue Squadron based on Okinawa, I asked him if he remembered any Jewish-oriented stories. He said he was a loner, kept to himself and didn't attend religious services. Then he remembered the story of two Jewish brothers in his squadron who brought their trumpets overseas and played music to pass the time. It was an innocuous story that a Borscht Belt musician might have re-told back in the day.

Then Tendler recounted a story of two other Jews in his squadron, men he said he sharply avoided. He told me that they were from Brooklyn. They searched the beaches and caves of Okinawa looking for skulls of Japanese soldiers who had been killed in battle. They would kick in the teeth and steal the gold fillings.

I interviewed others who searched Okinawa for souvenirs. They brought back Japanese rifles, flags and the like, but this desecration was far different. I felt deep shame, something I had not felt with any other remembrance in this book.

Jews and African Americans

There was never any intention of writing stories about American-Jewish and African-American relations as part of this book. Yet the connections that emerged from the interviews were so strong that to ignore them would be disrespectful to the memories of both the Jewish bomber crews and the pilots who helped save them.

The African-American pilots were officially designated the 332nd Fighter Group, but they came to be known as the Tuskegee Airmen. Any bomber crew whose lives were saved by the "Red Tails" will never forget them.[17] They were hailed as heroes and only the most intransigent of racists would fail to understand their contribution to the air war. For many Jews in combat, the Tuskegee Airmen were mirrors through where they could see reflections of themselves and their own struggles.

Norman Smeerin, a pilot with the 450th Bombardment Group, stated:

"We encountered lots of ground fire. By the time I got over there and started flying, which was January of 1945, the Germans had lost air control. Plus we had air cover, we had the P-51s, and most of the time they were from the black squadron, the Tuskegee Airmen, and they were fantastic. They would pick us up as soon as we got into enemy territory, they would fly cover for us until we got to the target.

"Over the target they would leave because there was no reason for them to stick around. You know, no enemy plane was going to come after us over the target because it was covered with anti-aircraft artillery—flak bursts. We were heavily shelled over the target. As soon as we got off the target, another group [of Tuskegee Airmen] would pick us up and take us out of enemy territory. But they were very good and they never left us. It never crossed my mind to admire them just because I was Jewish and they were black. I was so proud of them because I knew how hard they had to work to get where they were, much harder than I did. Everybody that I came in contact with just raved about them.

"One day at our base, when we weren't flying, one of the Tuskegee Airmen flew in on his P-51 and landed just for a visit. Everybody on our base just clobbered all over him—we were so happy. We had questions and looked at his airplane which was, you know a fighter plane. We were flying those big heavy big heavy B-24s, and here's this guy flying this single-engine P-51. It was the best combat plane they had in Europe at the time—that's the P-51 Mustang, single-engine, beautiful airplane—slick. We thought he was a hero."

Technical Sergeant Norman Zalkin was a radio operator with the 99th Bombardment Group that was based in Tortorella, Italy. It was part of the 15th Air Force. The 99th saw action throughout Europe and in virtually every country the Nazis occupied. The bombers would often return to based riddled with flak and crippled from fighter plane attacks.

"On several missions we encountered German fighters. I think I mentioned that I met the Tuskegee Airmen. We had two engines shot out. Our bomber was a four-engine plane. And we had to turn back and we were by ourselves. We were attacked by German Messerschmitts, and we called for help, and afterwards, we found out that the fighter group that came and shooed them away was the Tuskegee Airmen.

"They took us back to Italy—and they were black and we could tell by looking at them that they were the Tuskegee Airmen. On that particular mission, the Tuskegee Airmen saved our lives.

"At that time, they weren't called Tuskegee Airmen, I don't think. Black fellows at that time were Negro. They were college men who were allowed to enlist and make their own squadron or group, and they became the Tuskegee Airmen.

"A year ago, I went to my daughter's synagogue and met with several of them that were flying fighter planes during the war. They were only allowed to fly P-51s.[18] I didn't think much of it at the time. Now we think of it very much. I thanked them when we went to the synagogue. They went around to different areas giving lectures about the Tuskegee Airmen."

Technical Sergeant Frederick Bartfeld also knew what it was like to be saved by the Tuskegee Airman.

"About the flyers that nobody wanted, the Tuskegee Airmen, are you kidding? They always accompanied us to the target and back. When the German Messerschmitts attacked us—and I can still remember the first time the

Bf-109s came out of the sun to get us—and all of a sudden these P-51s [flown by the Tuskegee Airmen] were there knocking them out of the sky.

"You don't know how it feels—you can't possibly know that unless you were in combat in the air. You don't know what that feeling is of a plane coming down on you. I had a turret shot off of me.[19] I got hit in the head with flak. We had to ditch one time, we crash-landed one time. So you know, I went through a lot. It sounds like I'm bragging, but this is the story of my life. It was a fighting life, which I can't understand.

"I flew 45 combat missions. I was lucky until the P-51s came and took the Bf-109s out of the sky. They were able to do it because they discovered that you could put [auxiliary fuel tanks] on it, and drop them off your wings in flight.[20] They escorted us right to the target.

"I never did meet the Tuskegee pilots, but I thought it was the greatest thing. I wanted to go over and see them, but we had a couple of southerners on our crew who said they weren't particularly anxious to mix with 'coloreds.'"

First Lieutenant and navigator James Ruttenberg of the 461st Bombardment Group was on a mission to Zagreb. The 461st frequently went after targets such as oil refineries, bridges, railroad marshalling yards and German troop concentrations. All of the targets were heavily protected by anti-aircraft and German fighter plane support. It was on a mission to Croatia when he encountered the Tuskegee Airmen.

"And our plane on that bomb run got shot up pretty badly. We lost most of one of the tails. Do you know what the B-24 looks like? The bomber has two tails, with two rudders on its tail. At any rate, one of our rudders was very damaged and we had also lost an engine.

"So my pilot asked me for a heading to the nearest airbase that we could get to on the other side of the Adriatic. I gave him a heading from Yugoslavia to the Tuskegee Airbase, which was our farthest northern airfield at the time. And we went across the Adriatic with three engines, then lost our second engine when we were almost all the way across.

"About halfway across the Adriatic, the P-51s from the Tuskegee Airmen picked us up and flew cover for us, because a single bomber flying by itself, especially a wounded one, was a real easy target for enemy fighters. So they picked us up and escorted us all the way to their airbase. I was on the radio when we were coming into the airbase, and you never heard such wonderful jive talk. Those guys have a very soft place in my heart.

"I felt a very strong kinship to these guys because they were going through the same sort of things because of their race that I went through my whole life because I happen to be born of Jewish parentage. When we stayed there overnight and had dinner with these guys, the conversation went along the lines of an apology. I guess I more or less apologized for the rest of my citizens in the United States. I wanted them to know that everybody didn't feel the same way.

"When I got out of service I had always wanted to hitchhike across the country and here was the perfect opportunity. I got picked up in Needles, California by a black couple who were from Texas, but who had been living up in Seattle working in a bowling equipment factory. That work was over for them and they were going back home. They were pulling a little trailer with their stuff. I went a long ways with them—I think two days of traveling.

"We stopped in Kingman, Arizona at a motel, and it was that same sort of thing I would later experience [for being Jewish]. I registered with the clerk and got a room. When they went up to register, they were standing next to me. The desk clerk said, 'I'm sorry, sir, but I don't make the rules here, but we're not allowed to register you in this motel.' I said, 'But yeah, they're driving me—I'm their passenger.' And nothing cut any ice. So I said, 'Tear up my registration card and tell us where they can stay.' And he gave us the name of a motel down the road, and the three of us went down there, and I stayed where the black people could stay. Not being a hero, but who could not do that under those circumstances?

"My first objective [after my discharge] was to get an education, to develop some kind of proficiency so that I could earn a living and get someplace. I chose accounting, because it was shorter than law, it was shorter than medicine. So I was in a hurry and had to make a choice so I made that choice and I went that direction.

"Now at that time, in my mind, the best accounting school in Chicago was at Northwestern University. So that's where I went to enroll to go to school. The GI Bill was paying for everything, so this wasn't a case of money. My high school grades were good, way above average, and I had a financially rich uncle ['Uncle Sam'] that was paying for everything for me! So I thought this would be a slam-dunk.

"I went and registered and selected classes. I never got the notices as to my being accepted and enrolled. I made inquiries and time went on, and it was getting close to the semester beginning, and so I went to the university and started making inquiries in person. I was finally told ultimately, 'Mr. Ruttenberg, I'm sorry to tell you—I'm just an employee here—I don't make the rules for the university—but the university has a Jewish quota, and our quota for this semester was filled before your application was put in. We cannot accept you for this semester's work. If you would like to apply for next semester, I can almost guarantee that there'll be a spot for you next semester.'

"I'm still in uniform, I just came back from fighting the war, and I was a man in a hurry. A semester is a whole big thing out of my life—I've already lost three years—I needed to catch up. Well, there was nothing I could do about it—I went out of there mad as hell.

"I called DePaul University which is in downtown Chicago, and the Catholic priest said, 'Sure, you got money? Come on, we'll take you.' So that's where I ended up going to school, to a Catholic university. I got a good education, it was fine. It's just that it was not the university of my choice; but still at that time, there was a Jewish quota—you were not considered like everybody else—you were handled differently.

"So the world that we left, we came back to. But you know, it has been getting shaved down and shaved down and smoothed down. Over these 85 years that I've lived, I've seen a lot of changes, but I don't know that we'll ever really get there, the 'there' that we want."

Stories of Healing

Captain Yale Trustin, served as a pilot with the European Air Transport Services. It was the first "European airline" if you will, as the war transitioned to civilian life.

In late 1945 into 1946, Europe bore witness to masses of humanity who were displaced, alone and impoverished; no people in this "sea" were more lost than the survivors of the concentration camps. Yet even in the worst of times, blessings could be found.

"I normally flew out of Rhein-Main Air Base near Frankfurt-am-Main, Germany. I think it was early in 1946, I was driving a jeep toward my base, and I picked up a displaced person who was just hitchhiking.

"His name was Julius J—and he was going to Zeilsheim and that's where they had made a displaced person's camp.[21] At this

Captain Yale F. Trustin (courtesy Yale F. Trustin).

Zeilsheim, they confiscated some apartments, and they put them in there, just to temporarily take care of them, until they could go either to the States or Israel, or even some of them went back to their homes [in Europe].

"So this fellow showed me where Zeilsheim was. I met his brother Fred and his brother's girlfriend, and I befriended them as well. [In time] I would get them clothing and things like that from my friends back in the States.

"Later on I found the Jewish Welfare Board. The way I found it was that one of my passengers on one of my flights was a rabbi named A—. He was a Jewish chaplain during the war and he was on his way to Israel, so I took him part way on our scheduled flight, and then he changed in Munich, I think. Anyway, I told him I was Jewish, and he said, 'Oh, have you been to the Jewish Welfare Board?' I said, 'No, I don't know—what's that?' That's how I found the Jewish Welfare Board in Frankfurt.

"We visited the camps as volunteers from the Jewish Welfare Board and on Sundays we would take a truck that was loaned to us by the military. We would take food and clothing and so forth that was sent to us from our friends, and we would distribute them at these DP [Displaced Persons] camps. We'd go to a different camp almost every week.

"The refugees weren't in rags, but just clothes that people gave them. They would trade one thing for another, and if somebody had a watch, he'd trade it for something else. Cigarettes took on monetary value. They could get things—like for a pack of cigarettes, they could get two or three suits of clothes."

On one of his many trips to the Jewish Welfare Board, Trustin would be rewarded for his good deeds.

"My wife was raised in Vienna, Austria, she and her sister lived a middle-class life. Then in 1938, I believe it was, one of the husbands of my wife's mother's sisters was picked up off the street and sent to a concentration camp. They sent back his ashes. The rest of the family, of course, was shocked. They knew they had to do something, but they didn't. They just felt that it just couldn't happen to them and it was just one time [an isolated incident].

"When the Kristallnacht came with all the destruction of Jewish enterprises and synagogues and so forth, that's when my wife's mother said, 'Somebody has got to do something.' She had been a nurse in World War I in the Austrian Army. For some reason, at that time, the Nazis allowed—if there was a place that they could go to, the people that had served in the Army in World War I for Austria were allowed to leave. She found that England needed nurses and so she was able to go through the Quakers to England.

"She got to England and was able to get passage for her children because there were Quaker families who volunteered to take the children in their homes. They were able to go to one of those homes.

"Right after the war, they needed interpreters in Europe, and so she and her sister went back and took the job, along with many others who were from Germany or Austria. I met my future wife at the Jewish Welfare Board."

Julius, the man whom Trustin met on the road, married and eventually came to West Hartford, Connecticut. He was sponsored by Trustin's parents. Fred J—, Julius' brother also came to America and married. The brothers remain in contact with Trustin to this day.

About the same time, half-way around the world, Saul Nova's P-38 squadron, had been moved from the tiny island of Ie Shima off the coast of Okinawa, to the Japanese mainland. He became part of the army of occupation. His was the first P-38 squadron to be based in Japan and they were assigned to Ashiya Air Base in Kyushu.

His commanding officer decided it would be a good idea to have each officer take turns as officers-of-the day (ODs); it was in this capacity that Nova created an international incident where he showed mercy toward a peasant who had been accused of stealing food for his family, instead of allowing the local police to deal with it. The peasant would have been severely beaten by the police had Nova not intervened.

When I first interviewed Saul Nova, I asked him what he was doing when he heard the news of Pearl Harbor. He was playing basketball in a school yard with friends who would also join the Army Air Corps. As with many other young men, Nova loved sports. He remembered the following story nearly 70 years after the fact:

"We had a Japanese house boy who took care of our room where we were billeted. He was 18 years old and we became friends. Somehow we learned to communicate. As the war was ending, he was in training to become a *Kamikaze* submariner.

"Evidently, the Japanese had invented a torpedo that a person could sit in and drive into the side of a ship. They were [presumably] planning to use this weapon when [if] the invasion of Japan began.

"In April 1946, I was on my way back to a meeting in a part of the country I had never visited. I came upon a brick wall that was at least 30 feet high and 300 feet long. I could hear people screaming on the other side of the wall. I turned my jeep around and drove into an opening in the brick wall. It was a baseball game! I didn't know the Japanese played baseball.

"I stopped to watch the game and a man came running out of the stands. It was my house boy! He grabbed my arm and insisted I join him in the stands. He introduced me to his friends and each extended their hands to shake. The line of people who wanted to shake hands began to grow; it grew from five to 10 to 20 and kept getting longer. I couldn't stay because I was already late for a meeting.

"I could tell from some of the things they were saying that my house boy had told them that I was the American who refused to turn the peasant over to the local police for a beating. By that time these peasants were now citizens of a democratic Japan. Their future and the future of their children had changed. The caste system was gone forever.

"And we loved each other. They loved us because of how we had changed their lives and we grew to love them because of what they were doing with this opportunity of freedom. I am certain that experience has turned me into an optimist."

At the start of this book, I talked of my uncle, Laurence Wolk, a B-24 ball turret gunner who had been with the 467th Bombardment Group, 791st Squadron. What I would officially learn of his service was graciously offered by Andy Wilkinson, the historian of the 467th.

Laurence Wolk was a member of original 791st Squadron. His pilot was Lt. Lowell J. Hanna, and they were the first air echelon of the squadron arriving at Rackheath, England, even before combat operations commenced. They completed their tour in October 1944. My uncle had survived the worst of it, when the 8th Air Force was decimated by flak and lack of fighter cover.

In March 2015, one of the veterans I had interviewed, Leon Waldman, gave me a referral to another Jewish veteran, SSGT Morton Schechter. As this book would unfold, Schechter would be my last interview. He had been a tail gunner on a B-24 with the 467th Bombardment Group and 791st Squadron, the same as my uncle.

Schechter flew his first mission on D–Day in a bomber named *Belle of the East*. On D–Day, the 467th BG was busy as hell; the group flew three missions to Colleville, Villers and Pontaubault, France. The 467th was going after bridges and marshalling yards to prevent the Germans from re-supplying themselves their French coastal emplacements.

On D–Day, Schechter and Wolk had to have been in the air at the same time. Who knows how close their two aircraft came to one another in formation? Did the men pass each other on the flight line? Did they nod to each other from time to time? Did they eat their powdered eggs in the same mess hall?

I asked Schechter if he knew my uncle. At first he thought my uncle's name sounded familiar, then he wasn't so sure. He had a listing of many of the names of the airmen in the 467th. However, my uncle was not among them.

I wanted to know about bomb runs that stood out in Schechter's memory. He remembered a rough run to the outskirts of Berlin in February 1945, and then on March 1, 1945, where he said the flak was so horrific he did not know if he would make it back. I imagined my uncle on similar runs. My

Staff Sergeant Morton R. Schechter (left) with other Jewish war veterans in 2014 (courtesy Morton R. Schechter).

uncle, hanging down in the ball turret bubble, hoping his ass would not get blown away by flying pieces of jagged metal and fighter plane attacks.

Schechter flew on another B-24 called the *Also Ran*. They went on a mission where they were forced to return with a full bomb load. I thought this did not happen, but he explained that when they flew over France they could not drop bombs, undoubtedly to protect Allied troops from "friendly fire." Upon landing, the wheels of Schechter's plane collapsed with the full load of bombs. Though they had put the pins back in the bombs to keep them from exploding, landings with bomb loads were always risky. It only took one bomb to set off a massive explosion. Schechter said they returned with bombs on three occasions.

Schechter's interview was brief and it was long distance. It was hard to make a personal connection; still, through Schechter's words I was able to understand my uncle just a bit better. I was able to get a peek into what was behind the young faces in his book of snapshots. For all I know, Schechter was one of them.

•• 7 ••

The Return

We owned our first business in the USA—what a country!
                                                    —Manfred Loeb

Homer Goodman, the man who crawled back to Allied lines, described himself prior to the war in this manner:

"I was a spoiled, punk kid who didn't understand what was important. I thought cars and expensive clothes were important. They're not. Family is important, people are important."

His sentiment was shared by nearly every other veteran I interviewed.

Several of the Jewish veterans were modestly successful in the business world. They opened retail outlets and sold everything from Chardonnay to toilets. They fixed watches, made furniture, labored in machine shops and painted houses. Not surprisingly, many followed in the footsteps of their parents and worked in businesses connected to the needle trades; they became dry cleaners, furriers, pattern makers, haberdashers and the like. A number climbed corporate ladders to become directors, sales managers, manufacturers, real estate developers and builders.

Many took advantage of the GI Bill and became professionals in medicine, law, psychology, engineering, architecture, advertising, education, finance, accountancy and other white-collar trades. Some were career military, serving all the way up to Vietnam—the war of my generation.

They married, and most marriages were successful. A high percentage joined synagogues or even founded them. Several became active in philanthropic causes.

Not all their stories were warm and fuzzy. More than a few drifted, often crippled by severe depression, alcoholism and post-traumatic stress.[1] They were not immune from firings and lay-offs. They lost businesses and squandered opportunities. A few had minor scrapes with the law. There were broken marriages and bitter divorces. Some buried children. A number of them

166

would experience life-long problems from diseases or injuries incurred while in the military. Some of the injuries prevented them from resuming their pre-war professions.

Upon their return from the service and certainly up until the passage of stronger civil rights legislation, the veterans could experience anti–Semitism in housing, education, social organizations and in their professions.

The veterans whose words form the soul of this book came home as changed men and women; in turn, they had no choice but to be transformative. Their imprint remains on everything from the United Nations to the personal computer. A common thread in regard to the veterans wasn't the fact that they were part of what is referred to as "The Greatest Generation." That tagline is a burdensome mantle, even they admitted it could be hyperbole.

What *was* evident throughout these interviews was their lack of narcissism and self-indulgence, diseases that run rampant in present-day society. They realized they were once a part of something much bigger than themselves. They frequently downplayed their role in the conflict.

What of their lives after the service, as both Americans and as Jews? While it was impossible to review all of their postwar stories, I felt it interesting to explore some of their accomplishments.

Bernice "Bee" Falk Haydu: "Fighting for Recognition"

On July 1, 2009, President Barack Obama signed bill S614, awarding the WASP, the Women Airforce Service Pilots, the Congressional Gold Medal. In attendance were Bernice "Bee" Falk Haydu, Elaine Danforth Harmon and Lorraine H. Rodgers. They were among the few surviving WASP physically able to attend such a ceremony.

The medal would be presented by Congress on March 10, 2010. It is the highest honor our country bestows upon civilians. The medal symbolized the conclusion of a long fight undertaken by Ms. Haydu and a small cadre of other WASP pilots.

During World War II, the WASP were called upon to test repaired aircraft and ferry fighter planes, transport planes and bombers to duty stations across the United States. They instructed new USAAF pilots in instrument flying and delivered aircraft to crews preparing to go overseas. It was also the WASP who took many aircraft on their first "shake-down" flights after the aircraft had left the factories or had been repaired after being damaged in training or crash landings.

WASP Bernice Haydu saluting General Norton A. Schwartz (courtesy Bernice "Bee" Haydu).

The WASP pilots were thought of as dispensable; 37 WASPs were killed as the result of their duties. They had no rank and no military benefits, only vague promises of recognition that were swept under bureaucratic rugs. There is absolutely no doubt that the WASPs received a raw deal.

Bernice "Bee" Falk Haydu, a graduate of WASPs Class 44–7, received her wings on September 8, 1944. She was just beginning to fly missions from Pecos Army Airfield (Pecos, Texas) as an engineering test and utility pilot when rumors arose that the U.S. Government was going to disperse the organization.

On December 7, 1944, the third anniversary of Pearl Harbor, General Henry H. "Hap" Arnold, who would later become General of the Air Force, addressed what was to be the last class of WASP. Though General Arnold was a strong advocate of the WASP program and praised the organization to the skies, he could do nothing to stop the dissolution. The WASP were gone by the end of 1944. Hundreds of skilled pilots, who happened to be women, were suddenly out of work.

The former pilots tried to do whatever they could to cling to flying. Some started aircraft ferrying services for industry, or they worked as charter pilots, or they sold aircraft or worked as air traffic controllers. Most were forced from even those jobs when men returned to the workforce following World War II.

Ms. Haydu continued to fly private aircraft for the rest of her life. She has had a long marriage, children and grandchildren. Though her remarkable exploits as a civilian pilot and instructor earned her an induction into the Aviation Hall of Fame & Museum of New Jersey on May 11, 2000, she continued to fight for a wrong that needed to be corrected.

In her book, *Letters Home 1944–1945*, she stated:

"At the 1975 Reno, Nevada, WASP reunion, I was elected president of our organization … it was during my two terms as president 1975 to 1978 that we made our concerted effort to gain recognition as veterans from Congress. Leading us every step of the way was Colonel Bruce Arnold [the son of General Arnold]."[2]

Ms. Haydu further explained that committees were set up to list the WASP accomplishments, to prove they had been treated as military and to compare their training and monetary compensations to their male counterparts. "Bee" and other former WASP worked tirelessly with any Congress people who could help their cause. They were aided by the late Senator Barry Goldwater, who was himself an Air Force pilot. It was Senator Goldwater who would champion the granting of veteran's benefit status for the WASP.

Along the way, the WASP would pick up support from Air Force Major Nicole Malachowski, the first female Thunderbird pilot who drafted the bill in its initial form. Support for the bill was bipartisan and it ultimately passed in both the House and Senate more than 30 years after Ms. Haydu took up the fight.

Stuart Reichart: "General Counsel"

Stuart Reichart's start in life was about as humble as any veteran interviewed for this book. He would overcome his challenges to reach a level that few people in his profession have ever achieved.

"I grew up in Brooklyn, New York. My mother died from tuberculosis when I was quite young, about eight years old, and really the only recollection I have of her was visiting her twice in the hospital. There were three children; myself and my two sisters.

"It was at the height of the Great Depression and my father had lost all of his money. Though he was unable to take care of us, we remained in contact with him. For a while my older sister and I went from one foster home to another. We did that for about four to five years. Ultimately, we were placed in the Brooklyn Hebrew Orphan Asylum and I was there from the age of eight to 17.

"In retrospect we were better off in the Orphan Asylum during the Depression than a lot of kids who were not. While I was in the home it was not an unpleasant experience. We went to school, we had band lessons and it's where I learned to play football.

"I graduated from Thomas Jefferson High School and was given a football scholarship to Memphis State. I had completed two semesters of my freshman year by my 18th birthday, and when I was 18, I joined the Army Air Corps. I enlisted in November 1942 as an aviation cadet."

Reichart became a navigator-bombardier who served on a B-29 crew flying out of Saipan. He experienced intense combat, especially in performing low-altitude daylight firebombing raids over Japan. He earned the Distinguished Flying Cross and Purple Heart.

Sturart R. Reichart, New York City, July 1944 (courtesy Stuart R. Reichart).

"I was discharged 10 days after my 21st birthday on November 28, 1945. I went back to school to NYU. While in the service I earned college credits, including those while I was a cadet at Syracuse University. By the time I was discharged I had three years of college credits.

"Immediately after the war, law schools permitted students to apply after only three years of college. I entered law school in September 1946. We were permitted to take three semesters a year and I was able to finish law school in September 1948.

"During the time I was in law school I stayed in the Air Force Reserve. After being admitted to the bar, I practiced law in the New York area from 1948 until the Korean War broke out in 1951. I was recalled to active duty in April 1951. In December 1952 I was transferred to Japan for three years.

"Japan was a delightful three-year tour of duty. Before leaving the States I was engaged, and I was married while I was in Japan. In Japan all you had to do was to go to the clerk's office, open a book, sign a family page, pay the equivalent of twenty-five cents in Japanese yen and you were legally married. We were married in Japan on a Friday. My wife and I didn't feel right from a Jewish point-of-view getting married in such a fashion, so we went looking for a rabbi. The following Monday, we found a young Navy rabbi in Yokohama and it turned out that we were the first couple that he married.

"After Japan, other tours included San Antonio, Texas, Dayton, Ohio, Germany and Washington, D.C., all in the Judge Advocate's Office.

"I specialized in the government procurement area in the U.S., Japan and Germany. I initiated different kinds of procurement procedures that saved multi-millions of dollars, such as multi-year contracting. Whenever there was a serious problem with a contract they would call me in to be the 'fireman.' These multi-million dollar contracts could involve anything from missiles to aircraft to a closed circuit color television system for my old boss, General LeMay. In fact, as a Major I was given the task of telling General LeMay, who by then was the U.S. Air Force Chief of Staff and a four star general, that there would be a significant delay in delivering the television system he was anxiously awaiting.

"For six years, I served as an administrative judge on the Armed Services Board of Contract Appeals. We heard contract cases from all around the world. I retired from active duty in October 1971. I was by then a full colonel. I was asked to work in the Air Force General Counsel's office as a civilian lawyer. I was working in the General Counsel's office for a couple of years when the Deputy General Counsel left and I was promoted to that position. A couple of years later, the General Counsel left. Secretary of the Air Force Stetson said, 'Stu, I want you as my General Counsel.' It was a political appointment.

"In 1978, I was appointed the General Counsel of the Air Force. For three years, from 1978 to 1981, I headed up the entire Air Force legal department during President Carter's administration.

"As General Counsel of the Air Force, one of my additional duties was Governor of Wake Island. Ever since WWII, the Air Force General Counsel had the added duty as governor. I had that honor from 1978 to 1981. In all I served a total of 40 years in the Air Force on active duty and as a civilian.

"After I retired from the Air Force in January 1982, an award was named after me. The Stuart R. Reichart Award is funded in perpetuity, given out each year to the outstanding senior lawyer in the Air Force. To be eligible for the award the attorney must have at least 14 years of service in the Department of Defense. It is considered the most prestigious judge advocate's award in the Air Force because it is based on what a person does over the course of their career, not just for one year. There is a plaque for the award in the Pentagon and Maxwell Field, Alabama.

"I had a fantastic career. But I was also very lucky. I think back to the daylight bombing mission I flew over Tokyo on April 7, 1945 where I was almost killed, and I also reflect on my childhood in the orphanage and I realize just how lucky I have been."

Gideon Lichtman: "The Israeli Air Force"

After training as a fighter pilot, Gideon "Giddy" Lichtman was assigned to the Pacific Theater of Operations. It was one of the greatest disappointments of his life. He wanted to fight the Nazis and to pay them back for what they were doing to the Jews of Europe. He received a second chance to help the Jewish people through his flying by being one of the founding members of the Israeli Air Force.[3]

"Giddy's" interview is raw and to the point; it reflects anger and a resolve that is refreshing in its purpose, especially following a Holocaust where much of the world stood by and did nothing.

"After the war, I was very anxious to get into a university and get a law degree. I had a bunch of friends who were going to Upsala College in New Jersey, which was an excellent school. At that time, the schools were loaded with veterans. I went to Upsala for a year and then transferred to NYU. That move turned out to be a disaster. After the war there were so many veterans they didn't call you by name, but by a number.

"In the meantime, I kept going to Zionist-type meetings. I liked listening to a Conservative Rabbi by the name of Rabbi Joachim Prinz who was

First Lieutenant Gideon Lichtman (courtesy Gideon Lichtman).

the head of the Conservative Rabbis.[4] He came to the States from Germany and spoke with a thick German accent. He and my father were on friendly terms and they were both quite active in the Zionist movement. My father was principal of a Hebrew school in New Jersey.

"I went and heard Rabbi Prinz at Congregation Sinai in the Newark area this was sometime in March or April of 1948. Rabbi Prinz was an excellent speaker. After his speech, there was another speaker who had been a crewmember on the ship the *Exodus*.[5] The ship had attempted to bring Jewish refugees into Palestine, but they were intercepted by the British and put into prison on Cypress. The refugees went from the concentration camps of Europe to British prison camps, complete with barbed wire and guard towers.

"The [*Exodus*] crewmember gave an inspiring speech. I approached him and told him that I wanted to volunteer to rescue Jews from Europe. The speaker told me to contact a newspaper named *Land & Labor*. I wrote them a letter and they sent me back a mimeographed form. At the end of the form they asked questions as to whether I had served in WWII. I wrote on the form that I had been a fighter pilot.

"One or two days later I received telegram indicating that I should call a telephone number. They set up a meeting with a guy who would have a red rose in his label. No names were exchanged. It was all very secret, but the FBI was fully aware of this recruitment organization. So I met this guy. He didn't give me his name, but he said he would contact me soon and that there was a need for fighter pilots and that Israel was setting up an air force. He was an American guy who had been stationed in Egypt. I asked him what type of fighter planes the Israelis had, but he didn't tell me. I asked him again and he said something I was to hear many times: 'Leave it to the Jews. The Jews will take care of everything.' He told me to go home and they would contact me.

"They contacted me several times, and they always met me on West 57th Street in New York City, but with different guys. After I returned home from meeting with one these guys one evening, my parents told me that somebody had called. I called them back and they said that I would receive a certified letter with tickets to Rome. The flight would go from Amsterdam to Geneva to Zurich, and finally to Rome. My father was kind of proud of me but also upset. When my mother found out, she said, 'You are not going anywhere!' This went back and forth, but I went.

"I had one suit to my name, by the way, and it was a zoot suit! It was deep blue with wide padded shoulders. I was walking around Europe in a zoot suit and drawing attention wherever I went. From Amsterdam, I went to Switzerland and I stayed for a while in Zurich with nothing to do. I remember that I bought a watch. In Zurich, somebody contacted me and said, 'You will be going to Czechoslovakia through Rome.' I asked, 'What will I do there?' They didn't tell me anything, but that I would be meeting with a Dr. Felix who was in charge of all the recruiting.

"While in Rome, I was to meet one of the most famous war aces of WWII, George 'Buzz' Beurling.[6] He and I became very friendly. 'Buzz' was Canadian but of German descent, and initially they wouldn't allow him in Canadian air force. He took a boat back to England, was accepted into the British Air Force, took a boat back to Canada and was finally able to fly for Canada.

"'Buzz' was also recruited into the Israeli Air Force. They had arranged for him to take a Noorduyn Norseman to Palestine. The aircraft was a single engine seaplane that had been donated to the Israeli Air Force. I called him up in the morning and I made the last contact with him. He took off and the airplane blew up. I am convinced the Arabs sabotaged the airplane.

"I asked the contact person in Switzerland where was my visa? I was told that Dr. Felix would take care of it. As I was landing in Czechoslovakia, the Communists had just taken over the country. As I went to get out of the airplane, Communist soldiers with Red Stars met me at the airplane and they asked me for my visa.

"I was placed under house arrest in a hotel. It was a cruddy hotel and I wasn't allowed to leave my room. We had to eat our meals at the hotel and we weren't allowed out of our rooms. There was a nice woman who was also put under arrest in the hotel. I saw her from my window and we smiled at each other. She couldn't speak English and I couldn't speak Czech, but anyway there was a ledge outside my window and I used to go out and over the ledge into her room.

"I'm there for a week and I hear nothing from nobody. I found this piece of paper in my shoe. It was the contact number I had been given while I was in Rome. I don't know why I kept it in my shoe; there was no reason at all. I had never done that before, but I'm stuck in this room with a carton of Nescafe coffee that I was told to bring to Dr. Felix from New York, I'm in my zoot suit and I'm stuck in my room. I called a guy in Switzerland and I said, 'Send me back to States. I'm tired of waiting around.'

"Shortly after my call, Dr. Felix finally met me in my room. He was a little, nondescript guy. Do you know what the first words out of his mouth were? 'Where's my Nescafe?' I said to him, 'Take this Nescafe and shove it up your ass!' I grabbed him by the collar and asked him what the hell was going on? We finally got things straightened out. I think he paid some people off. He told me that I'm going to Prague to check out an airplane. He got me on a train and I got proper papers and there were more payoffs.

"I get on a train in my zoot suit and I traveled to an airfield 30 to 40 minutes away from Prague.[7] It was a former Nazi air base. The Israelis had made a deal with the Czech government on some airplanes that we were to fly.

"Now I can fly anything, but these planes were horrible. I asked, what are these? The planes appeared to be German Bf-109s, which were formidable weapons during the war, but they didn't have the power and couldn't handle like Bf-109s. These were the first Czech Avia fighter planes and they used the Bf-109 fuselage but they put on a less powerful engine, which resulted in less horsepower and less maneuverability that made it all but un-flyable.[8] The Czechs had screwed Israel. Dr. Felix took this deal because the Czechs were going to train us to fly this thing. We didn't need training, we needed good aircraft. There was apparently a deal that was rejected where the Israelis could get American P-47s from a South American country. The P-47 was a great airplane and I would have loved to fly it. Dr. Felix knew nothing about aircraft. He was just a Zionist in the government. The only thing he knew about was Nescafe.

"In Czechoslovakia I met up with Maury Mann and Dov ben Zvi. We flew a small airplane, a Czech trainer called an Arado 96B, under the supervision of Czech instructors to refresh our combat training skills.

"I had actually flown an Bf-109 before, but the Avia was nothing like the Bf-109. In order to check out any plane you really needed about 100 hours. This plane was a piece of shit. I gave it the throttle. It was like a battle. There was a big problem with torque. I thought at the time that we're in big trouble. The cockpit instrumentation was in the metric system.

"I figured I'd get in 50 hours on this plane and I'll figure out where the levers are, but there were three of us and I knew I'm not going to have enough time to [train]. I almost crashed on my first take-off. I knew the Israeli air force was in deep trouble. I had anticipated flying surplus P-40s at the worst and P-51s at best. When I took the Avia up, I knew it was completely un-flyable.

"While we were still training in Czechoslovakia, somebody knocks on the door and says, 'You're leaving for Israel in 20 minutes.' The ground crew took apart the fighter plane and loaded it into a C-46 transport plane for shipping to Israel. They managed to put the Bf-109-Avia fuselage into the length of the C-46 and on top of that they put the wings and on top of that the pilot, me.

"We took off and we're flying toward Israel. As we approached what we thought was Israel we noticed what looked like firing Ping-Pong balls. We realized it was artillery. We were approaching a landing in Cairo instead of Israel! We immediately changed course and headed toward where Israel was supposed to be.

"We headed toward the Israeli airbase in complete blackness. It had to be done in secrecy because the British were still there. When you're flying in

Israel, the stars light up the whole sky. It's that way throughout the Mediterranean. As we were coming in, the Israelis took jeeps and automobiles and on a signal they all put their lights on and illuminated the runway. They didn't have proper lighting in those days in Israel. When the lights went on, it was probably the greatest feeling I've ever gotten in my life. We landed in Southern Israel in the Negev in Aqir, the site of an old RAF air base.

"I stayed there for a few days when Mordechai 'Modi' Alon woke me up early in the morning and told me to get ready immediately.[9] I think he said something like, 'Get your ass up and get ready!' They were afraid that four Egyptian Spitfires, we called them 'Spits,' had taken off and that they were probably heading toward Israel to strafe Tel-Aviv as they had done a few days before. The Israelis had developed a secret way of finding out when the Egyptians fighters were taking off. This was probably done by the Hagana.[10]

"I'm grabbing my clothes and shoes. By this time, I had gotten rid of the zoot suit and they had given me brown overalls and then they're driving me to the airfield to get to my fighter plane. There were a few Avia S-199s that had already been assembled. In the early days, there were probably never more than four Avia's operational at any time.

"In those days, we needed a big strong mechanic to crank the plane. The engine starts to turn over and the pilot pulls a lever.

"Modi takes off before me and I have no clue as to where I am. The only thing I know is where the Mediterranean is. I didn't know how to read the metric instruments. Also, in the springtime in Israel there may be a fine powder in the air from the sand. You don't get into clear skies until 8,000 feet to 10,000 feet. Finally it got clear for me around 8,000 feet and we're looking around for the Spitfires and for each other.

"Basically air combat breaks down to an element leader and wingman. Modi is my element leader and I am trying to follow him. He was in a big hurry to get off the ground. He takes off into the haze full throttle instead of waiting for me. When I did see him I only saw a dark shadow. He was about a quarter of a mile away and finally he slowed up for me and I caught up with him right away.

"We had agreed as we were running to our aircraft that he would take his arm and circle it around and point to enemy aircraft. There was no radio communication between our aircraft. We were only two ships and my eyes were glued onto my element leader. My primary focus, therefore, was on Modi's aircraft.

"Way ahead of us we see four aircraft which turned out to be Egyptian Spitfires. There were only two of us. Also, I had a [faulty] instrument panel I don't know, which was a situation filled with possible disaster. I had some vague idea where the gun switches were. You have to arm the guns with one switch, then you put the gun sight on the target and it lights up a piece of glass with a circle of light. You have to take a lead depending on an enemy aircraft based on your level of attack and your air speed. Your angle of attack is changing constantly. I had to estimate.

"So now I'm in deep crap. I want to have guns working. The Spitfires were below us and way ahead of us and I don't know where the fucking switches are or where the gun sights, guns are! I am going full throttle and I've only got 35 to 40 minutes worth of fuel. Modi makes a pass at them, guns blazing and disappears into the mist. They break off and into the haze in four different directions.

"I finally find the gun switches but I've used up a lot of fuel and my fuel gauge is low. I maybe have 15 to 20 minutes worth of fuel. I see a shadow below me. I engage him in a dog fight. He is a lousy fighter pilot. Instead of turning into me as you're supposed to do, he turns away. I get him into my sights and pull the trigger and I see a piece of metal breaking off.

"Then the Spitfire disappears into the mist again. Just as I'm nearing the base. I see another Avia that has joined us. I follow him in and it's Ezer Weizman.[11]

"After we landed, he said, 'You shot down the first Egyptian fighter plane in the history of the Israeli Air Force.'

"Ezer once told me that he would sometimes take Coke bottles and throw them out of the window during ground battles. The Coke bottles would whistle just like a bomb and could halt Egyptian troop movements. But prior to that, there had been no fighter planes in aerial combat. Modi Alon had previously shot down two Egyptian transport planes, but not fighter planes.

"One day, I said to that we should name the 101st Israeli Fighter Squadron and make up a logo. I suggested the name should be Malach Ha-mavit, 'The Angel of Death.' I got the idea from the skull and crossbones like you see on a bottle of iodine, which was the only medicine we had. The logo was designed by Stan Andrews on the back of a cocktail napkin."[12]

Ira Weinstein: "A Promise Kept"[13]

Ira Weinstein, the former POW shot down during the catastrophic Kassel Mission, would become the successful head of a Chicago-based advertising agency. He started his business literally by going door-to-door asking for business. However, immediately following the war, Weinstein felt compelled to make right an oath uttered over the bodies of the dead crewmembers he was forced to bury.

Weinstein and another POW, Eric S—from the same mission, were marched to the crash site (see Chapter 5). They were ordered to strip off the workable machine guns and bury the dead.

"And one of the ships I came across was my own ship. I knew it was mine because of the insignia on it, but I didn't know any of the kids who were on the plane. I knew the pilot got killed. I didn't know where the navigator was, but I knew he had bailed out and there was another guy—I forget who it was, on the ship. The five other guys were all burned to a crisp. I had to take them out and bury them right there."

His interrogators never searched him to discover his pilot's dog-tags.

"I really don't remember how I managed to keep Lieutenant D—'s dog-tags. Once I was in regular [German] army POW hands, they never searched our pockets. I might have just kept them in my pocket during the interrogation. I don't remember them ever stripping me of the contents of my pockets. When they took our clothes for the shower, I believe they just chemically cleaned our clothes. After the war, I sent the dog-tags to the War Crimes Commission. I advised the War Crimes Commission and they sent two agents from Washington to Chicago to interview me. I can't be sure of this, but I sort of remember I heard they did find them [the farmers] and prosecuted them.

"When I got back to the States I said to my wife, 'You know, those parents must wonder what happened. All they get is a KIA [Killed in Action] notice, nothing else, no explanation from the government. I think I'm going to go visit all those parents.'

"I got the addresses and names of the crew and I went and visited all those parents. I didn't tell them the gory details, but I told them that the kids were in battle and it was terrible and they were probably shot during the battle, and that I buried their bodies and this is where it is [the location] and so forth.

"I am not religious; no, not at all. Well, I was bar mitzvah'd, and I used to be more active when I was younger. When my children were growing up, I was active in a very Reform temple. But how can I refute what I call God? Is there a God? I never get into that with anybody because I don't know the answers for it. I know that there's something that's made me so lucky.

"I don't think religion motivated me to do what I did. It just bothered me. I didn't really know those boys. It was a strange crew that I was flying with that day. But I was reading in the paper about what families went through. So maybe it was about God—I don't know—maybe there was a touch of that in it. Who can tell?

"You know, there were more than 200 guys down on the ground out of those airplanes [after the Kassel Mission]. So the Germans were up there all the time looking for survivors. When the American Air Force used to come over during the day when I was a POW, I'd look up at the airplanes, I'd think, 'I [wish] to hell I was up there.'"

Irwin Stovroff: "A Prisoner's Gift"

"Immediately after the war I went into the furniture business. But I didn't do it in my hometown of Buffalo, New York; I went to Youngstown, Ohio. I would move on from there to a major furniture company and I was employed by them for more than 40 years. I went from being a field salesman to the head of international sales, plus having responsibilities for three domestic territories. I was able to travel all over the world. I would still be with them had they not forced me to retire at 75.

"Based on my own experiences as a POW and unfortunately the post-traumatic stress that followed, I became an advocate for POWs at the Veterans Administration Center in West Palm Beach, Florida. I'm a national service officer for ex-POWs, and have been for more than 13 years. Two years ago, I was recognized by the national POW association as their outstanding member. We recognized that ex-POWs needed help. They didn't know about the benefits the government offered either medically or for mental health claims. I helped process more than 400 claims, allowing POWs to get pensions and other help. As much as I enjoyed this kind of work in terms of helping, it is obvious that the number of POWs from WWII, Korea, and Vietnam has diminished.

"However, while I was working for the VA, I became aware that an important and unmet need had developed for veterans returning from Iraq and Afghanistan. I was encouraged by the VA to tackle the issue and to do something about it. I discovered in 2007 that our government had no funds for our disabled and blinded veterans coming home, who were in need of a dog. The only way they could get a dog was through private donations.

"At first I became affiliated with the guide dog foundation in Smithtown, New York, and with their kind support, I created my own organization and began soliciting and raising funds for the young heroes coming home. I just felt it was something that needed to be done and should be and can be done. It fell on me to do it. I started an organization called 'Vets Helping Heroes.'[14] On the website, it tells what we're doing, why we're doing it, how we've done it, the amount of money we've raised, the goals that we have, and the media attention. We've raised more than two and a half million dollars by now.

"I will tell you that after a couple of years of trying to raise money on my own, I started contacting members of the U.S. Congress. I only heard back from one U.S. Congressman and he was Jewish—Democrat Ron Klein from Florida's 22nd District. Representative Klein pushed a bill through Congress that was part of an overall military spending bill. He stood up in front of Congress and told them he was motivated by me.

"Initially, we were granted $5 million, and then they cut it to $2 million. To this day we have not seen a nickel of that money. We will keep on going.

I'm hearing from people all over the country. I've heard from every state including Alaska. I've had people send me dog food, covers, blankets, money. I'd say this is probably one of the most satisfying things I've ever done.

"Of course I was motivated in part by my experiences in the service and I think probably part of it is being Jewish. It's the way we think. Within the last year or so, I came to the [following] conclusion: when I talk to these young veterans, often men and women who are without arms, without legs, without eyes, without brains anymore, because they're having seizures—that's what these dogs are for, I realized that I guess I'm doing this because I went through quite an experience myself.

"In the big picture I didn't go through anything much different than a lot of guys now or then. It was quite an experience. But I came home with my arms, my legs, my brains, and everything else. I'm doing all of this because I became a very lucky person to not only go through all that, but come back and take all the advantages there was to be given or got. I'm now 89 years old—that's not bad. It's nice to be recognized for my work, but the really important thing is that we have placed more than 55 dogs."

Herb Kaster: "Family Diaspora"

Herbert Kaster was an aircraft armament officer with the 303rd Bombardment Group. He witnessed dozens of aircraft crash land, often with loss of life of the crewmembers. He and his men helped rebuild the destroyed B-17 bombers. It was Kaster who was given a photograph of a concentration camp by his commanding officer with the admonition to always tell people what had happened to the Jews.

After Kaster left the service he would become a chemical engineer. He was involved in building manufacturing plants in the United States and Europe. Every time he traveled to the Munich area, he would schedule side-trips to the Dachau concentration camp.

"Yes, my family lost relatives in the Holocaust. As to my mother's family, I don't know [what happened to them]. My father's family lived in the Ukraine not far from Rovno[15] [Rowno] and he was one of eight brothers. When the Germans invaded Russia, they passed through their area in September of 1940. My father lost several brothers.

"The remaining family disbursed east all the way back to the Ural Mountains. In 1989, I went to Russia with a cousin of mine, specifically looking for relatives. I had an old friend who was Russian who served as a tour guide taking tours through Russia. We arranged for a tour to go to Moscow, Yalta, Kiev and Leningrad.

"We made arrangements to meet the remaining family members closest to my father's relatives in Kiev. My aunt came with her daughter. She was married to a Russian. A cousin of one of the brothers who was killed also came with his mother, sister and his wife. When the plane landed in the airport in Kiev, they were standing waiting in the terminal. By the family resemblance to my father and uncles and so forth, I immediately knew who they were. So I took pictures and everything and I brought them up-to-date. They were just as thrilled as we were.

"We all went to Babi Yar, where all the Jews in Kiev had been murdered. There was a big memorial there for them. They rounded up all the Jews and marched them down this main street out to the suburbs to this park. There was a big gully and they put them in the gully and machine-gunned them. Over the years, the rain and the water washed away a lot of the covering soil. The bones came up from under the ground, and that's how the people realized what had happened there.

"We spent several days with these distant relatives and we enjoyed ourselves. My aunt was just eight years old when all her other sisters went sent to Israel [in 1936]. They corresponded. In the early 1990s, the Russians started to let the Jews leave and go to Israel if they wanted to do so.

"My family here in America rounded up a few thousand dollars, and we sent it to the relatives in Israel who lived on a Kibbutz. They arranged for my aunt and her daughter to visit Israel for 30 days. So that was a mitzvah [a good deed] for all of us to perform, you know.

"In 1945, a third brother from my father's family was brought over by the Jewish immigration agency [HIAS]. He had been in the Russian Army. I guess he was asked if he had any relatives in the United States, and he said yes, he had two brothers.

"This brother was the youngest and they brought him over, so there were now three brothers in the United States. The three brothers were continually writing letters back-and-forth [to Russia] until my grandmother and grandfather passed away. My father would always try to remain close to them. He sent them money going back to the early 1900s. Whatever money he had, he used to send it to them. I never knew my grandparents.

"My father visited Israel in the 1950s. We were brought up in a Jewish household and we were very close with Israel. I have always been fond of Israel."

Manfred Loeb: "The Deluxe Bake Shop"[16]

Manfred Loeb and his family were barely able to leave Germany before all routes for Jews attempting escape were blocked. In a most improbable scenario, once they got to this country, he and his family would initially live and work on the Van Eeden agricultural settlement, a farming commune in North Carolina that was accepting and nurturing of German Jewish immigrants.

Loeb gained his U.S. citizenship while in Army Air Corps training, serving his time in the military with the famed "Flying Tigers" in the CBI campaign. He was part of a crew that transported supplies to troops fighting the Japanese. This is the story of how Mr. Loeb would become one of the nation's most celebrated kosher bakers.

"Before the war I went to trade school in Bridgeport, Connecticut, which was about 45 minutes from where my parents were living. I got into the trade school to became a tool and die maker. While I was going to trade school, a friend from Germany helped me find a room in Bridgeport and get into the school.

Corporal Manfred Loeb in China with Flying Tigers (courtesy Manfred and Ann Loeb).

"I had to earn a few dollars to pay for my room, which I think was six or seven dollars a week, and [find] food to eat. I was able to get a job in a bakery at night. I would go to school during the day, and then when I got out of school, I would walk to the bakery and work there until 11 p.m. or 12:00 a.m. at night. Then I went to my room and slept for a few hours.

"The fellow who owned the bakery got to like me, and he took me under his wing. He always told me, 'Take something home so you have something to eat tomorrow.' I'd take a little bread, some donuts or what not. And so I

Corporal Manfred Loeb in China with Flying Tigers, c. 1944 (courtesy Manfred and Ann Loeb).

worked in that bakery, and I advanced in the bakery business there too. I learned and I did well.

"I got out of trade school, and I worked in a machine shop in Bridgeport. Though I worked in the machine shop during the week, I still worked the weekends in the bakery. Before I went into the Army, the gentleman who owned the bakery said to me, 'What do your parents do?' And I told him, and he said, 'What did your father do in Germany?' And I told him, and he said, 'Well, I'll tell you what—I have a branch store, and I could use somebody like your parents, both of them, to manage the store. They could run that store and learn about the merchandise.'

"That was a good deal and they started in the bakery there, and they did alright. Those were the war years, and where this store was, within I would say a mile-and-a-half radius, there was Singer Sewing Machine and Bridgeport Brass and General Electric, and all these people that were involved in manufacturing ammunition, machinery and things that we needed for the war effort. Everybody was working and doing well.

"Then when I came back from the service, every ex-employer had to offer you your job back—that was the law. So I was offered a job in the bakery and a job in a machine shop.

"Mr. Z—was only too happy to have me back in the bakery on a full time basis. I started as an apprentice. I learned a lot and remembered every recipe I could. I had to scale the ingredients and mix the doughs but the foreman in the shop would only tell me a couple of the ingredients at a time and in between he gave me other jobs to do; but I would finally have all the ingredients in the mixer.

"After working there for about six months I left the job on a full-time basis and I enrolled in the Culinary School of New York. My aim was to become a good cake decorator and learn more about fancy cakes and pastries. My schooling there was paid for by the government under the GI Bill of Rights. We went to school five days a week and on Saturdays and Sundays I worked at Z—'s bakery. I did this schedule for about 8 months, after which I went back to work full time in the bakery.

"I first met my future wife in Van Eeden in January of 1940. It was a commune in Penderlea, North Carolina. I was 16 years old at the time and she was 14 and we became boyfriend and girlfriend. My family eventually left Van Eeden, as my parents got a job at a boarding school; but my mother and Anne, my future wife, kept in contact. One time the two of them spoke and my mother encouraged me to call her. Anne had been taking accounting and bookkeeping courses in North Carolina. We started to correspond. When I turned 22 and she was 20, she came to visit us in Connecticut. I showed her around the bakery.

"I spoke to the owners of the bakery about a job for her. Mr. Z—, my original boss, had sold the bakery a couple of years before and the new owners were in the process of enlarging and were in need of a larger staff, bookkeeper included. They offered Anne a job in the office and she decided to move to Bridgeport and take the job. A friend of ours, who lived two blocks away from us, rented her a room and she went to work in the bakery.

"The room she had rented was only for sleeping, the rest of the time, when not working, she spent at our house with my family. We were together every day and we grew very fond of each other. On March 18, 1947, after things got a little more serious, we decided to become engaged.

"Eventually I met Fred S—, an Austrian Jewish refugee who had also barely escaped the Nazis with his father and the rest of his family. He owned a pastry shop in New Haven, Connecticut and he wanted me to work for him, which I did. It was a good move for me since I learned a good bit about the fancy pastry business.

"In June 1948, Anne and I decided to get married. We did so on the 27th of June. We started to look for our own business. All the help was lined up. Anne was the bakery office person, my parents could sell baked goods and my brother wanted to work in the bakeshop. I was fully confident that I was capable of doing the job."

"We scraped all our money together. Anne had a little, I scraped up all

I could, my parents had some and my father's brother loaned us a little for a short time and we owned our first business in the USA—what a country! It was a large retail bakeshop with a delicatessen in Norwalk, Connecticut. We bought it at auction as one unit, as the other bidders were only interested in buying piecemeal.

"We cleaned up the place and we all worked hard. We placed our orders for raw materials, flour, shortening, sugar and whatever we needed. We advertised a little, stocked the delicatessen part of the business and opened up the store.

"Much to my surprise I had an unexpected helper when we started. He was my first employee. There was an Italian man working at Z—'s when I started working there. He was an excellent baker who did not speak English too well. He left Italy before the war but he still had his family there. He sort of adopted me as someone he wanted to make into a baker. Shortly before we opened the store in Norwalk, he called me up to tell me that he heard that we were opening a bakery. He then informed me that he was going to come and help. I told him that I thought we could do it on our own and I was not sure that I could afford to pay a baker at this time. His answer was, don't worry we will make it and you really need me.

"Well, the day we opened he was there ready to get to work and work he did. He taught me a lot in the trade and he was one of the most kind-hearted people that I have ever met. Every penny he earned in the U.S. that he did not need for his living expenses he sent home to his wife and children. His name was Ernesto G—, and he came from Milan, Italy. He always sang while working and he sang operatic arias, therefore, everyone only knew him as 'Caruso.' He stayed with us as long as we were in Norwalk. Business started out pretty good. We all worked very hard and long hours every day except Mondays. Everything was going along fine, business was increasing and we were able to pay Caruso a salary.

"After about two years we decided to open a branch store. We found a nice location in a neighborhood shopping area in East Norwalk and we rented a small store, big enough for what we needed. We purchased a well-used small panel truck, which we needed to carry our merchandise to the new store and to make deliveries.

"Things were going well until the fall of 1951. A third of the working population in the Norwalk area was employed in the hat industry. Fashions were changing. Most men, and some women, stopped wearing hats. Business was going down. Our plan was to find a new location.

"Our cousin Otto had opened a very successful German restaurant called "The Old Europe," in downtown Washington, D.C. Otto told us about something new happening there and we had to see it. It was called a 'Shopping Center.' It was in the suburbs where everyone was moving to. This would be a great opportunity to open our business. We loaded all of our earthly belongings on to a tractor trailer and went to Takoma Park, Maryland.

"A few days prior tour opening I received phone call from my mentor, helper and adopted family member 'Caruso.' This was the last thing I expected. He said I am coming to Washington, you need me. Rent me a room and I will call you when I arrive. There was no argument from me. That was the end of the conversation. Without any reservation I must say he was the best strudel baker I have ever met. We opened during the first week of April in 1952, under the name of Deluxe Bake Shop.

"Today, 55 years later, the name still brings back sweet and appetizing memories to lots of folks in Washington, D.C. area. The business started out well and within a few weeks we developed a sizeable Jewish clientele. The word spread of this nice Jewish bakery and one day a young man introduced himself to us, Mr. Charles S—, a kosher caterer. He was interested in our products, he liked what we produced and wanted us to do the baking for all his affairs.

"He and I went to the Rabbinical Council of Greater Washington, and asked them to approve us as a kosher bakery. They sent us a list of demands, which we had to adhere to, and we had to buy some additional equipment. We were now a kosher baker under the supervision of the rabbinical council. We were able to serve all the synagogues in the entire greater Washington, D.C. area, including Maryland and Northern Virginia. We supplied several other kosher caterers as well and even supplied baked goods to kosher dinners prepared by the U.S. Government for receptions when kosher goods were needed. Once there was a reception in the White House to honor Golda Meir. At that time she was still the Prime Minister of Israel. We baked 3,000 pastry shells for them.

"We were contacted by Rose S—, a caterer in Washington, D.C. She was asked to do a private party for Chief Justice Earl Warren, marking the publication of an encyclopedia to the bible, written by 12 rabbis from Israel. She requested that we make a kosher, very large fancy challah, small rolls, and strawberry shortcake. My wife and I delivered the baked goods personally and the meal was a great success. Following the meal, the Chief Justice, who was apparently familiar with the kosher laws wanted to know how the caterer could serve whipped cream with chicken. We told him [we used a vegetable base] and then he wanted to know if we could send him some more.

"Besides having been able to do so much 'kosher business,' we also did some everyday wholesale. We solicited restaurants, luncheonettes, and diners, anyone that wanted better baked goods. This way we were able to employ more people and we worked around the clock.

"Around that time there was a large Jewish population movement from the city to the suburbs. A Jewish community started four or five miles north of us and Anne wanted to move there.

"A short while after we moved our store to the White Oak Shopping Center. It was only about one mile from what would soon be the Washington Beltway. A year later our new synagogue was built one block from the store. At the height of our business we employed eight bakers, including a German pastry chef that I brought to the States from Germany.

"I was more than 62 years old when the shopping center owners said they wanted a 10 year lease. Anne and I decided we were too old for that. Consequently on the 12th of April 1987 we closed the doors.

"We kept enough equipment to furnish a small bake shop in our basement ... and our first job in the 'underground bakery' was to bake challah [breads] for us, our children and some of our neighbors. Things worked out perfect. We had our own baked goods again!

"Lots of friends and neighbors called and begged us to bake challahs for them for Shabbat including some rabbis and cantors. The following year I had a couple of jobs doing some consulting and teaching to young bakers for a large bakery chain.

"I took on another 'job,' I taught challah baking at the Jewish Community Center. It was hard to believe that so many people wanted to learn how to bake challahs!

"Joan Nathan, the well-known Jewish Cook Book writer, was one of my Deluxe Bake Shop customers ... she asked me to make challahs with her. She wrote about our bakery many times. I taught all her children how to make challahs. They all made their own challahs for their bar and bat mitzvahs. She published what became her best-selling book, *Jewish Cooking in America*, where she gave me a page spread including a picture of me with her children and of course the recipe for the 'World's Best Challah.'"

Loeb was only 14 when he fled Germany in 1939 shortly after kristallnacht. He didn't know what the future held.

"I didn't know, not to the extent of all the killing would I have imagined. In the last few years I've been reading more about the past. In Germany, there were a lot of people out of work—things were tough when Hitler first came in. All the things he said sounded good to them, and they started to believe him. I think they got suckered into this, I'm sorry to say. But there were still a lot of good Germans there too, but they kept their mouth shut—they were afraid.

"I went back to Germany a couple times and I took my children there. I also went back with my wife. I met an old neighbor who lived near to where my parents once owned our house. They lived across the street from us and they were very religious Catholic people. Our neighbor's daughter said she was glad to see us. She asked how my parents were doing, and I said they were still alive. This family was very quiet during Hitler's rise to power, and they didn't do anything … you didn't see them running around and hollering 'Heil Hitler!' and things like that.

"But there was a lady living across the street who was probably the biggest Nazi in the world, and my neighbor told me that this lady's husband passed away, and that her son had gotten killed. Both of them lost their lives in the war.

"My former Catholic neighbor said, 'Do you want to go over and see her?' I said, 'No, I don't want to see her, but you can do me a favor? Tell her I was here, that I'm doing quite well, that my parents are doing very well, and so is my brother. I can't say that I'm sorry about what happened to her.'

"She said, 'I will deliver that message.'"

Epilogue

My mother is now 97, and is one of a handful of former riveters still living who built the P-40 fighter plane. She worked for Curtiss-Wright aircraft in Tonawanda, New York. She married in May 1943, moved away from Buffalo and settled in Hempstead, New York.

Hempstead's Jewish community was vibrant in those days. There was a deep inter-connectedness of families. Mom developed a new circle of friends. One friend was a newlywed named Ruth, who had married an accountant. The man was about to be drafted and everyone thought it was a shame as Ruth had just found out she was pregnant and he would not be of help when the baby came. Mom remembered playing cards with them. As the accountant shuffled the deck he said, "What do I know about war?" He went into basic training certain he would be a paper-pusher. He was shipped off to Europe in time for the Battle of The Bulge, and was killed within 100 days of entering the service.

Shortly after the war, my mom was wheeling me in a baby carriage when she met a woman named Lorraine who was also wheeling a newborn. From that chance meeting, they would become life-long friends; to me, she was always Auntie Lorraine.

Phil, Lorraine's husband, had seen combat in the Pacific. The night before a bad mission, the company commander said that most of them would probably not survive the next day's battle. The formation broke up; somebody called Phil a dirty Jew. Maybe the guy expected different, but Phil started to beat the man. After they broke it up, Phil went off and stayed awake all night. He said *Kaddish* for himself. At daybreak, the battle orders were rescinded.

When the men and women came back from war to Hempstead, there was a social gathering of the Jewish community to honor the veterans. Not surprising, the accountant's family and Lorraine's family knew of one another. An argument broke out between the two families because Phil had lived and the other man had died. The rift never healed.

Mom remembered a New Year's Eve party 15 or 20 years later. Phil got loaded with my father and some other friends. They were horsing around outside, saluting each other like they were in the military. A heavy snow had blanketed Long Island just a few days before. All of the men came into the house except for Phil. Where was Phil everyone wanted to know? Phil was found marching in the snow, shouting cadence, glassy-eyed, rigid and upright.

Uncle Larry got into pointless arguments and fights well past middle age. I witnessed his temper when it flared. I believe he suffered from PTSD. No ball turret gunner ever returned the same, especially those who flew with the Mighty 8th from the start of the war through D–Day and beyond, as did my uncle.

I remember Eddie R—, a salesman for the dry cleaning supply company. Eddie called on my father's store about once every two weeks. He made jokes with Yiddish phrases. In those days the dry cleaning business was predominantly Jewish, a carry-over from the needle trades. Dry cleaning and tailoring have always been the businesses of immigrants. Eddie was a glad-hander who dressed as sharp as a tack, but mom told me he could quickly turn bitter and sad. Eddie also saw action in the Bulge. He took a tree-burst in the gut and spent the rest of his life doubled over from the pain and surgeries.

Mom grew up poor in a large family that had been slammed by the Great Depression. After high school she took jobs as a sales clerk making a quarter an hour plus commissions. She quit to build aircraft, where she made the first real money of her life—as much as $60 per week with overtime. She got her father a job there too; he pushed a broom and swept up the trash. He was an upholsterer who had been laid off from the Pullman Company.

Shortly after she started at the factory a supervisor questioned her. "What are you doing here?" he asked. "You people are all rich." She looked at him like he was crazy, "What do you *think* I'm doing here?"

Mom said that in the noise and commotion of the factory when no one was looking, she would walk past the assembled P-40s, lightly touch the fuselages and pray that the pilots would safely return.

There was no Jewish Quartermaster Corps. Jews were never assigned to guard Coney Island and there were never easy hand-picked assignments. There was just blind luck. Those who made it back were granted a precious piece of knowledge: there are no guarantees in life, not for success or love, good health or even for happiness. However, they also learned that hope can exist in the most hopeless of situations and, God willing, there can always be redemption.

Appendix I:
Roster of Interviewees

Of the approximately 110 veterans interviewed, 103 consented to be included and they are listed in the following table. Wherever possible I have given their ranks, job descriptions, units, branch of service and other pertinent information. Ninety-nine veterans were mentioned by name in the text or were directly quoted in regard to their wartime experiences. For the most part, the interviews were professionally transcribed from audio-files. Releases were signed either by the veterans or their surviving family members.

Captain Norman Y. Harris was a Fiscal Officer with the Army Air Corps. He spent most of the war years in several stateside posts. In civilian life, he became a very successful businessman. Mr. Harris, the son of a Polish-Jewish immigrant, was so affected by the horrors of the Holocaust, he would fund the Harris Center for Judaic Studies at the University of Nebraska–Lincoln in an effort to help fight anti–Semitism (courtesy Norman Y. Harris).

Last Name	First Name	Branch of Service	Theater	Rank	Military Occupational Specialty	Assigned	Bombardment Group	Squadron
Ashkinaz	Maurice	Army Air Corps	ETO	1st Lt.	Bombardier	8th AF	448th Bomb Group	
Bailen	Nat	Army Air Corps	ETO	1st Lt.	Bombardier	15th AF	455th Bomb Group	741st Bomb Squadron
Bartfeld	Frederick	Army Air Corps	ETO	TSGT	Flight Engineer	15th AF	459th Bomb Group	757th Bomb Squadron
Baskin	Horace	Army Air Corps	ETO	TSGT	Radio Operator	8th AF	489th Bomb Group	844th Bomb Squadron
Benjamin	Alfred	Army Air Corps	ETO	1st Lt.	Navigator	8th AF	384th Bomb Group	544th Bomb Squadron
Berman	Len	Navy	PTO	PO 3rd Class	Gunner	USS Wasp		
Bosley	Dick	Army Air Corps	PTO	Corporal	Truck Driver	20th AF	504th Bomb Group	359th Air Service Group
Codman	Murray	Army Air Corps	ETO	TSGT	Flight Engineer	8th AF	447 Bomb Group	710th Squadron
Cohn	Robert	Army Air Corps	ETO	1st Lt.	Pilot	8th AF	452nd Bomb Group	
Crane	Sidney	Army Air Corps	PTO	Captain	Pilot	5th AF	Headquarters	
Dubinsky	Maury	Navy	PTO	Lt. JG	Pilot	USS Intrepid		
Dulberg	David	Army Air Corps	Domestic	Captain	Training Officer	Peterson AFB	Headquarters	
Eder	Bernard	Army Air Corps	ETO	1st Lt.	Pilot	15th AF	483rd Bomb Group	
Eininger	Daniel	Navy	Domestic	ARM/2C	Radio Operator			
Feingold	Yale	Army Air Corps	ETO	SSGT	Gunner	8th AF	95th Bomb Group	336th Squadron
Fields	Milton	Army Air Corps	Persian Gulf Command	1st Lt.	Investigator			

Last Name	First Name	Branch of Service	Theater	Rank	Military Occupational Specialty	Assigned	Bombardment Group	Squadron
Frankel	Leon	Navy	PTO	Lt. JG	Pilot	USS Yorktown		Torpedo Squadron 9
Freeman	Marvin	Army Air Corps	ETO	SGT	Cryptographer	8th AF	385th Bomb Group	Headquarters
Friedlander	Sidney	Navy	Domestic	AMM/3C	Machinist Mate			
Friedman	Robert	U.S. Marines	PTO	Captain	Pilot			VMB 423
Fuenfer	Albert	Army Air Corps	ETO	SGT	Radar Technician	8th AF	490th Bomb Group	
Garber	Max	Army Air Corps	ETO	1st Lt.	Navigator	15th AF	459th Bomb Group	
Gasser	Sidney	Army Air Corps	ETO	1st Lt.	Pilot	9th AF	441st Troop Carrier GP	302nd Troop Carrier Squad.
Goodman	Homer	Army Air Corps	ETO	SSGT	Gunner	8th AF	100th Bomb Group	418th Squadron
Goodman	Sherwin	Navy	PTO	AOM-2C	Gunner	USS Independence		
Greenburg	Mark	Army Air Corps	PTO	SSGT	Radio Operator	5th Air Force	375th Troop Carrier GP	56th Squadron
Greenberg	Barton	Army Air Corps	Domestic	Corporal	Meteorologist			
Greene	Bernard	Army Air Corps	PTO	1st Lt.	Navigator/Bomb	20th AF	39th Bomb Group	61st Bomb Squadron
Greinsky	Ira	Army Air Corps	Western Technical Training Command	SSGT	Instructor			
Harris	Irvin	Army Air Corps	ETO	1st Lt.	Pilot	9th AF	441st Troop Carrier GP	302nd Troop Carrier Squad.
Harris	Norman	Army Air Corps	8th Service Command	Captain	Fiscal Officer			
Haydu	Bernice	WASP	Domestic	No Rank	Pilot	WASP	44-4	

Last Name	First Name	Branch of Service	Theater	Rank	Military Occupational Specialty	Assigned	Bombardment Group	Squadron
Horn	Harvey	Army Air Corps	ETO	Flight Officer	Navigator	15th AF	463rd Bomb Group	772nd Bomb Squadron
Isenstein	Harold	Army Air Corps	ETO	Corporal	Armorer	15th AF	455 Bomb Group	740th Bomb Squadron
Israel	Morton	Army Air Corps	ETO	SSGT	Gunner	8th AF	446th Bomb Group	706th Bomb Squadron
Kailo	Norman	Army Air Corps	PTO	SGT	Crew Chief	20th AF	462nd Bomb Group	769th Bomb Squadron
Kaster	Herbert	Army Air Corps	ETO	Captain	Aircraft Armament	8th AF	303rd Bomb Group	560th Squadron
Kaufman	Paul	Army Air Corps	ETO	2nd Lt.	Navigator	8th AF	388th Bomb Group	867th Squadron
Keller	Marshall	Army Air Corps	PTO	1st Lt.	Bombardier	7th Army	494th Bomb Group	37th Squadron
King	Jerry	Army Air Corps	ETO	Private	Crew Chief/Mechanic	9th AF	316th Troop Carrier Group	
Kozatch	Isadore	Army Air Corps	ETO	TSGT	Flight Engineer	15th AF	485th Bomb Group	830th Bomb Squadron
Latkin	Jack	Navy	PTO	Ensign	Pilot	US Navy		
Lazarus	Melvin	Army Air Corps	PTO	1st Lt.	Control Tower Officer			
Lerner	Robert	Army Air Corps	ETO	SSGT	Gunner	9th AF	386th Bomb Group	386th Squadron
Leventon	Marvin	Army Air Corps	PTO	TSGT	Radio Operator	5th AF	345th Bomb Group	500th Bomb Squadron
Levitan	Lee	Army Air Corps	ETO	SSGT	Radio Operator	9th AF	387th Bomb Group	
Levitt	Lester	Navy	PTO	Lt. JG	Pilot	USS Yorktown		

Last Name	First Name	Branch of Service	Theater	Rank	Military Occupational Specialty	Assigned	Bombardment Group	Squadron
Lichter	George	Army Air Corps	ETO	1st Lt.	Pilot	8th AF	361st Fighter Group	
Lichtman	Gideon	Army Air Corps	ETO	1st Lt.	Pilot	5th AF	3rd Air Commando Gp.	
Lockshin	James	Army	ETO	PFC	Driver	102nd Infantry		
Loeb	Manfred	Army Air Corps	CBI	Corporal	Crew	14th AF		27th Troop Carrier Squad.
Luck	Leonard	Army Air Corps	ETO	1st Lt.	Navigator	9th AF	15th Troop Carrier Group	50th Troop Carrier Squad.
Luterman	Paul	Army Air Corps	ETO	SSGT	Instructor	8th AF	301 Bomb Group	419th Squadron
Macfadden	Jack	Army Air Corps	Domestic	Private	Air Cadet Program	Training		
Mandel	Burton	Army Air Corps	Caribbean Defense Command	PFC	Clerk	6th AF		
Mascott	Florence	WASP	Domestic	Cadet		Training		
Mechlovics	David	Navy	Domestic	Y/2C	Yeoman	USS Pee Wee River		
Meyers	Louis	Army Air Corps	ETO	SSGT	Ball Turret Gunner	8th AF	385th Bomb Group	549th Squadron
Newman	Saul	Army Air Corps	PTO	PFC	Quartermaster	8th AF		
Newman	Stanley	Army Air Corps	ETO	1st Lt.	Pilot	9th AF	10th Photo Recon. Group	162nd Tac Recon. Squad.
Newmark	Harold	Army Air Corps	PTO	Corporal	Engine Maintainence	13th AF	Air Sea Rescue	
Nilva	Samuel	Army Air Corps	Domestic	Investigator		Provost Marshall		
Nova	Saul	Army Air Corps	PTO	2nd Lt.	Pilot			80th Fighter Squadron

Last Name	First Name	Branch of Service	Theater	Rank	Military Occupational Specialty	Assigned	Bombardment Group	Squadron
Paluch	Raymond	Army Air Corps	ETO	Private	Clerk	15th AF	33rd Fighter Group	60th Fighter Squadron
Pearlman	Herbert	Army Air Corps	ETO	1st Lt.	Pilot	8th AF	379th Bomb Group	526th Squadron
Penzer	Edward	Army Air Corps	CBI	SGT	Communications	14th AF	4th AACS	
Pfister	Elizabeth	WASP	Domestic	No Rank	Pilot	WASP	43W5	
Reichart	Stuart	Army Air Corps	PTO	1st Lt.	Bombardier/ Navigator	20th AF	497th Bomb Group	870th Squadron
Rose	Leo	Army Air Corps	PTO	1st Lt.	Bombardier	20th AF	498th Bomb Group	875th Squadron
Rosen	Leon	Army Air Corps	PTO	Flight Officer	Navigator	20th AF	29th Bomb Group	6th Squadron
Rosen	Ellsworth	Army	ETO	SSGT	Infantry	7th Army	36th Infantry	
Roth	Irwin	Army Air Corps	ETO	SSGT	Flight Engineer	15th AF	5th Bomb Group	
Ruttenberg	James	Army Air Corps	ETO	1st Lt.	Navigator	15th AF	461st Bomb Group	767th Squadron
Sabol	Allen	Army Air Corps	ETO	SSGT	Gunner	8th AF	492nd Bomb Group	856th Bomb Squadron
Schechter	Morton	Army Air Corps	ETO	SSGT	Gunner	8th AF	467th Bomb Group	791st Squadron
Schwartz	Sol	Navy	PTO	ARM/1C	Radio Operator	USS Quincy		
Shafer	George	Army Air Corps	Domestic	Corporal	Clerk	6th Svce Command		
Shafner	Sid	Army	ETO	Corporal	Infantry	7th Army	42nd Infantry Division	Regimental Recon. Unit
Shafner	Sol	Army Air Corps	PTO	SSGT	Crew Chief	20th AF	346th Bomb Group	463rd Bomb Squadron

Last Name	First Name	Branch of Service	Theater	Rank	Military Occupational Specialty	Assigned	Bombardment Group	Squadron
Shanken	Courtney	Army Air Corps	ETO	1st Lt.	Navigator	15th AF	450th Bomb Group	722nd Squadron
Shanker	Herbert	Army Air Corps	ETO	TSGT	Flight Engineer	8th AF	303rd Bomb Group	359th Squadron
Simon	Robert	Army Air Corps	ETO	1st Lt.	Navigator	8th AF	401st Bomb Group	613th Squadron
Sherman	Arthur	Army Air Corps	ETO	1st Lt.	Bombardier	15th AF	464th Bomb Group	779th Squadron
Sherman	Alvin	Army Air Corps	ETO	1st Lt.	Pilot	8th AF	96th Bomb Group	337th Squadron
Smeerin	Norman	Army Air Corps	ETO	2nd Lt.	Pilot	15th AF	450th Bomb Group	720th Squadron
Sorkin	Jack	Army Air Corps	ETO	2nd Lt.	Navigator	8th AF	92nd Bomb Group	325th Squadron
Spector	Morris	Army Air Corps	ETO	SGT	Radio Operator	9th AF	9th Troop Carrier Command	301st Troop Carrier Squad.
Stein	Sidney	Army Air Corps	ETO	SSGT	Gunner	8th AF	93rd Bomb Group	
Steinberg	Harold	Army Air Corps	ETO	Captain	Pilot	9th AF	365th Fighter Group	386th Squadron
Stovroff	Irwin	Army Air Corps	ETO	2nd Lt.	Bombardier	8th AF	44th Bomb Group	506th Squadron
Tendler	Sidney	Army Air Corps	PTO	SGT	Radio Operator	7th Emergency Rescue Squad.		
Teitelbaum	Robert	U.S. Army	ETO	Captain	Pilot	5th Army	985th Battalion	
Toppston	Arthur	Army Air Corps	ETO	TSGT	Radio Operator	8th AF	93rd Bomb Group	328th Squadron
Trustin	Yale	Army Air Corps	ETO	Captain	Pilot	ATS		

Last Name	First Name	Branch of Service	Theater	Rank	Military Occupational Specialty	Assigned	Bombardment Group	Squadron
Tulper	Leon	U.S. Army	ETO	SSGT	Radio Operator	3rd Army	260th Infantry	
Wagner	Bill	Army Air Corps	ETO	TSGT	Radio Operator	8th AF	457th Bomb Group	749th Squadron
Waldman	Leon	Army Air Corps	ETO	SSGT	Gunner	15th AF	483rd Bomb Group	840th Squadron
Weinstein	Ira	Army Air Corps	ETO	1st Lt.	Bombardier	8th AF	445th Bomb Group	
Wirtzer	Louis	Army Air Corps	CBI	2nd Lt.	Navigator	10th AF	7th Bomb Group	
Witt	Bernard	Army Air Corps	ETO	SSGT	Gunner	8th AF	487th Bomb Group	839th Squadron
Wolk	Laurence	Army Air Corps	ETO	SSGT	Gunner	8th AF	467th Bomb Group	791st Squadron
Worth	Karen	Army Air Corps	Domestic	Occupational Therapist				
Zalkin	Norman	Army Air Corps	ETO	TSGT	Radio Operator	15th AF	99th Bomb Group	348th Squadron

Appendix II:
An Interview with
Philip L. Elbaum, LCSW

Philip L. Elbaum, LCSW, is a retired Veterans Administration clinical social worker who is now in private practice. He has an interest in the problems of veterans who were World War II prisoners of war. His interest in the topic was sparked by Steven Spielberg's work interviewing Holocaust survivors. He wanted to understand if the POWs he was treating were similarly traumatized.

Elbaum videotaped 115 World War II POWs and his work resulted in a larger research project: "Persistence of Traumatic Memories in World War II Prisoners of War," Lance S. Rintamaki, Ph.D., Frances M. Weaver, Ph.D., Philip L. Elbaum, LCSW, Edward N. Klama, LCSW, and Scott A. Miskevics, MA, *Journal of the American Geriatrics Society,* Vol 57, No. 12, December 2009, pages 2257–62).

Mr. Elbaum graciously allowed me an interview for this book.

BRUCE WOLK: I was amazed at how many World War II POWs never even discussed these experiences with their families once they left the service.

PHILIP ELBAUM: *Well, it was the culture at that time that people should just "suck it up." There wasn't a discussion with the families when they came back home. People just kept things to themselves and didn't discuss anything. So one of the things we found when doing this project, is that when we interviewed the POWs, it was the first time that many of the families learned what had happened to these men was when they were finally able to look at the videotapes.*

BW: In an editorial describing your research, it was stated: "Patients may feel shame that they are emotionally weak if they're starting to recall memories."

PE: *At that time, a large number of the casualties in the Second World War were psychiatric casualties. We now call it post-traumatic stress disorder, PTSD; then it was called "battle fatigue." In fact, in the Army Air Force a significant number of the casualties were experiencing battle fatigue in terms of missions. People would be so traumatized. Until the Army Air Force developed long range fighter protection, the losses on a mission could be 40 percent to 50 percent. There was also tremendous fear of survival when you bailed out of a plane, especially those who were fearful that they might became POWs. In the present day, the armed forces have debriefings and we help them understand mental health support is not a stigma. We work with patients of all ages to help them realize they should not feel shame at these recollections.*

BW: Most of the POWs I interviewed experienced terrible casualties in their bomber groups.

PE: *Psychological trauma causes physiological changes in one's brain. The development of trauma depends on three factors; one of which is the duration of the trauma, number two is the severity of the trauma, and number three is the person's resiliency. So if a person has an isolated trauma, they may be able to cope better. For ex-POWs, it was an ongoing trauma.*

BW: What about prisoners who were segregated as Jews?

PE: *In my opinion, it was a much added stress. A number of Jewish men specifically wanted to fight the Nazis because they heard what was going on in Europe. There was also an added pressure being Jewish; the fear of being captured. This fear was reality based. Aside from the expected Nazi anti–Semitism in the Stalags there was a special concentration camp called Berga, a sub camp of Buchenwald for Jewish POWs where some were sent and treated as slave laborers. The fatality rate at Berga was nearly 20 percent, which was the highest of any POW camp where American POW's were held.*

BW: The POWs I interviewed told me of recurring dreams and thoughts, some are now in support groups.

PE: *Well, what happens with people as they get older is that their social support system diminishes. And they are not taken up with working all day and the hassle of having kids and families … people have a lot more time to obsess about things that happened previously. There's a lot more unstructured time, so this is not at all unusual with trauma … it doesn't go away, and as people grow older, they will re-experience the trauma … there's less diversion in their lives. If you've ever been in a life threatening situation, you feel a sense of numbness, and then you repress it just as you were trained to do. And then the memories resurface as repression often fails.*

BW: If you know someone who was a World War II POW, it must be important to be supportive.

PE: *I think that's the very thing that should be practiced. The veterans should be treated with dignity and respect in terms of what they went through. Human nature is that when the war is over, the war is over, and to just to move on. Even right after the Second World War, there was a lot of ambivalence about returning veterans getting special treatment. The POWs should use VA services. There's a VA outreach in terms of POWs. They are certainly entitled to them and they should be using them.*

Appendix III:
The Fate of Downed Allied Airmen in Germany in World War II

The presumption among many of the Jewish airmen was that they would have been singled out and summarily executed if captured by the Waffen-SS on German soil. It is difficult to say, as the SS seemed to have looked for any reason to kill downed airmen. It is not improbable that in their eyes, Jews should be the first to go. On the other hand, and in that particular setting, it may have made no difference—a "terror flier" ("*Terrorflieger*") was a terror flier.[1]

In terms of the accounts told by the former prisoners of war interviewed for this book, it was evident that the Jewish airmen were consistently saved from enraged townspeople and the SS by the Luftwaffe, Wehrmacht, elements of the Volkssturm (the People's Army) and many citizens who had not lost their compassion.

In the course of writing this book, I was fortunate to make contact with Herbert Weber of Iserlohn, Germany, who, along with Willi Wachholz and his wife Monika, created the website http://www.flieger-lynchmorde.de. The site was devoted to the documentation of lynched, allied airmen downed in Germany during World War II. They pursued this research as an act of healing and for historical accuracy.

According to Mr. Weber—who as a German teenager fled for his young life during the Swinemünde Raids—about 350 lynchings of Allied Airmen have been documented. Sadly, Willi Wachholz passed away on June 28, 2013, after a long illness. The website went inactive, but the paper records remain stored in Berlin.

Policies had been established for permitting the populace to take matters into their own hands. It is also apparent that the Waffen-SS was in full support of the policies. However, there does not appear to be an official policy *specific* to Jewish fliers. The development of an official, specific policy was unnecessary.

The following excerpts, reprinted by permission of Mr. Weber, show the abandonment of any pretense to the Geneva Convention as the war was reaching its inevitable conclusion (translation by Dr. Michael Wachholz).

1. "Heinrich Himmler, leader of the SS and, since 1943, when he became Minister of the Interior (and) Chief of the German Police, issued an order on 10 August 1943 which stated that it could not be the responsibility of the police 'to interfere with confrontations between German citizens and English and American terror airmen.'"

2. "Sporadic demands of lower-ranking party cadres to the effect that captured British pilots were to be shot on the spot had been heard since the spring of that year [1943].... It was to be Himmler's privilege to be the first to allow for, if not approve officially of, the lynching of hostile airmen."

3. "General Field Marshall Keitel, Chief of the Supreme High Command of the German Armed Forces [Oberkommando der Wehrmacht (OKW)] ...on 9 July 1944 ... sent out secret orders forbidding German soldiers to intervene against civilians who 'in their justified anger help themselves against Anglo-American terror airmen.'"

4. In a 26 February 1945 communication sent to the German Home Guard, the *Volkssturm*, "...the pilots of shot down fighter-bombers are to be left in the hands of the furious people. I expect from all party authorities ... that they do not seek to protect these gangster types. Authorities counteracting the healthy reactions of the people, will be brought to account."

5. "There may in fact be quite a few Allied airmen buried as 'fallen soldiers' who—according to the official version—were lethally injured in the crash of their plane or when landing by parachute, but who in truth perhaps became the victims of infuriated and fanaticized men."

Chapter Notes

Chapter 1

1. Courtney Shanken qualified to be an Olympic gymnast for the cancelled 1940 Olympics. Nat Bailen, Leon Rosen, George Shafer and others were scheduled to go to college on football scholarships. Morton Schechter played semi-pro baseball before the war, and after the war he was recruited by major league farm teams. Physical Therapist Karen Worth was a prodigy; she studied at the Philadelphia Academy of the Fine Arts and became a sculptor. George Lichter spent his summers playing clarinet in a jazz band that toured the Catskills. He had aspirations of becoming a professional musician. Len Berman, played in a jazz band into his 90s.

2. Navy Aviation Machinist Mate Sidney Friedlander and all six of his siblings volunteered for military service. One of his brothers was killed in combat. Sgt. Marvin G. Freeman was in college on December 7, 1941 soon after, his entire Jewish fraternity, *Zeta Beta Tau* enlisted. One of his fraternity brothers died in combat as an infantryman in the Pacific, one of his brothers was in the Army Air Corps and was shot down in a raid on the Ploesti oil fields. Soon after Cpl. Dick Bosley enlisted, his father, a WWI veteran re-enlisted. Elizabeth Haas Pfister, a WASP pilot, enlisted after her fighter pilot brother was shot down and killed in the Pacific. Pfister and brother were Jewish.

3. Staff Sergeant Sol Shafner was growing up in Philadelphia at that time. He said that the Jewish community went crazy at the news and that people were "pulling their hair out" in anger. Though he generally liked Roosevelt, he never forgave Roosevelt.

4. Abraham H. Foxman, www.adl.org/immigrants, 2008.

5. Jewish War Veterans of the United States of America. See also American-Jewish Historical Society, *American-Jewish Desk Reference*, The Philip Leff Group, Inc. (1999).

6. *Jews in American Wars*, by J. George Friedman and Louis A. Falk, Jewish War Veterans of the United States of America (1954).

7. The Sixteenth United States Census, conducted by the U.S. Census Bureau.

8. American-Jewish Historical Society, Fall/Winter 2003.

9. The statistics do not include ground accidents, stateside accidents and transport accidents.

10. The Pacific killed in action casualties included more than 3,600 Naval personnel and approximately 5,700 Army Air Force personnel. For additional information consult Aviation Personnel Fatalities, 1941–1946, Navy Department Library and Army Battle Casualties and Non-battle Deaths of WWII (June 1, 1953).

11. Men who flew as artillery spotters were Army as opposed to Army Air Corps.

12. Bureau of War Records cited in AJHS Newsletter (Fall/Winter 2003).

Chapter 2

1. Hyman George Rickover, a four star admiral, was recognized for the development of the world's first nuclear-powered submarine. Rickover was Jewish, born to parents who escaped the pogroms of Poland. He himself was an immigrant.

2. At the request of Sidney Crane, the captain's name was changed.

3. Crane was a licensed plumber in civilian life. While in training on the B-17, there was a well-known engineering flaw to the hydraulics. Using his background as a plumber, he recommended a design change that was adopted throughout the Army Air Corps. He joked that everyone on base knew that it was "Jew Crane" who designed the modification.

4. Initials are used to protect the identity of those referred to by the veterans.

5. Interview notes of August 16, 2012 and excerpts by permission from the author's self-published book, "Herb P. Flyboy, *The Journey from WWII Pilot to German POW*," by Herbert Pearlman (2005).

6. Spector arrived in Berlin as Swastikas and Nazi statuary were being ripped down from buildings. A buddy of his was killed by a former German Army "terrorist" whom Spector referred to as a "Werewolf."

7. The term "White Jew" does not refer to skin color but of a Jew who is perceived by the anti–Semite as being a "different kind of Jew," a "good Jew" who didn't look Jewish and wasn't "pushy."

8. There was a complement of 1,142 officers and enlisted men aboard ship; Jews comprised less than 2 percent of the personnel.

9. "Starting in 1942, the United States sent thousands of troops to Iran and Iraq specifically to transport war Materiel to Russia. Iran was already occupied by British and Russian troops who were guarding the oil fields and keeping more than a watchful eye on the pro–German Iranians (Persians)." By permission, Webmaster, Persian Gulf Command website. www.pgcvowwii. homestead.com.

10. Though Mr. Shanker was obviously proud of the number of Jews in combat with the 303rd Bomb Group, in searching the BG website, it seems unlikely that an inordinately high percentage of the navigators in the group were Jewish.

11. "Ikey" was a variant slang for "Kike," for being Jewish and was derogatory.

12. Sergeant Edward Penzer, recalled a cartoon someone handed to him when he was in advanced training in Sacramento, California. It showed a hook-nosed soldier guarding an island, with the caption: "Jews guarding Coney Island, It's All They Can Do!"

Chapter 3

1. The P-51 was also known as "The Mustang," a long-range fighter plane built by North American Aviation. It was primarily flown in the European Theater of Operations.

2. There is a variation in this remembrance as others have reported smaller bombs so as to allow ground troops easier movement. The difference was most likely due to the different targets the bombers were assigned. Goodman's 18th birthday was June 3, 1944, making him one of the youngest members of the group.

3. Luck would also be involved in dropping the first Pathfinders into Rome.

4. The Channel Islands have a fascinating history. They are "protected by" the United Kingdom, but they are close to the Normandy, France beachhead and were occupied by the Germans.

5. The French Legion of Honor is France's highest award and is being awarded to living WWII veterans who participated in the Liberation of France.

6. St. Lô in Northern France was devastated during the Normandy invasion. It had been in German hands prior to the invasion.

7. General Leslie McNair, a Lieutenant General, was killed during the battle along with hundreds of American Infantry troops.

8. From the certificate: "This signifies membership in the Lucky Bastard Club of SSGT Bernard Witt who has completed 34 successful round trips over enemy territory to deliver the H.E. Mail to Der Feuhrer for the Eighth Air Force a principal agent for the United States of America."

9. Notes from Bernard Witt: *"This is a diary of John Gibbs [Co-Pilot]. He flew 32 missions. I completed 34. I am not sure which 2 others I flew."*

10. Neunkirchen was a major iron producing area of Germany in the Saarland region.

11. Most likely Ramitelli Airfield, near Termoli, on the Adriatic coast.

12. The Tuskegee Airmen were the first African-American pilots in the USAAF. They formed the 322nd Fighter Group, comprised of the 99th, 100th, 301st, and 302nd fighter squadrons. They first flew P-40s, P-47s and finally P-51 Mustangs. They were known as "Red Tails" for the color they

painted their rudders and propeller spinners.

13. SSGT Leon Tulper, who with Patton's 3rd Army and a Dachau liberator stated that his cousin was a glider pilot who had been killed over Holland.

14. Ironically, the number "18" is symbolic in Judaism as "*Chai,*" a symbol of life and of good luck.

15. The average squadron was 12 to 14 planes. On this day, about 40 percent of the planes were lost.

16. Kozatch said the naming of a plane or nose art was a kind of Hollywood affectation. Several of the veterans felt the same way and said it was silly and unnecessary. However, other crews attached great affection to naming their planes.

17. The Website of the 483rd Bombardment Group details the Memmingen Mission, with permission.

18. More than 50 aircraft were destroyed and 600 airmen were reported as dead.

19. Ted "T." was picked up by the German Army and transported to a hospital. He and Sabol remained friends for many years after.

20. During the Korean conflict Teitelbaum was recommended for the Silver Star.

21. Regensburg was a major target for many Bombardment Groups as there was ball bearing production vital to the German war effort.

22. See the earlier interview with PFC Burt Mandel who was assigned to the Caribbean Command.

23. The most serious of the Schweinfurt Raids were carried out in October of 1943. There were 77 Allied bombers that were either lost over the target or crash landed a short distance away from the target due to damage from flak or German fighter planes. While the mission was deemed a success, with many ball bearing and other factories destroyed, close to 600 airmen died, with about 65 airmen taken prisoner.

24. The Norden Bomb Sight, initially a highly classified instrument, was first delivered to the USAAF in 1943. Despite its improvement over the British Mark XIV bombsight, the Norden bomb sight, used under combat conditions, had a CEP (Circular Error Probable) of 1,200 feet. World War II Encyclopedia.

25. The Battle of Arnhem (Operation Market Garden) occurred in September 1944 and was the subject of the movie, "A Bridge Too Far." The British would eventually surrender to the Germans.

26. Given they were told there was a POW camp nearby, they may have been on a mission to Moosburg in Bavaria.

27. General Adolph Galland, the German fighter pilot "Ace," was a strong advocate for using the jet aircraft against the superior Allied forces. The jet mentioned was most likely the Me-262.

Chapter 4

1. General Joseph Warren Stillwell, also known as "Vinegar Joe," was a four star General who commanded the 7th Infantry Division of the China-Burma-India Theater of Operations. He had a tremendous love for China, the Chinese people and for the enlisted men under his command.

2. The PBJ-1 was the Navy's version of the USAAF B-25.

3. Espiritu Santo is a large island in the New Hebrides chain of islands in the South Pacific.

4. Rabaul was a township in Papua, New Guinea.

5. Flight Officer was a USAAF World War II rank equivalent to a Warrant Officer junior grade (W-1).

6. According to the military criteria for the award of the medal: "*The performance must have involved personal hazard or danger and the voluntary risk of life under conditions not involving conflict with an armed enemy....*"

7. A Naval Lieutenant Junior Grade (JG) is the equivalent to a Second Lieutenant in the other services.

8. The Battle of Luzon began early in January of 1945. Luzon is the largest of the Philippine islands. Mr. Levitt was probably on this mission in November or early December of 1944.

9. Strafing, simply put, is going after a target on the ground with machine gun fire from the aircraft. It is one of a number of skills that must be mastered by fighter pilots and is extremely dangerous as it puts the strafing aircraft well within the range of smaller caliber ground-based anti-aircraft artillery.

10. The Lingayen Gulf is the body of water in the South China Sea off of Luzon.

11. Levitt is referencing a book by James Bradley entitled *Flyboys: A True Story of Courage*, where American flyers who were taken prisoner in the vicinity and sent to Chichi-jima and were subjected to unspeakable atrocities. Chichi-jima Island is approximately 150 miles north of Iwo Jima and was important during the war for Japanese communications.

12. Canton, a city approximately 75 miles from Hong Kong, is more officially known as Guangzhou. The Japanese occupied Guangzhou from 1938 to the end of WWII. There are numerous stories in regard to the brutality with which the Japanese treated their Chinese prisoners.

13. The Doolittle Raid took place on April 18, 1942. It was regarded as a morale boosting victory rather than a military success.

14. For a good summary of this information with primary sources: http://www.cv6. org/1945/tokyo/tokyo_2.htm.

15. The Yamato was a "monster," with a length of nearly three football fields and powerful weaponry. It was the pride of the Japanese Navy. Fully loaded it weighed more than 71,000 tons.

16. For a synopsis of Mr. Frankel's award: http://www.homeofheroes.com/members/ 02_NX/citations/03_wwii-nc/nc_06wwii_ navyE.html.

17. *Terry and the Pirates* was a popular comic strip of the WWII era. It was created by Milton Caniff in 1934. Though controversial at the time, Mr. Caniff foretold of the Japanese invasion of China and the Pacific.

18. The 3rd Air Commando Group was part of the Fifth Air Force in the Philippines. The fighter pilots flew P-51 Mustangs. They attacked Japanese positions throughout the Philippines and Formosa (Taiwan).

19. The Salween River Campaign was fought by the Chinese against Japan from the summer of 1944 through 1945. The Japanese had blockaded this trade route to India between China, Burma (Myanmar) and Thailand.

20. The pilot ran from the plane and jumped into a 40mm gun bucket to stop the gunnery crew from firing on a Navy TBF Avenger. In the gunnery crew's excitement they were shooting at everything with wings coming toward the ship.

21. *Negros* Island is one of the largest islands in the Philippines.

22. Halmahera is an island in the Pacific south-southwest of the Philippines, while Palau is an independent island country southeast the Philippines. Both were occupied by the Japanese.

23. Harbor located on (then Formosa, now Taiwan) used by Japanese shipping.

24. Panay Island is a small island in the Philippines.

25. Dubinsky was trained on a rocket called "Tiny Tim," a weapon specifically intended for situations where the enemy was dug into caves such as on Okinawa. This was in preparation for an invasion of Japan.

26. The Yamato was, in a sense, on her own *Kamikaze* mission when she was sunk in early April 1945. Her final duty was to defend Okinawa until she, herself, was destroyed. More than 2,000 Japanese naval personnel died on the Yamato.

27. In regard to the Intrepid, Dubinsky recalled that there were several types of squadrons arranged around certain tasks: the fighter squadron, dive bomber squadron, torpedo squadron, night fighter squadron and fighter- bomber squadron.

28. Usa Prefecture, despite popular legend, was not the name of a city where they made cheap toys. The name was well in use many centuries ago.

29. Radar Rope was most likely a form of chaff—aluminized strips of foil used as a counter measure to jam enemy radar.

30. Ie Shima is an island off the coast of Okinawa that was used as an airfield. It was taken over by the U.S. in 1945.

31. Tinian Island is in the Northern Marianas chain of islands.

32. *Bockscar* was the name of the B-29 that dropped the bomb on Nagasaki.

33. Mr. Nova may have been referring to Chiang Kai-shek.

Chapter 5

1. This was later changed to "J" for Jewish.

2. The total chaplains as of May 1, 1945 in the European Theater of Operations was 2,796, and of that number, only 67 were Jewish. WW2 U.S. Medical Research Center. See also Derek J. Penslar, *Jews and the Military*, Princeton: Princeton University Press, 2013, P. 210.

3. Traditional or Orthodox congrega-

tions specify the Minyan should be ten men who have been *bar mitzvah'd*, However, in many Reform and egalitarian congregations, it is 10 Jews, either female or male, who have gone through the bar mitzva or bat mitzva.

4. The Jeep with the flag is commonly known as the "follow me" vehicle that would lead landing aircraft to a parking spot on the ramp.

5. This topic is explored more fully in Appendix III.

6. Lichter, must have meant "P" for Baptist. There were only three designations on dog tags: Protestant ("P"), Catholic ("C") and Jewish ("H").

7. Teitelbaum competed on an Army pistol team.

8. In re-creating Mr. Weinstein's comments, I supplemented my interview of January 3, 2010, with an interview Mr. Weinstein conducted with Aaron Elson on April 17, 1999 for the Kassel Mission project.

9. www.kasselmission.com.

10. Several veterans have described the flat spin; the laws of physics trapped many men to their deaths and destroyed numerous aircraft.

11. This fact has been confirmed by authors Willi and Monika Wacholz and Herbert Weber who manage a German Website, www.flieger-lynchmorde.de, devoted to documenting cases of lynching's and murders of downed Allied airmen. Notes taken from documents graciously compiled by Herbert Weber will appear in Appendix III.

12. Ira Weinstein interview, April 17, 1999, with Aaron Elson. Permission granted by Aaron Elson.

13. Loosely translated from the Yiddish, it means "Blessed Destiny."

14. After the war, Ira Weinstein made good on a personal vow, and visited the five families whose sons he buried to offer comfort and closure.

15. In many instances, *Terrorflieger* were not afforded the Geneva Conventions but considered by the SS as criminals and spies.

16. As the war progressed, and fighter support improved, the number of required missions increased from 25 to 50.

17. Standard Operating Procedure for all prisoners was to strip search them, then place them in solitary during the interrogation process.

18. Undoubtedly to kill the airman as was the case with Ira Weinstein's Crew.

19. Leck is a small town located in Northern Germany.

20. The police turned Sabol over to the military, as they were Army Air Corps, most probably they were turned over to the Luftwaffe.

21. The Five Books of Moses found in virtually every synagogue. It is the Torah in book form, both in Hebrew and English, with extensive commentary.

22. One of the Jewish infantrymen interviewed for background information, SSGT Leon Tulper was a radio operator with Patton's Third Army. While atop his jeep he heard a strange "whoosh" sound and was so shocked, he said he "soiled his pants!" The jet passed so close he could see the pilot's face smiling at him. At that point in the war the Germans had run out of ammunition for the Me-262.

23. In September 1944, the Me-262 equipped Kampfgeschwader 51 (Fighter Squadron 51) "Edelweiß" was based at Hopsten, which was protected by approximately 500 AAA guns in the vicinity.

24. USAAF Statistical Summaries, World War II. Note that more than 4,500 aircraft were lost in combat in the Pacific.

25. Army Battle Casualties and Non-Battle Deaths (1953).

26. National Museum of the U.S. Air Force. Note: Japan captured 5,436.

27. Stalag is a German acronym for Sträflings Lager or prisoner's camp.

28. After 1945, Sagan was transferred back to Poland and became Zagan.

29. Red Cross food packages were essential to supplement diets, as the camp diet, in and of itself was insufficient.

30. Kriege was the American abbreviation for the German *Kriegsgefangener*.

31. Research compiled by William Newmiller for use by the United States Air Force Academy.

32. Alternative: Grosstychew, Poland.

33. www.b24.net, Stalag Luft VI and IV; Capt. Wynsen, Medical Corps; Deposition of Capt. Henry J. Wynsen for the Judge Advocate General's Investigation. This website is an excellent resource for anyone wishing information on B-24 crews.

34. For an excellent account of the mis-

treatment of Allied prisoners at Heydekrug, read "The Heydekrug Run" by Greg Hatton, www.b24.net.

35. Lerner is referring to the forced evacuation march of Stalag Luft IV.

36. www.b24.net. From the excellent research archives of the 392nd Bombardment Group Association.

37. Taken with permission, Irwin Stovroff, January 2010.

38. Kaufman most likely meant Oberst (Colonel) Warnstadt instead of von Warren. Warnstadt had replaced Oberst Sherer in 1945. See www.b24.net.

39. Fairly common rest and recuperation area for former Allied POWs, located in Paluel, France.

40. There is a huge discrepancy in the number of Jews that were believed to be segregated.

41. Personal correspondence, Aaron Elson, February 11, 2015.

42. *Obergruppenführer* Gottlob Berger, the man in charge of all of the POW camps, claimed at his Nuremburg war crimes trial in October 1945 that Hitler also considered using the POWs as human shields.

43. Captain Leslie Caplan, M.D., "Death March Medic," *Air Force* magazine, November 1945, Vol. 28, No. 11.

44. Notes originally prepared by the Military Intelligence Service of the War Department, compiled and presented by Greg Hatton.

45. The most accurate date for the camp departure found in my research was February 6th, however, it is entirely possible that another section of the camp left earlier in that month.

46. In Harvey Horn's interview, he talked of a German officer who rode in the same railroad car with the prisoners and their guards; with tears streaming down his face, he pleaded with the Americans to join forces with the Germans against the Soviets. He did not know that Horn was Jewish.

47. Sabol remembered Lerner's attempted escape. He said it was a "stupid thing for Lerner to do!" Lerner would undoubtedly agree!

48. The woman was probably a collaborator or was trying to gain favor with the Nazis.

49. The German officer intentionally changed Roosevelt's name to a much more Jewish sounding name: Rosenfeld.

50. Numerous stories appear online in regard to Leslie Caplan, M.D. He is revered among the ex-prisoners of war of Stalag Luft IV. Recommended reading on Dr, Caplan and the forced march is a self-published book (2004) by Laura Caplan entitled: "Domain of Heroes—The Medical Journal, Writings, and Story of Dr. Leslie Caplan."

51. Testimony of Dr. Leslie Caplan: The Evacuation of Luft IV for The War Crimes Office, Civil Affairs Division, WDSS, 31 December 1947. http://www.stalagluft4.org/Testimony. See also Captain Caplan's "Death March Medic," *Air Force Magazine*, Vol. 28, No. 11, November 1945, Page 12.

52. Claude Watkins, Ex-POW Bulletin, April 2000 placed the number significantly lower.

53. The People's or National Militia formed near the end of the war.

54. Moosburg Online Website, though other references place the number as high as 130,000 (www.b24.net). The discrepancy may be that a large number of prisoners were assigned as factory workers, and therefore, off the site. The number of American troops was estimated at 30,000.

55. Apparently, 700 prisoners reportedly escaped en masse, in an effort to meet up with the British. There are reports that some of the POWs who left the camp were killed by advancing Russian forces simply due to the confusion in the liberation process.

56. The town has passed into Croatian hands, and has been renamed Rijeka.

57. *Lili Marlene* is a German love song that was recorded in 1939. It was translated into English and became very popular throughout Europe. It is a sad and wistful song and talks of war's futility.

58. In personal correspondence, April 14, 2011, Mr. Horn stated that the Brenner Pass was typically bombed by B-25s which was a medium range bomber that bombed from lower levels than a B-17.

59. Personal communication, Larry Grauerholz, Air Forces Escape and Evasion Society, May 25, 2010, Nichol, John and Tony Renner, *Home Run: Escape from Nazi Europe*, New York: Viking Books, 2007.

Chapter 6

1. In June 2009, twenty veterans were accompanied to Normandy Beach by stu-

dents from College of the Ozarks. Two of the veterans interviewed for this book, Harold Steinberg and Homer Goodman attended the commemorative event.

2. Some of the Jewish Army Air Corps veterans interviewed were critical of the rabbinate for what was considered a lack of volunteerism for overseas assignments.

3. *Aliyah* has two broad definitions: the most popular definition may be thought of as the return of Jews to Israel or "to make *aliyah*," However, there is also the honor of being called to read a passage from—or to say the blessings before—the reading from the Torah during religious services. In this manner, a Jew renews a commitment to return to the teachings of the Torah.

4. Dreidels are four-sided spinning tops with numerical values on each facet. Playing the dreidel is normally done around Chanukah time.

5. The sabbath, starting on Friday nights after sundown is marked by the commandment to light candles.

6. From official General Orders, Headquarters Twentieth Air Force, September 17, 1945, forwarded by the veteran.

7. Refers to General Earle Gilmore "Bus" Wheeler who would later serve as Chairman of the Joint Chiefs of Staff.

8. There was no reference found to Tendari. The veteran most probably meant, Kendari in Indonesia, which was the site of an airbase that the Japanese had captured from the Allies.

9. Axis Sally was the name given to Mildred Gillars, an American-born language teacher who moved to Germany prior to WWII and became a broadcaster and propagandist for German State Radio. Her role was to demoralize Allied troops and to convince them that Germany was their friend.

10. The five Sullivan brothers all served aboard the Navy ship USS Juneau, which was sunk by a Japanese torpedo in the Battle of Guadalcanal. All five were killed. A policy was put into effect that from that point forward, brothers were prohibited from serving aboard the same ship.

11. Using numerals on the clock face was an easy and accurate method of describing direction in relation to one's aircraft. 12 o'clock meant straight ahead, 6 o'clock was directly behind, 3 and 9 o'clock were to the right and left respectively. An attacking aircraft's location and altitude could then be called out as 3 o'clock high or 12 o'clock low.

12. The pilotage navigator was responsible for calling out checkpoints on the ground. The head navigator was responsible for the mission. The radar navigator was used in case the plane hit bad weather, the so-called "Mickey Radar." On extremely important missions there were three navigators on the lead plane. On this particular mission Shanken's bomb group flew over Allied troops for morale purposes and obviously it was extremely important to carefully observe position and to be on course.

13. This was not part of the famed "Kinder Transport," but was a group sponsored by "Youth *Aliyah*," another rescue operation founded by Henrietta Szold. The children at the service would settle in Palestine.

14. Possibly referring to Piardoba Air Base in West Bengal, India.

15. The advanced glider training field was most probably in Stuttgart, Arkansas, which would later become Stuttgart Municipal Airport.

16. Mountain Home, Idaho and Fort Sumner, New Mexico, were Army Air Corps training bases.

17. The Tuskegee Airmen painted the tails and propeller spinners of their P-51 fighter planes red.

18. The Tuskegee Airmen (the 332nd Fighter Group and the 477th Bombardment Group) actually had flown several different types of fighters before the P-51. They first flew the P-40 "Warhawk," the Bell P-39 "Aircobra," the P-47 "Thunderbolt," and then in July 1944, they received the P-51 "Mustang." The 477th Bomb Group flew the B-25 "Mitchell" medium bomber but never saw combat.

19. On a B-24 Liberator in a combat situation, the flight engineer would sit in a "bubble" that protruded from the top of the aircraft. In addition to his technical duties, the flight engineer would also take up a gunnery position. When Bartfeld understatedly recalled having the turret shot out, he was describing a situation where by the luckiest of margins he escaped a mortal injury from machine gun fire and flak ripping through the Plexiglas bubble.

20. Both the Germans (1940) and English (1942) developed auxiliary fuel tanks to

extend the range of their fighter aircraft. The Americans adopted the technology later in the war making it possible for the P-51 fighter plane to protect bombers for longer distances.

21. Zeilsheim was a district of Frankfort that had a large displaced persons camp.

Chapter 7

1. A veteran interviewed shared the sad story of a good friend, also Jewish, who had been a star football lineman at a New York university. The men enlisted together for the Air Corps but went to different bomb groups. His friend had the dream of attending medical school. When the friend returned he suffered from what was then called "shell shock" from combat. The man struggled to hold a job and finally became a car salesman. He had what was described as a "lousy marriage" and died from a disease related to obesity.

2. Haydu, Bernice "Bee" Falk, *Letters Home 1944–1945*, Riviera Beach, FL: Top Line Printing and Graphics, 2003.

3. The story of the founding of the Israeli air force is not without its share of controversy. There are those who have made claims as to their exploits but their claims are without first person corroboration. Lichtman stands by his role in the formation of the 101st.

4. Rabbi Joachim Prinz, a German immigrant, was an ardent Zionist who warned German Jewry of the dangers of Adolph Hitler's message as far back as the early 1930s. In 1937, he immigrated to the United States where he became an outspoken critic of the Nazi regime and a strong believer in the return of the Jewish people to (then) Palestine. He served Temple B'nai Abraham as their rabbi starting in 1939. Over time, he became very active in the civil rights movement, seeing the plight of African Americans in the United States as being similar to the Jews in Germany.

5. The original name of the ship was the SS President Warfield; it was re-named the Exodus 1947.

6. "Buzz" Beurling is a WWII hero and without question one of Canada's greatest fighter pilots with more than 30 "kills" to his credit.

7. Etzion, was the codename for the Israeli Air Force base in Žatec, Czechoslovakia, in the 1948 Arab–Israeli War.

8. The Aircraft was an Avia S-199, a Czech version of the Messerschmitt Bf-109G-14. The plane had difficult handling characteristics and very unforgiving controls. As a result, it was nicknamed "the mule." Jewish Virtual Library, http://www.jewishvirtuallibrary.org/jsource/History/avia.html.

9. Mordechai "Modi" Alon was the first commander of the 101st Fighter Squadron. He held the rank of Lieutenant Colonel and died in a combat-related flying incident not long after the incident that Mr. Lichtman described.

10. The Hagana was the organization that was the forerunner of the Israel Defense Forces (IDF).

11. Ezer Weizman would eventually go on to become Commander of the Israeli Air Force and after that President of Israel.

12. Stan Andrews had been a B-25 medium bomber pilot during WWII and in civilian life he was an artist. Recruited into the Israeli Air Force in 1948, he was killed in action a brief time after he joined the forces. His designs endure on every plane in the 101st and 105th squadrons.

13. Ira Weinstein's story was constructed from three sources: personal interviews for this book conducted on January 3, 2010, personal correspondence on May 22, 2010, and the interview conducted between Weinstein and Aaron Elson on April 17, 1999 for the Kassel Mission Historical Society. I am indebted for permission granted by the "Society" to reprint parts of Mr. Elson's interview. Verification of this story is confirmed by a "Request for Casualty" document from the War Department (provided by Weinstein) dated July 12, 1945. For more information on the Kassel Mission, please go to www.kasselmission.com.

14. For more information, please go to: www. Vetshelpingheroes.org. This book lists the website as reference; it does not constitute an endorsement.

15. Rovno, or Rowno, had a centuries-old Jewish community that was steeped tradition, worship, and a love of learning. The community was virtually wiped out by the Nazis with the complicity of anti–Semitic elements who were only too willing to destroy the relatively large Jewish population.

16. This story is based on personal interviews with Mr. Loeb, as well as memoirs dictated to his family, "Opa's Biography."

Appendix III

1. There are many references to flyers who were shipped to the Buchenwald concentration camp between the periods of the late summer of 1944 to the fall of 1944 with the intention of the execution of these men as spies. Ultimately (and with pressure from within the German ranks), the men were transferred to Stalag Luft III. There are some key points of distinction from these notes: the flyers who were shipped to Buchenwald were apparently caught in civilian clothes and treated as spies and hence, not protected in the same manner under the Geneva Convention and second, the group was composed of fliers from many countries. We will never know the possible fates of Jewish airmen who were caught as "spies."

Bibliography

American Jewish Desk Reference: The Ultimate One-Volume Reference to the Jewish Experience in America. New York: Random House, 1999.

Caplan, Laura. *Domain of Heroes: The Medical Journal, Writings, and Story of Dr. Leslie Caplan*. Edina, MN: Jerry's Printing & Design, 2004.

Crane, Sidney. *Tales of a Clam Digger*. Sylva, NC: Old Mountain Press, 2002.

Fredman, J. George, and Louis A. Falk. *Jews in American Wars*. New York: Jewish War Veterans of USA, 1954.

Freeman, Roger Anthony. *The Mighty Eighth: A History of the Units, Men, and Machines of the US 8th Air Force*. London: Casssell, 2000. Print.

Haydu, Bernice Falk. *Letters Home 1944–1945: Women Airforce Service Pilots, World War II*. Riviera Beach, FL: TopLine Print and Graphics, 2003.

Horn, Harvey S. *Goldfish, Silver Boot: The Story of a World War II Prisoner of War*. Jacksonville, FL: Fortis, 2010.

Nichol, John, and Tony Rennell. *Home Run: Escape From Nazi Europe*, International Edition. Amazon.com: Books, 2008.

Pearlman, Herbert. *Herb P. Flyboy: The Journey from World War II Pilot to German POW*. Self-published, 2005.

Index

Numbers in **bold italics** indicate pages with photographs.